VICTORIAN BRITAIN:
THE NORTH EAST

VICTORIAN BRITAIN:
THE NORTH EAST

FRANK ATKINSON

DAVID & CHARLES
Newton Abbot   London

British Library Cataloguing in Publication Data
Atkinson, Frank
  Victorian Britain: the North East.
  1. North-east England, 1837–1901
  I. Title
  942.8081

  ISBN 0-7153-8747-2

Typeset by Typesetters (Birmingham) Limited
Smethwick, West Midlands
and printed in Great Britain
by Butler & Tanner Limited, Frome and London
for David & Charles Publishers plc
Brunel House Newton Abbot Devon

CONTENTS

1

THE VICTORIAN
NORTH EAST: TODAY

We were too close to the Victorians until the middle of this century fully to appreciate their remarkable achievements, and indeed I can remember from my own childhood in the 1930s, how things Victorian were rather disdained; their furnishings were dowdy, their paintings completely outmoded, their buildings fussy, their way of life stuffy.

Now we can look back more comfortably from a greater distance and surely no-one has helped more in this rehabilitation than John Betjeman.

However, in this work I have tried neither to praise nor to criticise our forbears - after all they had so many problems and so little to help them in coming to terms with enormous industrial developments, amazing scientific discoveries, entirely new methods of transport, novel sources of power and huge urban expansions.

It was these urban expansions which created so many of the problems which beset the Victorians and yet which stimulated so many of their great improvements: crowded housing and lack of water and drains resulted in cholera and ill health, yet led to the Public Health Acts, sewerage, better plumbing and improved street layouts; overcrowded church yards led to Burial Boards; overworked young children led to Mines Acts and to Factory Acts; overcrowded prisons led to improved prison conditions, an inadequately educated population led to Education Acts, and the onset of gas, electricity and tramways led to facilitating legislation.

Although all this expansion and change resulted from and led to considerable movements of people, it has to be noted that there was not much transfer of occupation, from one place to another in the region. Within mining there was the absorption of unemployed lead-miners into coalmining, but the majority of those entering the region during the mid nineteenth century came without particular skills of use in their new environment, being generally unskilled labourers. Yet it was from such an unpromising labour force that the tradition of machine skills was built, which we, today, think of as having been such a pronounced feature of the North East.

Throughout this book I have tried to weave together two different series of strands. On the one hand I have endeavoured to analyse what it is that we feel is so typical of the Victorians. My chapter headings: 'Thriving Industries', 'Expanding Towns', 'Increasing Mobility', 'Living and Dying in Towns' and so on attempt to epitomise both the joys and the horrors of that period. I have tried to emphasise these stand-points, whether they were the first fumbling attempts at mass education, the squalor of children catching rats from the cholera-ridden sewers, the exciting benefits of electricity or the philanthropy of the well-to-do, helping their less fortunate fellow-men.

On the other hand I have pin-pointed North-Eastern examples of today's material remains of the period, generally those which were once typical, though now often minimal and curious: public buildings, houses great and small, schools, chapels, bridges, roads, pottery, glass and paintings. In this way we may relate the North East to the national picture and see the broad issues as they affected our region, looking at what remains of the 19th century in our towns and countryside today not just as 'period remains', but as specific pieces of history, with valid reasons for their creation, even if it is only by chance that they survive today.

There are so many remains to be found, around which we can build our story. Some are only names: Pandon Bank which reminds us of the ancient Pandon Dene, changed into a sewer around 1850; some are relatively unspoilt like Grey Street in Newcastle, whilst others have been partially destroyed (one is tempted to say 'wantonly'), like Eldon Square. Some have been preserved in a special way like Francis Street from Hetton-le-Hole; an 1880s pit row now rebuilt at Beamish (The North of England Open Air Museum). A memorial stone in Barnard Castle churchyard reminds us of the terrifying cholera outbreak of 1849. Durham Shorthorn cattle at Beamish (now on the way to becoming a 'Rare Breed') recall the first attempt at in-line breeding (a deliberate seeking to 'improve' the breed) carried out along the banks of the River Tees at the very beginning of the nineteenth century. A tall 'gothic' churchyard memorial to the oarsman Harry Clasper reminds us of a Tyne river sport long forgotten. A Board School, of the 1870s, calls to our notice the beginnings of free education for all.

The railway lines, often still following their original routes, with others barely traceable on the ground and marked on maps as 'old track', may help us to recall the problems of Victorian finance: sometimes shaky capital funding by dubious characters like George Hudson who yet built up so much of the North Eastern Railway's routes, and without this chicanery it may never have come to pass. We may see Robert Stephenson driven to a rather unhappy deal to save himself from financial ruin, and yet going on to construct a fine bridge over the Tyne which today, more than a century and a third later, is carrying heavy modern traffic, both road and rail. And the Armstrong Building in Newcastle tells us not only of the beginning of Armstrong College later to become King's College and thereafter the University of Newcastle upon Tyne, but of Armstrong himself – the 'great gun-maker' and notable industrialist who was responsible for Elswick's growth along the north bank of the Tyne (now demolished to clear land again) and who then built Cragside for his own use, in the Northumbrian hills.

8

It has been said that Sir Walter Scott's greatest contribution to historical understanding was his remark that our ancestors were once 'as really alive as we are now', and we should try to apply this truism when considering the lives of our forbears. In this way we might look at the lives of several northern Victorian people who have had such a long-lasting effect that we can still identify their benefits today. The Reverend John Hodgson for example, whose outspoken sermon published after the 1812 colliery explosion led directly to Sir Humphrey Davy producing his Safety Lamp, and in a modern version this is still used today for gas-testing by the 'Pit Deputy'. And if that were not enough, Hodgson's volumes on the *History of Northumberland* are still held as standard works of reference, a century and a half later.

John Dobson, architect, partnered by Richard Grainger the builder, left the face of Newcastle more dramatically and indeed more attractively laid out than when he found it, and Thomas Bewick's engravings are to this day frequently used for all kinds of illustrations, for his acute observation of the countryside is as valid as when he worked nearly two centuries ago.

All these and many more objects and facts are there to be sought and interpreted. For just as the Victorian 'narrative' painters would have every picture tell its story, so we may compose our own picture of Victorian North East England around buildings, machinery, photographs, names, memories . . .

However, so many aspects of British urbanised life which we take for granted today can be shown to stem directly from actions taken, often by Parliament, perhaps a hundred and fifty years ago, and it would be parochial in the extreme to write about the Victorian North East, significant though it was at certain points, without highlighting national decisions which have so shaped our own lives.

By 'Parliament', one is often intending also to refer to those officers – the early forerunners of today's 'Whitehall Civil Servants' – who played such a part in either preparing Commissioners' Reports and Bills, or in responding to the subsequent Acts.

It is in this context that one introduces Edwin Chadwick who in 1833 became a Commissioner of the Poor Law Commission, a large part of whose Report he had drafted. He was particularly responsible for those parts which formed the basis of the Poor Law Amendment Act of 1834. Chadwick also framed the Factory Act of 1833, which was put into effect by Inspectors. It has indeed been considered that these Inspectors and the Poor Law Commissioners represent the very beginning of the modern Civil Service. Moreover Public Audit started with the audit of the Poor Law Authorities, imposed by the Poor Law Amendment Act of 1834 and the grant-aid of rates, with grants to Local Authorities (to subsidise the expense of prosecutions), effectively began in 1833.

Finally, as to the book itself, the author has to confess to a predilection for 'things', whether they be buildings, machinery or pots and pans – not surprising in one who has spent his working life in museums, and is concerned with the material culture of the region. But material culture is just so much miscellaneous 'junk' if it lacks associated data, and so recollections, contemporary descriptions and Parliamentary Reports have been invoked to produce a more human approach to the dry and dusty objects which museums were once supposed to hoard.

To end on a personal note I should mention that more than once, whilst drafting this text, I have thought of the kind of letter which so many of us in museums, archive departments and libraries receive frequently from young students: 'I am studying Victorian England – please tell me everything you know . . .'!

It rapidly became clear to me that one just could not write with any degree of clarity and interest on such an enormously wide subject, within one volume, even when restricted to the region and the period. Instead I have chosen a number of topics which I hope will illuminate my subject, and then written essays within this framework. I hope that the result will stimulate readers to follow up some line or other, and the brief classified Reading List may help here.

2
THRIVING INDUSTRIES (I): MINERALS AND ENGINEERING

COAL MINING

Much of modern North East England, contrary to a belief still held elsewhere in the country, shows little sign of having been black and grimy and dotted with coal pits and pit heaps. One can travel miles without seeing either. The colliery buildings have been demolished and grassed, or even built, over and the pit heaps have been graded down and planted too. The poor terraces of pit cottages have been demolished or 'revitalised' and the only coal-mining now carried out is at the coast, from modern structures looking more like contemporary factories than collieries.

Within a generation the coal-mining industry, for long seen as the staple industry of Durham and Northumberland, has undergone remarkable changes. At 'vesting date' (1948) of the new National Coal Board, there were a hundred and twenty eight pits where now there are only eight, all of them at or near the coast. Large scale transfer of mining populations was one of the more humane ways of ameliorating this rapid run-down, as families, and indeed whole communities were invited to move into Nottinghamshire and other Midland coalfields where expansion was still possible.

It is often forgotten that an extractive industry like coal-mining has a finite life in any area, and coal has been mined from the North East since well before Elizabethan times. Indeed it is mentioned in the Boldon Book (that later equivalent of the Domesday Book, which recorded the state of County Durham in 1183). There coal is mentioned as being used by the smith of Bishopwearmouth.

One very interesting area of ancient mining in south west Durham, now preserved as a site of archaeological significance, is Cockfield Fell near Bishop Auckland. Here are traces of centuries of workings, one cutting into another. Old mines, worked by drift (ie the entrance running gradually down into the hillside following the seam), sometimes come across even older workings where the coal has been partially extracted and the

PLATE 1 *Pitmen playing Quoits*. Oil painting by Henry Perlee Parker, 1840 (Photo: Tyne & Wear Museums)

mine then deserted. Other early sites are frequently exposed by the modern method of 'open-cast' workings where all the overlying rocks are removed by modern machinery, to facilitate the extraction of the underlying coal seam.

Another early area of coal-mining was along the banks of the River Tyne, where seams 'outcropped', or were exposed edge-on along the river banks. By the eighteenth century mining had advanced to shafts sunk inland on either side of the Tyne, to get at the deeper seams. By the nineteenth century miners were getting to grips with the hazards of the early miner: water and gas. The deeper workings filled with water and regular pumping, made possible by the Newcomen steam engine, was essential. Steam engine pumping-houses, as well as powerful windmills, were to be seen around these growing coalfields though the only traces today are of two ruined engine houses: one on the south bank of the Tyne east of Gateshead at Friars Goose and the other at Haswell near Easington in north east County Durham. This latter site also draws attention to the so-called 'concealed' coalfield of East Durham, where the coal measures are overlain by Magnesian Limestone, making their exploitation more difficult until 1835 when the first deep shaft was sunk into coal. Flooding here was a serious problem and could only be properly tackled as mining engineering improved and pumping rates grew.

Whilst water could be drained or pumped away at a greater rate by the more powerful nineteenth century steam engine, the danger of explosion was sudden and ever-present in the mind of the miner. The history of explosions did not stop when Humphrey Davy, simultaneously with George Stephenson, invented the so-called safety lamp. Before that date Dr Clanny (whom we shall meet again when we come to the dreaded story of cholera in the Sunderland area) had experimented with a rather elaborate safety lamp in which the air to be burnt by the lamp – and that left after burning – was pumped through water, thereby separating the flame from its surrounding explosive atmosphere. Not unnaturally this lamp proved too unwieldy for practical use.

A terrible explosion at Felling Colliery (on the south bank of the Tyne) in 1812, was publicised by a sermon by Rev. John Hodgson which was subsequently printed. This led to the formation of a *Society for the Prevention of Accidents in Mines*, which in turn invited Humphrey Davy, as the notable scientist of his day, to bring his mind to bear on the problems of explosions. Independently George Stephenson worked on the same problem and both men came up effectively with the same answer: separating the flame from the atmosphere by a metal gauze or sheet of perforated metal. John Buddle, a northern mining engineer of note, also pondered on the problem of gas and devised a system of driving fresh air round the coal workings by means of doors which blocked off shorter routes, thereby causing the fresh air to circulate up to each coal face and thus

13

PLATE 2 Dr W. Reid Clanny (1776–1850), designer of a safety lamp and author of an early description of cholera

ensuring a thorough ventilation through the workings.

Not every apparent benefit, however, is entirely beneficial and Buddle's system of 'traps' or wooden doors, though extremely helpful in improving air circulation, led to the need for 'trapper boys'. Young lads of ten or eleven years of age were required to operate those doors through which the 'putters' pushed their tubs of coal and hence a new class of young workers was created. Thus an improvement in safety had led to a demand for young lads to work long hours underground.

The prime method of moving the air in Buddle's design was a ventilation furnace: simply an enormous coal fire near the foot of the shaft, and contrived such that the rising volume of hot air carried with it air that had been routed round the workings. At the surface the furnace-shaft terminated in a chimney, cowled and fan-tailed to assist in the extraction of the foul air.

As the industrial development of the country expanded, so did the demand for coal increase through the century. The region's coal trade grew from two million tons per annum in 1800 to forty five million tons per annum by 1900. Workers poured into the area, not all of course for coal mining, for the iron and steel and shipbuilding and allied trades were all expanding around the same time. Men came from the surrounding countryside

14

Another more matter-of-fact memorial was an Act, passed in the same year, compelling all new collieries to construct two separate shafts, thus removing the chance of any similar accident being repeated.

Coking

Coal, particularly from seams in West Durham, was especially suitable for coking: the production of a relatively pure form of carbon which provided a smokeless fuel and was of growing demand in the steel industry as well as that other growth area of the nineteenth century – the brewing industry.

Since the seventeenth century coke had been made in the northern coalfield by heating coal in the absence of air, driving off the 'volatiles': chemicals in the form of gases such as methane, carbon dioxide and carbon monoxide, benzene, coal tar, ammonia etc. In the earlier years of the nineteenth century these fumes were still being vented to atmosphere, adding to the overall atmospheric pollution of the period. However it was eventually realised that these gases had a value of their own and by the 1880s coking ovens were being designed which collected these chemicals as 'by-products'. By so doing the whole construction of the ovens changed from the so-called 'beehive ovens' of the early years – like 8ft diameter upturned pudding basins of special heat-resisting brick – to the later vertical ovens which were almost continuous in their operation and permitted the gases to be efficiently drawn off, separated and purified. Only one coking plant of this kind still operates in the region, at the Monkton Works near Hebburn, on the south side of the Tyne. As for the beehive oven, a few ruins remain preserved in West Durham, for example at Tow Law and Butterknowle.

Coal Transport

As will become clear when the history of public railways is examined, the early transport of coal in North East England helped to encourage the development of railway systems. Because coal is bulky but relatively light, large wagons could be hauled across country by horses on well-graduated tracks, and these had become known as 'Newcastle Roads' by the eighteenth century.

Below ground, in the mine, the coal was at first transported to the pit-bottom by sledges, drawn by boys, but by the nineteenth century 'tubs' were being used: small four wheeled trucks just high enough to match the thickness of the seam and so save the expense of higher passages for their movement. At one time pushed by young men known as 'putters', these were later drawn by pit-ponies. Once they had been drawn to the surface

PLATE 5 A cokeman on the 'bench' alongside a bank of 'beehive' coke ovens in County Durham, c. 1900

by the steam-hauled 'cage', the tubs were tipped and the coal was sorted by hand, to remove pieces of stone. The coal was then run into bigger trucks which originally – in the eighteenth and early nineteenth century – would hold about 53cwts of coal, known as a *chaldron* (roughly 2.7 tonnes). None of these very early wagons exist, but by the second half of the century, a larger version was constructed which was suitable for haulage by stationary haulage engine or by early locomotive. Of these, only about twenty or so now exist out of thousands which were to be found only forty or fifty years ago. They are mostly preserved at Beamish and are used as the symbol of that regional museum.

These 'black wagons' or 'chaldron wagons' – once so typical of the region – were clearly so suitable that their use continued well into this century, carrying coal from the pit head to the coal staithes at river or port whence the coal was exported. Practically all trace of this enormous trade has also disappeared and one of the few remaining pieces of machinery is a *coal drop* from Seaham Harbour, once used to lower a coal wagon down to the boat, so as to minimise coal breakage. (This is preserved at Beamish, but not yet re-erected.)

The wagonways, or specially constructed rail-routes, from collieries to staithes criss-crossed the whole region and a few can still be traced on the map and identified by the persistent walker. One of the earlier routes, that of the well-known 'Stockton & Darlington' railway of 1825, can still be traced along its western stretch from Witton as far as Shildon and the stone abutments of the bridge which crossed the River Gaunless are still preserved. The bridge itself, the world's first iron railway bridge, is preserved at the National Railway Museum at York.

Once the coal wagons had reached Shildon, having been drawn there by a mixture of stationary haulage engines on the hills and horses on the level stretches, the wagons were made up into trains and drawn by steam locomotive ('locomotive engines' as they were originally called, to distinguish them from the stationary ones), along to the river at Stockton and later to Middlesbrough. The first locomotive to steam on this historic route was 'Locomotion', designed and built by George Stephenson. The original 1825 machine (a little altered over the years, of course) is preserved in the North Road Station at Darlington, and a replica can often be seen excitingly in steam at Beamish.

Housing the Pitmen
As the rate of coal-mining grew throughout the second half of last century, so new workers poured into the coalfield, as we have already seen. Housing had to be urgently provided and mine-owners often constructed this as they sank the shafts and built the pit-top engine-houses and workshops. Indeed the very stone which was dug out as the shaft was sunk was frequently used to construct the first nearby terrace of cottages and

the name 'Stone Row' or 'Sinkers' Row' may indicate this.

Although in later years it has become habit to decry the poor housing so provided, the fact remains that many of these cottages were – by the standards of the day – relatively roomy, often provided with adequate land for gardening and leek-growing and certainly well-heated with 'free' or concessionary coal. That they were often well-furnished is also now agreed, for many mining families spent money on furniture and furnishings of which they were proud. One witness, giving evidence to the Children's Employment Commission in 1842 testified that:

> within the last ten years collieries have been opened in very many places between the Weare and the Tees; and wherever a colliery has been opened a large village or town has been instantly built close to it, with a population almost exclusively of the colliery people, beer-shop people and small shopkeepers. The houses have either been built by the colliery proprietors, or have been so by others and let on lease to them, that they might locate their people.

The village of Coxhoe, close to Clarence Hetton Colliery, extends about a mile along both sides of a public road, but the houses are not continuous, there being a break every 10 or 12 houses to make a thoroughfare to the streets which run off right and left. Throughout the whole village there are seldom more than 10 or 12 in an unbroken line, so that it is easy to get from one place to another. The cottages are built with stone plastered with lime, with blue slate roofs, and all appear exceedingly neat, and as like to one another as so many soldiers are like to each other. There is no yard in front of any of them, or any yard behind, or dust-hole, or convenience of any kind, or any small building, such as is usually considered indispensable and necessary. Yet there was no unpleasant nuisance, no filth, nor ashes, nor decaying vegetables. All was swept and clean. It was explained that carts came round early every morning with small coals which were left at every house, and the same carts after depositing the coals at every door, moved round and came along the backs of the houses and received the ashes and all other matters, and carried them off and deposited them in a heap in an adjoining field.

The dimensions of the houses in this village were as follows: Front room, length 14ft × breadth 14ft 10in. Back room, length 14ft × breadth 10ft, communicating with which is a pantry 6½ft × 3ft. Upstairs is a bedroom partly made up by a wall and a sloping roof. The ground floor is made of clay, sand and lime. The height of the front wall is generally 13ft 10ins: the height of the back wall is less. The whole expense of erecting such a cottage is £52. It could be rented for £5 a year.

The population was estimated at about 5,000. The work people of several collieries live in the village. It was stated that there were altogether 30 beer-shops in the village. There was no Church of England church or chapel, but here as everywhere else in the collier district, the Wesleyans and Primitive Methodists had established their meetings, and had many adherents.

I was conducted into one of the cottages and it seemed very comfortable ... This house, like most of the collier's houses in the several villages, was very clean and well furnished. In fine weather the doors are frequently left open, and in passing along in front, in every house may be seen an eight-day clock, a chest of drawers, with brass handles and ornaments, reaching from the floor to the ceiling, a four-poster bed with a large coverlet, composed of squares of printed calico tastefully arranged, and bright saucepans, and other tin-ware utensils displayed on the walls. Most of the women take pains to make themselves, as well as their houses, look very agreeable. It must be admitted that there are exceptions and there are some women who are neither so attentive to themselves, their children or their houses, as their husbands have a right to expect.

In the collier villages are many little brick buildings used as public ovens. Small coals are put into them, and burnt until the ovens are thoroughly heated, and then the coals and ashes are swept out, and the bread put in, and by the heat of the bricks it is well baked.

Although there is not one inch of land attached to the houses in villages, there is frequently a large field divided by stakes of wood, into small plots of ground, which the colliers cultivate as potatoe gardens. The usual size maybe about a twentieth part of an acre.

A large number of these pit villages, especially in the Durham coalfield, having sprung up in the middle of last century, as pits were sunk, have now completely disappeared again. A few, chosen at random and still remembered by many people, include that part of Esh Winning where perhaps a hundred houses were built along three sides of a large square with the engine pond and allotments in the middle and the pit and part of its tip along the southern side of the square. Another was Leasingthorne where Stone Row followed round a bend in the local road, and nearby were four terraces of wooden-built houses (obviously not expected to last long, but occupied for the larger part of a century). Here were Oak, Ash, Yew and Thorn Terraces. On the other side of the A1 East Howle does not now exist even as a name on the map. Its pit 'fired' (ie suffered a tremendous explosion) in 1901 and never worked again, but the village lingered on for many years. Renee Chaplin remembers the village as a girl. It had two chapels – a 'Primitive' and a 'Wesleyan' as well as a 'tin' Church of England building. Here also were Bottom and Top Railway Streets, one of the latter with a shop in a front room run by a Mrs

Fairless. Pit Street had two rows; there was Front Street with a few rows of pit houses below, a shop in the corner of Front Street run by Manny Stevenson and a Good Templars' Hall (ie Temperance).

One could write at length about many more of these pit villages which appeared, flourished and have now disappeared. It is only possible to reconstruct this lost landscape (no thing of beauty it must be agreed) by reference to elderly memories, old photographs and early editions of large-scale Ordnance Survey maps.

IRON, LEAD AND STONE

Iron and Steel

Had one been writing about iron and steel in the North East only ten years ago, Consett Iron Works would have provided a central topic, continuously operational since 1840 and with early features and structures still to be seen, yet thoroughly updated in most essential respects. Sited high on a scarp the blast furnaces and coking plant could be seen from miles around, throwing out their dramatic clouds of smoke and steam.

Consett was the last of the great Durham and Northumberland ironworks to remain in production and linked back to that time a century ago when blast furnaces were to be found in so many apparently isolated places, usually attracted by the presence of coal or iron ore.

Throughout the first quarter of the nineteenth century the only blast furnace in the area was Lemington, founded around 1797 to use local ores. But from that time blast furnaces were established steadily: Birtley in 1827 and Wylam, Ridsdale & Bellingham in the 1830s; Stanhope, Brinkburn, Haltwhistle, Consett, Walker and Witton Park and Tow Law in the 1840s and Elswick, Newcastle (1864). Teesside's first blast furnace was erected at Middlesbrough in 1851 and by 1874 there were 139 furnaces in blast there and by 1896 Teesside was producing almost a third of the nation's iron output.

Essential ingredients of Victorian industrial growth were iron and steel: for rail track, for locomotives, for steam engines, for bridges, for ships. The need for the raw material was insatiable and the inauguration in 1868 of the Newcastle Iron and Steel Association was a token of the region's role in that industry.

One by one these huge works have closed and been cleared and today little remains to be seen apart from the occasional overgrown wasteheap of an earlier site such as at Spennymoor; later sites have been even more radically cleared. Consett Iron Works was the last to operate in Durham and Northumberland. At first it had its own ironstone shaft and coal was readily on hand, as the first blast furnaces were erected and rolling mills laid down. After a time, however, it was found that the local ironstone was becoming scarce and expensive to work and eventually Cleveland became

PLATE 6 Blast furnaces at Consett, c. 1880, with pig-beds in the foreground

the prime source. Yet the very existence of this large works encouraged its continuing use even many years later when practically all raw materials had to be brought by rail and the finished product was similarly removed.

Cleveland came a little later into the Victorian iron business, but rapidly caught up and overtook the rest of the region. In the 1830s small quantities of ironstone were brought from Grosmont, but it was not until the next decade that shipments became important. Bolckow and Vaughan, for instance (names we shall come across later in connection with Middlesbrough) put up new furnaces at Witton Park, Auckland in Co. Durham in 1846, originally to use local bands of ironstone, but soon supplied from the Whitby area. These works, incidentally, no doubt owed their construction to the rise in the price of pigiron (the raw product from the blast furnaces), which advanced in 1845 from 35s (£1.75) to £6 per ton, as new markets were opened up for railway construction, the building of iron steamships and even gas and waterworks. It was around this time too that the Derwent Iron Company built seven furnaces at Consett.

However it was in June 1850 that the Cleveland 'break through' took place when John Vaughan found a bed of ironstone sixteen feet thick in the Eston Hills. By September that year the first seven tons were brought down to the road nearby, carted to Cargo Fleet and sent by rail to the

Witton Park Ironworks. In January 1851 a railway line had been laid and become operational. Some idea of the rate of growth can be sensed from the fact that the Eston mines were originally required to produce 1,000 tons of ironstone per week, but before the permanent rails had been laid production was running at 10,000 to 12,000 tons per week. In that year the number of blast furnaces in the north east was 83, of which 66 were 'in blast', producing 8,490 tons of pigiron per week, from which 2,660 tons of malleable iron were being produced in rolling mills in the region. Cleveland's share was by then 3,970 tons of pigiron from 29 furnaces.

Apart from abandoned mines and spoil heaps and rapidly changing mining villages, little remains to reveal the Cleveland area's former significance though Rushpool Hall, near Saltburn on Sea, is constructed of ironstone blocks, having been built in 1862 for John Bell, one of the ironmasters. It is a rare monument to the industry.

Terraces of iron-workers' homes, now isolated at such places as Tow Law, Spennymoor, and Tudhoe in Co Durham, or Skinningrove in the Cleveland hills, have generally been 'modernised' and visually altered by the addition of larger windows, part-glazed doors and often new roofs too. The visual effect of the spectacular growth of Middlesbrough, to be referred to elsewhere, has also been negated by demolition.

At such rural backwaters as Bellingham or Redesdale in Northumberland, a few houses and ruins, some suitable for archaeological excavation, are all that remain of ironworks which flourished but briefly before Teesside overtook them, only to shrink in turn. The Redesdale ruins are probably the largest ironwork remains in the region, being one of the earliest (1839). It is often the case that remains on such a scale are early in date since later works are generally demolished as soon as they go out of use.

The Lead Industry

As we have already observed, modern industry strives to clear its sites at the end of their working life but, fortunately for the industrial archaeologist, this was not so in the nineteenth century and whilst many sites have, of course, been robbed of their machinery, the earth and stone work often persists. This has particularly been the case with the lead mining industry of the northern dales and the seeking-eye can trace much, from huge gashes on the hillsides where 'hushing' was done (washing away the soil and vegetation in the search for a lead vein), to tips indicating old mining sites and – most interesting of all – the long winding surface-tunnels of the lead-flues or 'pipes' which run up the hillsides from smelting works to the hilltops where the fumes would be dispersed (though not particularly healthily even there!).

We should not, of course, blame the nineteenth century employer for not carrying out safety requirements such as we would expect today, but it has to be noted that little care was expended on the health of work

PLATE 7 Outside Rampgill leadmine, Nenthead, c. 1900

PLATE 8 Lead smelting at Rookhope smeltmill

people and on the preservation of the environment. These flues typify this.

As lead was smelted (the process of extracting the metal from the excavated ore), the heat caused some of the metal to volatilise and dissipate along with the fumes. Since the fumes also contained sulphur dioxide, the resultant emission was poisonous in the extreme and areas of moorland, even now, are not good for sheep grazing. However, the cause of greatest concern to the industrialist was the loss of the volatalised lead and it was found that running a 'pipe' or long chimney-like structure up a hillside would cause the lead to cool and become deposited, along with the soot, on the walls of this flue. It was then a labourer's job periodically to walk down the flue (when it was not in use, of course) and sweep out the deposits which could then be retreated to extract the lead. Such men probably died early, for we now know that lead vapour is very dangerous.

A dramatic piece of Victorian machinery associated with the lead industry has already been mentioned : the large water wheel at Killhope in Weardale. This provided power, turned by water from a large reservoir uphill from the mill, for the crushing of the ore, before washing and then smelting. This site is now being preserved and partly restored and is well worth a visit. An adjoining picnic-site makes it into a good stopping-place for a day out, very different from a hundred years ago when men, women and boys toiled here, mostly out in the open despite the weather.

Stone Quarrying

Whilst much less significant nowadays, stone was an essential material in nineteenth-century England for building purposes, decoration and even, when cut into rollers or wheels, for crushing and grinding.

Limestone was burned in lime kilns to produce 'quicklime' which was then mixed with water for building purposes, or for use on the land as a relatively soluble fertiliser. Every building site would have a lime pit where the quicklime was 'slaked' with water and then mixed with sand to provide building mortar. Equally lime kilns were built on any limestone outcrop reasonably near a road or track. Many of these, quite attractive to us, now that they no longer smoke and pollute our atmosphere, can be seen in parts of Durham and Northumberland. Some would be purely local and used by farmers for their own and their neighbours' use whilst bigger ones – such as those not far from the railway line near Ferryhill – would serve much wider markets.

Another limestone product was the so-called Frosterley 'marble': actually a fossilferous and dark-coloured limestone. A very large quarry lies to the north of the main road through Weardale, as it passes the village of Frosterley and this highly decorative stone delighted the Victorian eye and was used for fireplace surrounds, special areas of paving etc. especially in churches and particularly Durham Cathedral. Pieces of it can still be found lying in the waste heaps at the foot of this quarry. Wherever a good quality sandstone outcropped, it would be quarried locally for building purposes and many large houses still have a small quarry nearby, whence the building materials came. Good examples are Blagdon and Belsay, where attractive gardens have subsequently been established in these sheltered hollows. At Slaley in Northumberland a particularly fine and very fissile flaggy sandstone is still quarried and used for special pavements and the like. A good example can be seen on the floor of the Waiting Hall of Rowley Station, as rebuilt at Beamish Open Air Museum.

However the stone which took the name of Newcastle over the world was a fine gritty sandstone quarried on either bank of the Tyne, but particularly on Gateshead Fell. The phrase, now little used today, but commonly recalled fifty years ago was 'A Scot, a flea and a Newcastle grindstone you'll find the world over'. This stone was cut in large bedded pieces and then shaped and pivotted to be used either as a 'pulpstone' for crushing such material as sugar cane, or for grinding and sharpening tools. We are fortunate to have an interesting recollection of an elderly quarryman of Gateshead: (Bill Louther, born 1900, recorded 1974):

There's 50ft of what we call Rag (stone – but not good enough to make building stone of) at Springwell before you come to the main rock – they used to borst it up for road making – give it some geligniting – smash it up – it was all handling then.

But when you got to the stone, it was all naturally flat stuff – maybe nine inches or a foot thick – they used to make grindstones out of it. You had to get deep down before you came to the big panels such as Kenton Stone which was a very coarse stone – not much good for pulp stones. Some stone was used in paper mills for crushing wood pulp, and they used to send them to Japan, early in the first war. But all that fizzled out and we started to send them to Norway – used to ship them to Bergen.

It was rough – now they've got the modern machinery – sometimes we had to drill the holes by hand in the rock – now they've got compressed air drills – they can drill a hole a foot a minute. On the main rock, if you wanted to cut off the face – you put your straight edge on: holes about 2 feet apart, 2 inch diameter holes and then you got them drilled to where you thought the bottom of the panel was – (beds for it to slide off). You had to put your reamer in – it was a flattened drill but you had an old drill machine with the ratchet taken out – it didn't revolve, it hammered down – it made a groove down each side of the hole – and when you charged the hole with gunpowder and get a bit grass: stuff it down the hole to about 18 inches off the charge, then stem it tight up to the top of the hole and when the powder was ignited it flushed up that cut and pushed the stone forward – may be one inch, or two inches – a whole block of stone. I've cut a piece 40 feet long off the face – then you had to cut crossover after that – just big enough for your crane to lift. [He remembers quarrying stone for various buildings – the biggest job of all was for the County Hall at Durham – he quarried all the stone for that – 'the last one I quarried was for a bank in Grey Street'.]

I was just getting the block stone – and then it was cut up in the big sawmill.

For grindstones, after you got your slab, you put them flat on the banker, put your compass on – then hammered it round with a square-faced hammer, just to that mark, and once you got that you had to scappell them down with a quarry pick, using a set square to make sure you didn't go in under the sides (ie kept the cut surface vertical) and when you got halfway down you got the crane to turn them over and then you hammered that other back – that was the quarryman's job on the banker – and the next job was to put a hole in the centre, take them down to the lathe, – put them on the lathe shaft – key things tight and the turner used to turn all the rough off it with a pointed steel bar, then a flat tool to plane it.

They used to send grindstones all over the world. They came from Springwell, Eighton Banks, Windy Nook – a nice grinding grit – especially Windy Nook. Scissor makers used to come to the quarry and run their finger over the stone to make sure of the grit – they didn't want to hone (polish) the scissor blades – they wanted to cut them sharp.

I started work at almost 14, at Eighton Banks at the beginning of the first war and worked in the quarries till October 1968 – 54 years. When I started you got 2d an hour – and you had to work till you were 21 before you got the full rate – 10d an hour (labourers had 6d). You started at half past six in the morning, till half past four at night – except Monday – and you started at eight on a Monday because they thought you might be in a bad fettle with the booze on a Monday. Quarrymen had an hour for their dinner, labourers had a half hour. You carried your sandwiches in your red bait hankerchief and got your tea warmed on the blacksmith's fire.

You had to work for your living – if you didn't work you didn't keep your job – you were pushed out and someone else came in your place.

Today a quarry on Wrekenton Fell produces small stone for decorative fireplaces and the like and this is the sole reminder of another prosperous Victorian industry apart from photographs and a preserved 'pulpstone'. This latter was found a few years ago when it was unearthed from a wasteheap on the Fell, during excavations for a new building. It is practically complete and is now preserved at Beamish, The North of England Open Air Museum.

ENGINEERS AND ENGINEERING

Unlike the coal industry, of which one might say that the history of the region was in large part the history of that industry, one cannot so readily claim the same for engineering, for names like Telford, Brunel or Whitworth have nothing to do with the North East. On the other hand, Stephenson (George and Robert), Armstrong, Palmer, Parsons and Hawthorn are only a few names of men who helped to build up this region as a centre of heavy engineering by the end of the nineteenth century. Apart from the armaments and hydraulic machinery produced by Armstrong's Elswick works, the emphasis tended to be towards either railways or shipbuilding: the two real strengths of the Victorian north eastern engineers. And both these stemmed from coal-mining: particularly the need to transport the coal away from the collieries and then away from the region.

For example a Newcastle colliery company decided to have constructed an iron collier, and the *John Bowes*, launched in 1852, was built by the General Iron Screw Colliery company which had been formed by Charles Palmer and his brother George. Although the first iron vessel had been built as early as 1787 and the first iron ship built in the North East was the *Star*, of South Shields (1839), it was a young ambitious man, Charles Palmer, who recognised that in iron vessels, propelled by steam, lay the future success of both the coal and the shipping industries.

Naturally not everyone was convinced and since the *John Bowes* cost £10,000 to build, as against £1,000 for a sailing collier, this is not surprising. However on her very first voyage to London, she proved her worth, for she was loaded with 650 tons of coal in four hours, took forty eight hours to reach the capital, one day to discharge and two days for the return journey. In five days she had done as much work as would have taken a sailing vessel two months.

The *John Bowes* was also an innovator in other respects, for she was the first such ship to use water ballast, pumped out by the engine which powered the screw. This not only reduced time and labour, for solid ballast was expensive to handle, but cut down the problem of the ever-growing ballast hills along the banks of the Tyne. This must also have had some effect on the subsequent shrinkage of the pottery and glass industries which had depended so much on cheap raw materials brought to the region as ballast.

Although many years later than the *John Bowes*, it is relevant here to mention *Turbinia*: another 'first' for the region, in the form of turbine propulsion. Charles Parsons, youngest son of the third Earl of Rosse, had served a four-year apprenticeship at the Elswick Works of Sir William Armstrong before joining the Gateshead firm of Clarke, Chapman and Company, where he was put in charge of their newly-formed electrical department. His first work on turbines was therefore in connection with

PLATE 9 'Turbinia' at speed, 1897; designed and built by Charles Parsons

electrical generators, but he soon seems to have appreciated the part that turbines could play in marine propulsion. In 1894, after a quarrel with Clarke, Chapman, he severed his connection and set up his own firm, The Marine Steam Turbine Company, at Heaton. By 1896 he had built *Turbinia*, yet although he had kept the Admiralty informed of his difficulties and his successes, their lordships showed little real interest, despite the remarkable speeds which had been achieved in tests. It is said that Parsons, therefore, decided upon a dramatic demonstration of *Turbinia's* capabilities and that his chance came with the Spithead Naval Review of 1897. There the solid pomp and splendour was shaken by his tiny ship whipping up and down the lines at the unprecedented speed of more than 30 knots. The Admiralty was convinced and turbine propulsion was soon accepted, though in all fairness one should add that perhaps this 1897 Review incident was not quite as 'cheeky' as is popularly supposed.

Over succeeding years the very future of *Turbinia* herself was in threat and in 1926 her after-half was cut off and sent to the Science Museum in London, whilst her bow, wheelhouse and boiler remained in Newcastle. After further vicissitudes her safety seemed secure when her after-half was reunited with her bow; a happy reunion which took place in 1961 and was celebrated by a special building constructed alongside the temporary home of the Newcastle Museum of Science and Industry. Since then that temporary building has ceased to house museum collections, and the future of *Turbinia* has once more been in the balance. At the time of writing one is hopeful that another, perhaps more permanent, resting-place has been found, but this is not yet certain.

As for mechanical skills doubtless in one form or another these have existed in the region for as long as coal-mining has required more than mere horses – and man-power. One of the earliest nineteenth century engineers here was Phineas Crowther who, in 1800, patented a particularly efficient stationary steam engine which was rapidly adopted for winding at collieries. Only one example now remains, though a hundred or more must have been built at one time or another. This is one built by Joicey and Company in 1855 which has been re-sited, in its original stone-built engine-house, at the North of England Open Air Museum at Beamish. It may once more be seen in steam there, having been extensively restored and fitted in late 1986 with a good steam supply.

By the end of the eighteenth and the beginning of the nineteenth century engineering works and foundries were beginning to be established in the north east. Amongst these were Hawks Crawshay (Gateshead, 1747); Murray and Company (Chester le Street, 1793); John Abbot & Co., (Gateshead, late eighteenth century); Losh, Wilson and Bell (Walker 1807); R. & W. Hawthorn (Newcastle, 1817); R. Stephenson and Company (Newcastle, 1823); Gilkes Wilson and Company (Middlesbrough, 1844); W. G. Armstrong & Company (Elswick, 1847); Morrison and Company (Newcastle, 1853); Thompson and Company (Newcastle, 1856); Joy and Company (Middlesbrough, 1862).

Little remains of most of these works and for evidence of their existence we must seek examples of their products, not all of course to be found in the region or indeed in this country.

R. & W. Hawthorn had a works on a very restricted site on the river banks below Newcastle. Although little can now be traced of these works, the magnificent beam engines still working (on occasion) at the Ryhope Pumping Station, are a tribute to their engineering skills. Built in 1868, these engines have beams over 33ft long and a fly wheel of 24ft diameter. They were built to pump water from the underlying strata, for the Sunderland and South Shields Water Company. They are preserved by a Trust and demonstrated from time to time.

Armstrong's works at Elswick, two miles upstream of the early stone bridge at Newcastle, built hydraulic machinery for the Tower Bridge at London (use now discontinued), the Douglas Swing Bridge in the Isle of Man, as well as the Swing Bridge at Newcastle. The actual Douglas bridge of 1895 was replaced in 1979, though the bridge still swings, and the

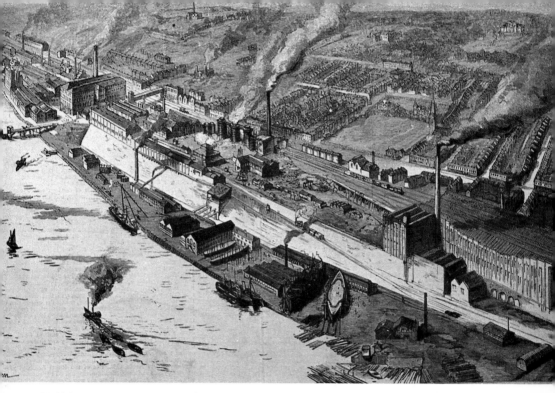

PLATE 10 Armstrong's Works at Elswick, west of Newcastle upon Tyne. From *The Illustrated London News*, July 16th 1887

original hydraulic equipment, supplied by Sir W.G. Armstrong, Mitchell and Company Limited was due to be modified in 1987. The Newcastle Swing Bridge replaced, in 1876, the old stone bridge and permitted vessels to travel upstream beyond the bridge, thus enabling Armstrong to begin warship construction at his Elswick Works. But the increasing scale of such work seems to have inhibited this once more and new works were established further downstream at Walker.

In addition, some of the more significant memorials on which we depend for reminders of this nineteenth century industry include the High Level Bridge at Newcastle (1844–9) and Newcastle's Central Station (1846–50). A few pieces of heavy machinery also survive such as 'Locomotion' at Darlington (1825), the Coal Drop from Seaham Harbour now at Beamish (c. 1860) and the giant water wheel at Killhope in Weardale (c. 1870).

Various pieces of hydraulic machinery exist around the region, one of the more unusual ones being an agricultural silo built with hydraulic rams to compress the silage, at a farm near Cragside. Off Howdon Road in Tynemouth is a hydraulic accumulator tower of 1882, built for the Tyne Improvement Commissioners. The equipment remains inside a sandstone tower and is now the only surviving example on the Tyne.

A small example of an agricultural steam engine by Gilkes Wilson

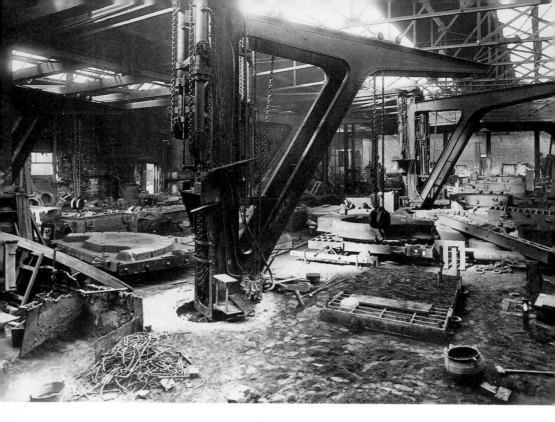

PLATE 11 An iron foundry, c. 1898, including two hydraulic cranes, at Swinney's Engineering Works, Morpeth

PLATE 12 Decorative cast iron at Tynemouth

FIG 1 Plan of 'The Lathe and Tool Shop of Stephenson's Locomotive Manufactory at Newcastle upon Tyne'. From *The Illustrated London News*, 1894

and Company of Middlesbrough of 1852 worked on a farm at St Helens Auckland until around 1900. It has now been dismantled and transferred to the regional Open Air Museum at Beamish where plans are now in hand for it to be restored and demonstrated once more. It is of an interesting 'upright' design, and a notable demonstration of how stationary engines had reduced in scale since the beginning of the century.

Following this observation for a moment leads one on to mention Professor Weighton, the first Professor of Engineering at Armstrong College (now of course the University of Newcastle). One of his strengths was the design of more efficient steam engines and he designed a superb four-cylinder marine-type engine, with multiple variability of adjustment. With the aid of this some significant research work was carried out in the early years of this century, on more efficient steam power – just at the time, however, that the internal combustion engine was replacing steam as a prime mover. This engine is now preserved by the Tyne and Wear Museum Service at Newcastle.

Yet despite all these scientific and technical developments, life in a nineteenth century factory could be remarkably dangerous. The illustration (Fig. 1) from *The Illustrated London News* shows part of Robert Stephenson's Locomotive manufactory: the lathe and tool shop in 1894.

PLATE 13 Machine shop, Shildon locomotive works

Amongst this moving mass of belts, pulleys and machinery, what could not happen! A vivid quotation from a Report of H.M. Factory Inspectors (republished recently to commemorate 150 years of health and safety inspection) makes clear:

> A man named Campbell, the overlooker of the room in which it happened, was mending a belt which was held for him by a little girl, another girl named Burns, 14 or 15 years old, incautiously running between them and an upright revolving shaft, got her clothes entangled with the shaft, and whilst Campbell was endeavouring to extricate her, the girl who had been holding the belt for him, being frightened, threw it down and ran away. The belt, getting entangled with the teeth of the shaft, caught Campbell also and both he and little Burns were drawn up, and before the machinery could be stopped almost crushed to pieces.

One of the few heavy pieces of manufacturing machinery to remain with us in the North East is a huge steam hammer used at Darlington Forge during the late nineteenth century. It was used to forge ship's rudders, having been built for this purpose at Glasgow in 1883. In 1901 it was sold to a works in Rotherham, but has now come back to County Durham, where it provides a 'ceremonial arch' at the entrance to Beamish, the Open Air Museum.

3

THRIVING INDUSTRIES (II): CHEMICALS, POTTERY AND GLASS

THE CHEMICAL INDUSTRIES

The Alkali Trade on Tyneside

Modern Tyneside no longer has any heavy chemical works. To the north, in south Northumberland, a number of pharmaceutical manufacturers have been established on 'greenfield' sites and Imperial Chemical Industries still thrives at Billingham and Teesside.

Yet though possibly the only remaining trace of a once great and successful, if unhealthy, Victorian Tyneside chemical industry is Proctor and Gamble's soap-works (originally Hedley's), there was a time when the 'alkali trade' seemed to have a great future there.

It is now generally supposed that one of the major features of the so-called Industrial Revolution in Britain was the application of mechanisation to the making of textiles. But it was not as simple as this, for the production of textiles required large quantities of soap, bleach and dyes. Moreover packaging in various forms expanded and glass bottles were needed in ever-growing quantities.

A little-known chemical revolution followed close on the heels of the better known Industrial Revolution and much of the pioneer work leading to the establishment of a chemical industry took place on Tyneside. Unfortunately for the purpose of this book it was an industry that has left little in the way of material remains, except perhaps for the occasional tips and spoil heaps which are nowadays opened up from time to time by accident during building excavations. One particular branch of the chemical industry was known as the alkali trade. The importance of this substance can be understood when one realises that *soap* was made with alkali and fat, and *glass* was made with alkali, sand and lime. Thus alkali lay at the heart of materials needed for the growth of so much industrial development at the beginning of the nineteenth century. Incidentally we may note here that the north east forged another link in all this, for the breed of Durham Shorthorn cattle was at first encouraged by the need for animal fat and the early examples of this once-well-known breed were enormous, in order to produce still more fat for soap and tallow (the latter for candles).

Turning now to Tyneside itself, it was – at the beginning of our period – a difficult and, in places, dangerous river for shipping. At its mouth lay a bar, in places no more than six feet deep, and even over the bar and into the river the narrowness of the channel and its twisting course made it difficult to navigate. The banks were not readily accessible to shipping, hence the use of keels and other small vessels plying between the staithes and the sea-going vessels, which had to wait further downstream.

Paradoxically it was probably the bad state of the river which encouraged new industries for, if river traffic had flowed freely much more of the mined coal from the northern coalfield would have been exported readily and fetched reasonable prices in London and on the continent. As it was, coal had to be literally handled from staith to keel and from keel to collier. Hence only large pieces were worth moving and the 'small coals' were left as near waste. From this sprang the cheap production of salt, by boiling seawater in enormous iron 'pans' and later the production of glass which could no longer be produced elsewhere by wood-fuel, as that grew scarcer. As we have seen glassmakers needed alkali and the early process for making alkali required coal both as fuel and as raw material. And once the alkali was available, the production of other chemicals followed.

Salt was a basic commodity for many chemicals and in the eighteenth century had been manufactured locally by boiling seawater. But the heavy tax on salt was very limiting. However the price of north eastern salt began to lose against that produced in Cheshire and after the repeal of the salt tax in 1823 rock salt from Cheshire was brought to the Tyne in growing quantities, by canal and sea. In the 1860s salt began to be worked in the Billingham and Haverton Hill areas and this may now be seen as the beginning of the movement of the chemical industry from Tyneside to the Tees.

Copperas or iron pyrites was an interesting raw material, sometimes called 'coal brasses' and known also as 'fool's gold' from its golden appearance. It is a compound of iron and sulphur and proved to be a source of sulphur, eventually used in the production of sulphuric acid; one of the most essential of basic chemicals to this day. In the older process pyrites were spread out on the ground to weather for several years before being roasted. In later years pyrites were heated directly in an oven, connected to lead-lined chambers in which the acid was concentrated.

Alkali resulted from two stages of chemical reactions: sulphuric acid and common salt produced 'saltcake', whilst freeing hydrochloric acid gas. The coal, limestone and saltcake were heated together to produce soda or 'alkali'. Because the evidence of the escape of hydrochloric acid gas was clear to the public, the manufacturers were obliged to deal with the problem. At first they attempted to suggest that not only was the gas harmless, but that it was indeed positively healthy. A remarkable plea is to be seen in a letter to *Chemical News*, 1860 from 'an old alkali manufacturer', under the heading 'Is hydrochloric acid a cure for consumption?':

> The foreman of our upper works had a lodger, a young man, by trade a ship carpenter, who was very ill and much reduced, evidently in a consumption. One fine day he asked leave to go up in the barge to the upper works, where he remained while the barge was being loaded, all the time breathing an atmosphere highly charged with hydrochloric acid gas. He experienced great relief from this, and often repeated his visit. He regained his strength rapidly, so that he was soon able to walk to the works, so eventually I gave him employment there and he became a strong robust workman . . .

Attempts were also made to bubble the gas through water to absorb it. But although the gas is relatively soluble, this method did not bring the gas into contact with the water long enough for it to dissolve fully. The problem was tackled particularly by Anthony Clapham of Friar's Goose and William Losh at his Walker works, but without success. Eventually William Gossage of St Helen's devised a tower packed with coke down which water trickled while the gas was passed upwards. These so-called Gossage towers were usually built of good flagstone and with the passing of the Alkali Act in 1863, their use became general. Indeed this Act is a good example of legislation following unofficial developments rather than being original.

The acid thus obtained was converted to chlorine and this was combined with slaked lime to produce bleaching powder: a substance in great demand from the textile industry. Although essential, bleaching powder was clearly unhealthy for those producing and handling it (see Plate 14, showing the crude flannel face masks worn by bleach packers at Gateshead in the 1870s).

At the heart of this industry was the demand for 'alkali' or soda, used both in the manufacture of soap and glass and both those industries also flourished in the north east at the same time.

But more than this, the men who were involved in these manufactures come through to us as being more than 'mere industrialists'. The most successful operators were not the one-product firms, but those who controlled a number of inter-related manufactures. There were several very practical men such as John Glover who designed and operated a particular recovery process which later spread to the continent, since he never patented it and showed it to all who were interested; there were men of high calibre like William Losh who had studied at Cambridge and Paris, Richard Hoyle who studied chemistry at Cambridge, and Hugh Lee Pattinson who was elected in 1852 a Fellow of the Royal Society. Probably

the northern chemical industry had only one non-chemical commercially able man, namely Christian Allhusen.

Together these men, known to each other through their various cultural, philanthropic, scientific and sometimes political organisations, helped to build up the industrial life and prosperity of their region.

The process at the heart of so much of this chemical manufacture was known as the Leblanc process after the French chemist who invented it in 1790. It commenced with sulphuric acid and salt and ended with soda crystals but was a rather complex and economically unstable process. It was wasteful, producing sulphur, nitre and chlorine as by-products and the whole operation had to be kept in balance. If one product decreased in value then the process could rapidly become uneconomical. Indeed in the 1870s bleaching powder became much in demand to such an extent that it was of more value than the soda, of which it was a by-product.

Sooner or later a new process was bound to come along and eventually in 1872 the Solvay brothers, working in Belgium, produced a process still known by their name. It used three raw materials: brine, carbon dioxide and ammonia and provided one useful product: soda. Thus, once this process was adopted, large quantities of coal were no longer required and the process was more economically sited much nearer to the salt deposits.

At first this process was slow to be accepted in England, but between 1882 and 1886 three Tyneside firms, Allhusen's, Tennant's and Jarrow Chemical Company established saltworks in the neighbourhood of Haverton Hill and in this they prepared the way for their own Tyneside destruction.

The decline, once started, was rapid. Between 1890 and 1891 the United Alkali Company was formed, all Tyneside firms were amalgamated into it and all but two were shut down and dismantled. Tennant's and Allhusen's survived for a time, but the eventual growth of the enormous chemical industry on Teesside finally took over completely.

Before leaving this fading Tyneside industry, mention should be made of soap manufacture which was fed by the alkali trade. Early in the nineteenth century a heavy tax on soap restricted its manufacture but although the Duke of Wellington by his personal example popularised daily baths among the upper and middle classes, among the working population the consumption of soap was still low because of its cost and the lack of good domestic water supplies. It was the cholera epidemics of mid-century which led to Gladstone, as Chancellor of the Exchequer, repealing the soap-tax in 1853. At its highest this tax had equalled the cost of manufacture.

PLATE 14 Bleach-packers, with flannel face-masks. At Allhusen's Works, Gateshead, c. 1870

Thomas Hedley, the son of a Northumbrian farmer was first employed with a firm of grocers, tallow chandlers and wine merchants in Gateshead. In about 1840 he entered into partnership with the firm, in establishing a soap manufactory in Newcastle. He eventually acquired the business and carried it on as Thomas Hedley & Company, and this prospered through the rest of the century, though perhaps not always due to what we today would call 'aggressive marketing'. For in the late 1890s Hedley's claimed to 'rely on *quality* rather than on *advertising*'.

Chemical Developments on Teesside
Meanwhile on Teesside the chemical industries had been increasing and expanding. The Egglescliffe Chemical Works was founded in 1833 at Urlay Nook for the manufacture of fertilisers and sulphuric acid. In 1860 William James and Company was established in Cargo Fleet Road to produce alkali and other products. It was one of the first firms registered under the Alkali Act of 1863. A larger works also in Cargo Fleet Road and which eventually absorbed James's, was that of Samuel Alexander Sadler (1842–1911), industrial chemist, Alderman and Member of Parliament for Middlesbrough. His statue now stands in front of Middlesbrough Town Hall, in Victoria Square Gardens.

Sadler was trained as a scientist, having obtained the degree of Doctor of Science at the University of London. For a time he worked for Messrs Chance, chemical and glass-makers and carried out investigations into aniline dyes. After 1856, when Perkins had discovered the possibility of producing synthetic dye, a demand for this rapidly grew. It was made from benzene, extracted from coal. In 1862 Sadler determined to commence business on his own at first in a small way and then, in 1869, at new works on Cargo Fleet Road.

Also at this time change was in the offing in the coking business. The beehive coke ovens then in use were allowing potential by-products such as tar and benzene to go to waste (and create considerable atmospheric pollution) and experiments had been carried out using special by-product ovens which collected this material. The first battery of by-product recovery ovens in Great Britain was erected in 1882 by Messrs Pease and Partners at their Pease's West Colliery at Crook in County Durham. They were Simon-Corvés ovens, based on a modified French design. Sadler founded and became chairman and managing director of the Bearpark Coal and Coke Company, which in 1884 built the second set of such ovens in this country.

An 1890 report says of Sadler's works: 'The Works of this company are the only establishment in Middlesbrough devoted to the distillation of tar and the manufacture of alizarine and aniline dyes.' The chemical basis of alizarine was a red-coloured substance found in the root of the madder plant and in the 1860s, a means of making it artificially had been devised, using sulphuric acid on anthracene, distilled from coal tar. Synthetic alizarine soon took over from madder and, as was said a little later, 'an industry of large monetary value passed from the field to the factory'. Clearly Sadler was well sited to move into this new industry.

As for the alkali and salt industries of Cleveland, these, as we have seen, gradually took over from Tyneside, as the chemical process changed, throwing the emphasis on to cheap salt. As far back as 1859 Bolckow and Vaughan, whom we shall come across again as ironmasters, had decided to free themselves from the grip of the newly formed Stockton and Middlesbrough Water company, and sank a well into the New Red Sandstone. After eventually striking fresh water, they proceeded to drill further and at a depth of 1,206ft (368m), they struck a 100ft (30m) thick bed of rock salt. Later, in 1874, the Bell brothers (who had originally been part of the Walker Iron Works partnership on the Tyne but had now set up their own ironworks at Port Clarence), put down a trial bore hole to the north of their works. They proved salt at a depth of 1,152ft (351m).

Thomas Bell suggested that water be introduced into the salt bed and the resultant brine pumped out. Thus in 1881 they became the first producers of salt in the Cleveland area. As we have already seen, they were followed by the Tyneside chemical manufacturers, Charles Tennant and Partners and Allhusen's, who then sank wells in the area. Thus began the great chemical expansion of Teesside.

Lead Products
Whilst the mining of lead was an occupation of the Dales, which effectively ended before 1900, the manufacture of lead products was to be found well into the present century in works along the northern bank of the Tyne, to the east and west of Newcastle. This also has been radically reduced in recent years as the use of lead in many forms has lessened.

Victorian architects found considerable uses for lead products: *cast* for ornate pump heads, rainwater hoppers and the like; *sheet* for roofing of large public buildings and churches; *pipe* for domestic water supplies. It is only in recent years that the danger of providing domestic water services in lead has become apparent, but until copper pipe and – more recently – plastic pipe became readily available, it was hardly feasible to find an alternative. Thus most buildings of last century will be found still to have lead piping for water supply as well as waste disposal from sinks, baths and wash basins. There are still a few men alive who could 'sweat' a joint: the necessary method of joining two lead pipes using solder in an almost plastic rather than molten state, and examination of the plumbing of older premises will bring to light several examples of this skill.

However two major lead products which were once manufactured on the banks of the Tyne have also now virtually ceased to be produced there. A lead-shot tower at Elswick was, until demolished in 1969, a striking landmark; the other works, near Willington Quay had a less dramatic shape, being a number of 'chambers' in which 'white lead' or lead carbonate was manufactured, by an intriguing and complex process. As a pigment this was an essential component of most paints until replaced by zinc and other products.

A valuable by-product of regional lead processing has been silver, for north eastern lead generally has a relatively high content of silver. The de-silvering of lead was greatly improved by Hugh Lee Pattinson of Newcastle (1796–1858) who observed, in 1829, that when lead is melted and allowed to cool slowly, crystals of pure lead form, near the melting point, and sink to the bottom. The still-fluid part above is consequently slightly enriched in silver-content. By suitable ladling from one shallow circular heated pan to another the silver/lead content could be gradually improved before a chemical process was used to complete the separation. This Pattinson process was patented in 1833. Pattinson became involved in a chemical company in County Durham and his name is commemorated today as that of one of the Districts of Washington New Town.

Aluminium Smelting
Aluminium produced from imported ore is currently smelted at Lynmouth on the Northumbrian coast, but surprisingly as far back as the 1880s the Alliance Aluminium Company had a works sited at Wallsend-on-Tyne, where aluminium was extracted from the ore cryolite by means of a process using sodium. However this process was quickly replaced by a superior one developed in 1891 and the works soon closed. Just before that Professor Bedson of the Chemistry Department of the Newcastle College of Physical Sciences (later to become Armstrong College and now the University of Newcastle upon Tyne) had arranged for several photographs to be taken and Plate 15 is one of this series, fortunately preserved.

Today, whilst an enormous range of chemicals is produced by the ICI complex around the Tees, the salt industry has shrunk and in the Tyneside area paint and particularly pharmaceuticals are the only remaining chemical industries of note. Perhaps it was James Crossley Eno (1820–1915) who encouraged the pharmaceutical development here. He was fortunate enough to serve an apprenticeship to a druggist on The Side – then the commercial hub of Newcastle – and after that he joined the staff of the Old Infirmary in the Forth as dispenser. In 1852 he set up as a druggist in the Groat Market, particularly offering a refreshing, effervescent drink made by stirring into water a mixture of sodium bicarbonate and citric acid. He actively 'pushed' sales by distributing free samples to ship's captains and in this way the fame of Eno's Fruit Salt was carried round the world. Eventually demand outstripped the capacity of his tiny Newcastle premises and in 1876 he moved to London. But he apparently never forgot the debt he owed Newcastle and when, in 1899, Sir Riley Lord, as Lord

PLATE 15 Molten aluminium being skimmed, prior to casting an ingot, Walls-end-on-Tyne, 1889

Mayor, put out an appeal for £10,000 to complete the fund for building the new infirmary, Eno sent a cheque for £8,500. For many years afterwards Ward 11 of the Royal Victoria Infirmary was known as the J.C. Eno Ward.

POTTERY MAKING

Another major industry once thriving in the North East, which has now disappeared, was that of pottery production. Along the Tyne riverside, this industry was encouraged by the proximity of cheap coal and of sand brought in as ballast by the returning colliers.

There were three main pottery producing areas in the north east during the nineteenth century; Newcastle, Sunderland and Middlesbrough. Of these Sunderland is perhaps the most widely known and 'Sunderland Ware' is a common term applied to a pink-lustred print-decorated creamware, overlooking the fact that such pottery was being made elsewhere in the country and moreover that not all wares produced in and around Sunderland were of this type.

The Wearside Pottery Industry

Newbottle, a village some four or five miles south west of Sunderland, seems to have pride of place as the first recorded pottery-making site in the region, for there is a reference to a 'kiln' existing there in a document of 1615 – though of course this could just have been a lime-kiln. More sure is the record of the 'High' Pottery having been founded around 1720 and by 1740 flint crushing mills had been constructed from which may be deduced that white ware was being made there. Flint, it should be explained, was first calcined, or brought up to red heat, thrown into water and then crushed before being ground to powder. This powder when added to clay, toughened the product and helped to reduce a tendency to shrinkage. One of these flint-crushing mills is now a small farmstead still known as Flint Mill, along the banks of the Beamish Burn below the village of Beamish in County Durham. Pieces of partially-ground flints with flattened surfaces have been found on the land around this farm. It was because of the relatively flat land between here and Sunderland, some twelve miles to the east, that flints were brought all this way to be crushed by a grinding mill driven by the fast-flowing Beamish Burn.

Over the next few decades pottery making grew from a rural craft to a mass production industry, for the increasing population, with its more varied diet and growing liking for drinks such as tea and coffee, stimulated the production of a greater quantity and variety of pottery.

By the beginning of the nineteenth century several potteries had been established on the banks of the Wear. This made obvious good sense since coal was being brought down to the river, for transhipment to sea-going vessels for export, and hence could be readily brought to the kilns. Moreover finished pots could be crated and loaded directly on to ships berthed nearby, for export down the coast to London or across to the Continent. And whilst brown clay was locally available, white clay from Devon and Cornwall could be bought in relatively cheaply as ballast. This need to import white clay arose as attempts were made to emulate the higher quality wares of Staffordshire. Flint, already referred to, was brought – also as ballast – from eastern England, south of the Humber, though by 1875 Moore's (*Wear Pottery*) and Scott's (*Southwick Pottery*) were also importing flint from France.

Up to the middle of last century pottery-making flourished on Wearside, but the decline set in and in the present century only three potteries continued to work, the last, Wearside Pottery, closing down in 1957 (though the manager then started a pottery under the same name near Seaham). It is more than probable that the death of this Wearside industry was partly attributable to the increase of railway networks. Certainly the railway system helped to strengthen the major English

PLATE 16 From a coloured packaging label, c. 1880 showing an 'improved view' of an early nineteenth century textile mill near Barnard Castle, County Durham. The railway line is entirely imaginary and never existed!

ceramic industry in Staffordshire and it became so much easier to transport Staffordshire wares to the north east, thus reducing the demand for the poorer local product. The Sunderland trade had largely provided local needs and some export to the continent and could not match either the quality or the competitive price of the Staffordshire product. Moreover the Wearside potteries found it extremely difficult to employ skilled labour in competition with the booming ship yards, where skilled artisans could – in the 1860s – be earning over 30 shillings per week (£1.50), whereas the usual wages of a pottery-worker would be well below a pound.

This labour situation resulted in still further depression for the less-skilled workers and children and elderly men were much used. For example the oldest employee at the 'High' Pottery at Newbottle in 1851 was aged 84 and in 1841 the firm had an apprentice of 8 years of age. Some of the young boys and girls working in Wearside potteries may well have been workhouse children, appointed by the Poor-Law Guardians. Journeymen throwers, who were paid by the piece, employed children – of any age – since the pottery owners had no control over this. These children brought clay to the potteries and carried away the finished pots. The Children's Employment Commission of 1841 received evidence of working hours for children in excess of a twelve hour day and of the pay they received. In the printing (ie transfer-printing) of pots, for example, the printer might receive 3d to 9d a dozen pots and would allow the girls he employed a few pence out of each shilling he earned. Those children employed in glazing pots frequently experienced nausea, headaches and tiredness due to lead-poisoning and if they remained in this branch of the trade many eventually lost the use of their limbs and suffered brain-damage. Turning from these hard facts to the attractive wares so produced, we find a considerable range, from brown kitchenware to creamware, printed tableware, and copper-, silver- and pink-lustre. The most famous product was the transfer-printed pink lustreware, now known as 'Sunderland Ware', though as we have now seen, Sunderland produced much more than this one eye-catching product, which itself was produced elsewhere at all the major pottery-manufacturing areas.

Sunderland pottery catered mainly for people with moderate incomes: the lustre-ware for example was made not for artistic effect but with a view to quick sales. Since popular appeal was the aim, decorations and verses were often of a rather bawdy nature. For instance a chamber pot of about 1840 in purple lustre is transfer-painted with a humorous verse on 'Marriage' and inside is a transfer-printed seated figure saying, 'Oh! Dear Me! What do I see?', with the rhyme:

> Keep me clean and use me well;
> And what I see I will not tell

The piece can be seen at Sunderland Museum.

The Newcastle Pottery Industry

The earthenware industry of Tyneside began around 1730 when a Mr John Warburton established his pottery at Pandon Dene. Twenty years later he moved to Carr's Hill near Gateshead. This pottery mostly closed down in 1817 though a small operation, making brown-ware, continued to the very end of the century.

Towards the end of the eighteenth century three important potteries were started at St Anthony's, Stepney Bank and Ouseburn. Other factories followed and Parson & White's *Gazetteer* of 1827 states that there were then about 20 potteries on the banks of the Tyne . . . 'Flint and potters' clay are brought from the south of England, in ships coming for coals and the chief materials used for colouring and glazing are procured in the neighbourhood'. Here, incidentally, is a reminder of the then flourishing chemical industry clearly capable of manufacturing specialist products for the pottery trade.

In the second half of the century the number of pottery firms was smaller, but those that remained had grown in size and efficiency. By 1893 there were six firms manufacturing white and printed wares, four white-printed and brown-ware and three brown-ware only. Together they

PLATE 17 A Sunderland-ware jug (ht 138mm) celebrating a local wedding and dated 1827, in the collections of Beamish, North of England Open Air Museum

employed some 1,200 hands and – for those who like statistics – they used 12,000 tons of white clay and 3,000 tons of brown, the Ford Pottery supplying 80 per cent of the jam and marmalade jars used in England and Scotland. By this time none of the raw materials were obtained in the neighbourhood, but came as ballast.

For some years a popular motif for the transfer-painted decoration was the High Level Bridge across the Tyne, just as the arched bridge over the Wear was popular with Wearside potters.

The family firm of Maling, which finally ceased trading in 1963, first established the North Hylton Pottery Works near Sunderland in 1762. However in 1815 the business was moved to Tyneside, possibly because

49

the clay deposits were becoming exhausted, and was established as the Ouseburn Bridge Works. Christopher Thompson Maling (1824–1901) took over these works from his father and it was under his control that the firm prospered and indeed grew to a size comparable to some of the largest of the Staffordshire potteries.

In 1859 a new pottery was built near to the Ouseburn works, and became known as the Ford Pottery. In its 13 kilns it produced some 750,000 articles a month, principally jam and marmalade pots, dishes for potted meat and cream, and ointment jars. It was written in 1863 that Maling were producing 'no first class goods', but that they were supplying 90 per cent of the jars for jam makers in England and Scotland as well as exporting to the continent and the Colonies.

Around 1900 the Ford Potteries (reputedly one of the largest pottery works in Britain) were employing over a thousand workers.

Outside our period, but worthy of recording, is the fact that in 1929 Maling began their long association with the tea merchants Ringtons Ltd and many Tyneside homes still possess one or more of the characteristic jars given away by Ringtons, in their sales drives.

The Linthorpe Pottery of Middlesbrough

Whereas the Sunderland potteries were producing popular ware for people of moderate means and the major Newcastle pottery, Malings, was concentrating on making food packaging jars and pots, the Linthorpe Art Pottery, founded in 1879, had a quite different market in mind as its title indicates.

This venture was jointly inspired by a local landowner, John Harrison and Dr Christopher Dresser, orientalist and architect, and one of the foremost influences in introducing oriental design into English fabrics, silver, glass and ceramics. The dual aim of this new works was to help alleviate some of Middlesbrough's unemployment (due to a 'trough' in iron and steel production) and to produce a type and quality of fine pottery not previously attempted in England or indeed in Europe.

Local clay was used at first – the same clay as was being used for brickmaking – and an artist Henry Tooth was brought from the Isle of Wight, after being sent to the Staffordshire potteries to get basic training in this industry. Dr Dresser acted as Art Superintendent for the first two or three years, various skilled workers were brought from the Potteries and fourteen artists were brought from London.

By 1885 the pottery employed between 80 and 100 workers and Dresser's influence could be traced in styles clearly based on Middle and Far Eastern designs. White clay was now being imported from Cornwall and glazes brought from the Staffordshire Potteries, though Linthorpe eventually mixed its own glazes too.

Because of its original concern to help the local employment situation, attention was paid to comfort, room, light and proper ventilation for working areas. There were separate painting rooms for male and female artists. Whether the works really alleviated local unemployment is difficult to establish, but certainly many of the employees had been brought from Staffordshire.

Exhibitions were held nationally and the Pottery was awarded a bronze medal at the 1884 World's Industrial Exposition in New Orleans. A gold medal was awarded at an Exhibition at Alexandra Palace, London, where Princess Alexandra purchased a turquoise vase, resulting in great public interest.

For some years the works were progressively administered, being the first Pottery in the country to use gas for firing the ware in the kilns. No seconds or poor quality work were allowed to be sold and the standard set was a high one from the start.

In the late 1880s however, the Linthorpe Pottery began to suffer difficulties, perhaps partly due to the rising cost of white clay. Moreover other potteries had begun to imitate the style of Linthorpeware, though cheaper and lacking in finish. By now, too, the quality of design had been lowered in an attempt to increase sales, and the end result was that the Pottery closed down in 1889.

Other Pottery Trades

Less well known than the major firms and products outlined above, was a very large manufacture of crude earthenware – items such as bricks, tiles and sanitary ware (ie pipes, gullies etc, used for water and sewage transmission).

Many remains of brick and tile kilns can be traced especially in south Northumberland, where local clays were particularly suitable and cheap coal was available nearby. Kilns can be seen, for example, outside Belsay and near Corbridge. The Corbridge Pottery is particularly interesting for it still demonstrates examples of three kinds of kilns: the so-called 'bottle' kilns, well known from the Potteries, circular kilns with domed roofs and 'Newcastle' kilns which are rectangular in plan with an arched roof.

One pottery still working is at Bardon Mill, where a modern demand for such items as strawberry-growing pots has been encouraged by a growing tourist trade.

From such large or relatively crude items it may be interesting to turn to small well-sculpted pottery items, namely clay pipes. Clearly a light industry, pipemaking required the minimum of equipment and was often a one-man job. An innkeeper may have become a pipe maker, since pipes were sometimes offered free as an inducement to clients to visit the Inn and records in the north east suggest that this was often the case. A close study of regional Gazetteers or Directories will produce many examples of local pipemakers and occasionally a pipe-bowl will be turned up in one's garden. A local writer has published, in the Transactions of the Society of Antiquaries of Newcastle upon Tyne (1964: J.E. Parsons), an impressive list of North East pipemakers, ranging in date from some of the very earliest in the seventeenth century.

GLASS

Apart from Corning Ltd. of Wearside, making 'Pyrex' glassware, Hartley Wood & Co nearby making window glass and GEC producing bulbs at Lemington-on-Tyne, another one-time north eastern industry has disappeared. Yet last century it was a large, prosperous and wide-ranging one. A good point at which to begin observing the scale of north eastern glass manufacture in the nineteenth century is in the introduction to Parson and White's *Directory & Gazetteer of the Counties of Durham and Northumberland*, published in 1827. After noting that the first glassworks on the Tyne were established in about 1619 and that since that time the industry had rapidly increased, we read:

> . . . there are on the river Tyne no fewer than 31 glass houses, viz, one for the manufacture of plate glass; fifteen for crown glass, six for flint glass; and nine for green bottles; besides which there are four green bottle houses at Hartley Pans; and three green bottle and one flint-glass house at Sunderland. It has been confidentially stated, that more glass is manufactured on the river Tyne than in the whole kingdom of France and about two-fifths of the English glass is said to be made in this district. In 1810 it was estimated that the 30 glass houses on the Tyne manufactured goods to the amount of £499,000 annually, of which the enormous sum of £181,000 was paid in duty. In 1812 the duties on glass were doubled since which the trade has experienced great fluctuations, though it is still conducted with considerable spirit, ingenuity and success.

Of all these glasshouses only one remains; a huge brick-built cone which may well date back to the later eighteenth century. It is situated on the north bank of the Tyne near Lemington, some five miles to the west of Newcastle and now scheduled for preservation. It can clearly be seen from a good distance in several directions. Such a building, looking outwardly not unlike one of the 'bottle kilns' which used to be so common in the Black Country, was constructed primarily to conserve working heat and to protect the operations from the effects of draughts. Within the circular space, enclosed upwards by a towering brick cone, would be the 'pots' where molten glass was held with fires beneath, ready for use. The glassblowers, each with a metal blowing tube, stood around the pots. Each

PLATE 18 A glass mug engraved in memory of the colliery disaster of 1862, in the collections of Beamish, North of England Open Air Museum

would dip his tube into the glass, draw out a 'gob' or globule and proceed to blow it to the required shape. This is now a rare skill, replaced by enormous machines producing bottles or other glassware at a considerable speed.

Writing some thirty years after Parson and White, in the 1850s, Fordyce in *County Palatine of Durham* describes the glass trade as he observed it at Sunderland:

There are sixteen bottle houses at which 60,000 to 70,000 bottles are daily manufactured 'they do a great stroke of business in the glass way' says Doctor Dibdin. 'My daughter was delighted with the different processes she saw; but almost screamed when she heard that an order had come down that morning for a *thousand dozen of gin glasses*!' The ordinary wine or beer bottle is the prevailing article of commerce in the glass way, but both here and in the immediate neighbourhood of Newcastle you shall see decanters, tumblers and wine glasses with all their accompaniments manufactured in a style of surprising great beauty and in endless variety.

In another part of the same work, Fordyce refers to the 'Great Exhibition' (of 1851) in the 'Palace of Industry' at Hyde Park. This exhibition, he asserts, 'could not have been constructed without the remission of the glass duty', and then goes on to detail items contributed by Messrs Hartley and Company of Sunderland:

Patent rough plate glass of improved surface, one-eighth of an inch thick, 30 ounces to the square foot; for ridge and furrow roofing of conservatories, factories and for general purposes. Larger sizes are obtainable in the rough plate than could previously be procurred in glass of similar quantity of less substance than a ¼in: models and c., illustrating the manufacture of crown and sheet glass: model of a glass-house, the 'cone' being made of glass, with model of an eight-pot furnace: melting pot, full size: specimens of the various stages of manufacture: model of a greenhouse on the ridge and furrow flat-roofed principal: specimen windows of patent rolled coloured glass: specimens of stained glass borders: various kinds of coloured glass: specimens of various articles for horticultural and dairy purposes: glass or railway purposes etc.

Messrs Swinburne and Company he adds, contributed:

Silvered, naked, rough and Venetian plates of glass: opaque plates of glass intended as a substitute for marble in articles of furniture: perforated plates of glass for ventilation: glass domes for skylights: opaque glass table: glass pipes for conveying water and other fluids: sets of chemical apparatus for manufacturing purposes: glass trays for dairy and domestic purposes: pressed and coloured plates of glass for church windows.

Fordyce's mention of the 'Remission of the glass duty' refers to the final lifting of an excise duty in 1845, which had been a source of concern to glass manufacturers for half a century. A markedly large duty had been imposed in 1812 after which the manufacture of glass fell by almost half. In succeeding years reductions were made in the duty, but it was not until 1845 that the restrictions were finally removed. As for the processes which were used to manufacture such ranges of products, these varied to a considerable degree. Bottles were being blown into metal moulds, which resulted in straight-sided bottles which could be packed more efficiently. Window glass was made from large blown cylinders which were then cut lengthways, re-heated and flattened out to make 'broad' glass, though before this process, blown bulbs of molten glass were spun out into disks from which small panes were cut, leaving the 'bulls-eye' in the centre as waste. 'Crown' or 'sheet' glass was an improvement on the 'broad' glass technique. High quality tablewares were also made, many engraved with famous views.

In 1847 Hartley's Glass Works at Sunderland introduced a cheap process of rolling plate glass which was used in the new railway stations, market halls and greenhouses: a case of new processes and new demands feeding each other. And after around 1860 bottles were blown in hinged metal moulds and table and decorative wares were 'pressed' in machines.

This process of 'pressing' combined the two processes of shaping and decorating the glass into a single operation. A 'gob' of molten glass was dropped into a mould and a plunger then lowered in, squeezing the molten glass to shape and – since both the mould and the plunger may have been patterned – giving the glass its decorated surfaces.

Two companies in Sunderland produced a wide variety of pressed ornamental table and glassware. Mathew Turnbull's Cornhill Works at Southwick is first mentioned in trade directories in 1865 (closed in 1965) and the Wear Flint Glass Works at Millfield was working around the same period and is now owned by Corning Ltd, producing today only heat-resistant glass such as 'Pyrex'.

On Tyneside Sowerby's of Gateshead were noted for their decorative pressed glass and continued, though attenuated and changed in emphasis, through into the 1970s. Today, for the collector, the name of Sowerby is virtually synonymous with press-moulded glass and their distinctive peacock's head trademark is a symbol of quality.

It was an expansion in the nineteenth century market for cheap utility glassware that helped Tyneside and Sowerby's in particular. Low manufacturing costs and the opening of a wider trade with North America and Europe, provided a good financial base. Glass ceased to be a luxury and became a utility. In consequence several luxury glass-producing companies in London and the Midlands went into a sharp decline and new glass firms in the North East – like Sowerby's – quickly expanded and developed, through the 60s, 70s and 80s. However by 1890 Sowerby's found their cheap lines less in demand and tried to move into more expensive products. They were facing stiff Belgian competition and although an attempt to beat this was made by erecting a glassworks at Hoboken near Antwerp in 1896, this proved unsuccessful.

Elsewhere in the region, the glass companies were collapsing for the sea-trade was no longer relevant when the railway network had been built up. Also, northern glass works were not as quick to modernise as in other parts of the country and window-glass manufacturers, as well as pressed-glass manufacturers, were hit by cheap imports from Belgium.

4

THE LAND

FARMING AND MECHANICAL IMPROVEMENTS

As already mentioned, County Durham with a reputation of being a heavily industrialised county in Victorian times, was – as recently as the 1840s – still predominantly rural in terms of the occupation of its population. And much of Northumberland has never been other than predominantly rural; similarly with the old county of the North Riding of Yorkshire. So whilst much emphasis must rightly be placed upon the new heavy industries and urban development which characterise Victorian change in the North East, we must remember that, for a large proportion of the population, change took place more gently and less dramatically.

There were, of course, periods of unrest, but we do not find anything like the 1834 Tolpuddle Martyrs of Dorset, for whereas those workers had 'combined' to resist wage reductions, agricultural wages in the North East were on the whole higher than average, probably on the account of well-paid work in the adjoining mining and industrial areas. Indeed at the very beginning of the century when the threshing machine, invented by Andrew Meikle in the Lothians in 1786, had begun to spread south, it was not treated as a threat to employment by the workers though much sought after by farmers as a means of reducing expenditure. This radical machine, which effectively and very rapidly replaced the considerable manual labour of hand-flailing, was driven by other machinery: water-power in hilly country, wind-power on an appropriate site or – most commonly – horse-power in the form of a 'gin-gan' or horse-engine. Elsewhere in the country the 'Luddites' were driven to take up their ill-fated destructiveness in 1812, being 'croppers' of woollen cloth who were being put out of work by mechanical replacements of their skills. Similar, if not so well known, bands of unemployed agricultural workers were fighting their hopeless battle in midland rural areas; destroying horse-engines and threshing-machines. In the north east however, this did not happen to anything like the same extent, since any unemployed agricultural worker could readily find work in the nearby coal mines, with the result that, today, we can still observe farms with 'engine-houses' or 'wheel-houses' attached to their barns: single-storeyed square, hexagonal or round buildings which once housed these wooden 'roundabouts' driven by plodding horses to power the threshing machines.

The north-eastern advance of Meikle's thresher seems to have begun fairly early, for in 1788 Arthur Young, a great reporter of rural activities,

PLATE 19 Sheep shearing at Nookton Farm, near Blanchland, County Durham

PLATE 20 Threshing by steam traction engine, at Woodhead Farm, County Durham

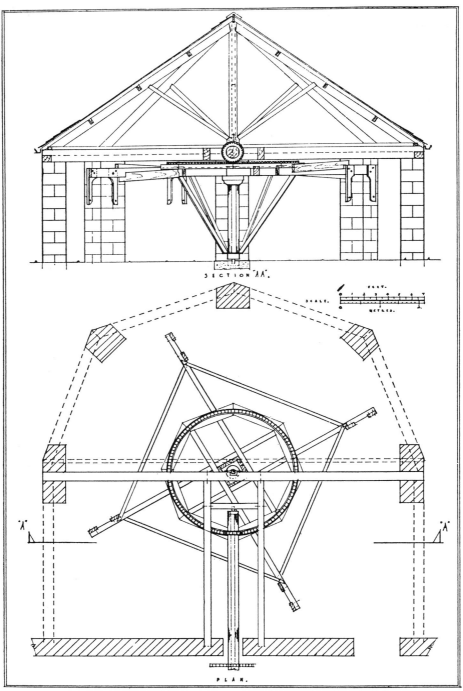

SECTION "AA".

SCALE.

PLAN.

FIG 2 The construction of an agricultural horse-wheel and wheelhouse, of about 1830

58

PLATE 21 Farm near Berwick on Tweed, with chimney for stationary steam thresher, c. 1870

mentioned in his *Annals of Agriculture* one of Meikle's mills erected near Belford in Northumberland and in 1805 Bailey and Culley in their *General View of Agriculture in Northumberland* reported threshing machines in general use.

Of course, as is so often the case with inventions for which a great need may be said to have existed (compare the miner's safety lamp invented simultaneously by Humphry Davy and George Stephenson), there were several claims to have produced the first successful threshing machine and the north east has its claims to put forward. John Rastrick, of Morpeth, a 'civil engineer and millwright' claimed to have invented the threshing machine and went so far as to engage in a long dispute with Meikle about patent rights, which ended inconclusively in 1799. Rastrick, although eccentric, was certainly a skilful mechanic and produced many inventions and improvements in farm machinery around 1800.

EXTRAORDINARY MILKERS : THE SHORTHORNS

It was not only through farm machinery that the North East made its name in agricultural circles, since towards the end of the eighteenth century, two Teesdale farming brothers made cattle-breeding history. Their breed, the Durham Shorthorn (often known today as the Dairy Shorthorn), exists to this day, though now in much reduced numbers. Following what would now be termed 'in-line' breeding of their cattle, Charles and Robert Colling, farming in lower Teesdale near Darlington, set out to produce a breed which would be a notable producer of fat meat. Until that time a farmer would put

PLATE 22 A Durham Shorthorn cow: 'Cambridge' at eight years old (1840) bred by Thomas Bates of Kirk Leavington near Yarm

a cow to a bull and be grateful for what appeared. But the Colling brothers brought breeding to a finer art, carefully selecting their breeding cows and their bulls in such a way that the progeny came closer and closer to their aim: a solid beast with a very heavy fat yield.

There had long been a Teeswater breed of short-horned cattle, so-called because they were to be found along the banks of the Tees. And even before the Collings' work they were noted as 'extraordinary milkers' though when put to fatten they were 'slow feeders, producing an inferior quality of meat'. William Youatt in his well-known book on *Cattle* (1831), and writing at a time when several of the early protagonists could still be remembered, noted that Mr Charles Colling 'manifested a superiority of skill as a breeder which, in a very brief period, secured him an ample fortune'. Colling's first bull was *Hubback*, as well-known for the shorthorn breed as is the Godolphin Arabian as the ancestor of so many racehorses. From him came the bull *Foljambe*; he in turn was the grandsire of *Favourite* from whom came the Durham ox and the famous bull *Comet*.

Who has not heard of the Durham Ox? There must have been scores of old English pubs of this name at one time, scattered over the country and recording the remarkable journey of one of England's most famous animals, which was toured far and wide in a specially constructed wagon behind horses. Charles Colling had sold the Durham ox locally for £140 and later a Mr John Day bought it and toured it for nearly six years, until

60

the ox unfortunately dislocated its hip and had to be slaughtered. This tour undoubtedly helped forward the fame of the breed to the great benefit of the Colling brothers; for when Charles sold up in 1810 his prize bull *Comet* sold for 1000 guineas at 6 years of age and his whole herd of 47 head totalled £7,114. Eight years later Robert sold his herd of 61 head and realised £7,484. These sales distributed the best of the breed far and wide.

The prints of the famous Durham ox, and of the bull 'Favourite' often with Durham Cathedral as background, and of other cattle from the same breed, are still to be found, though one should take the proportions of the beasts with a pinch of salt. Some of these are good examples of artist's licence, taken a little too far. Indeed we have a contemporary account from Thomas Bewick, the noted wood engraver who, in his *Memoir* (published posthumously in 1862), wrote about 'these fat cattle makers': ' . . . I would not put lumps of fat here & there to please them where I could not see it . . . Many of the animals were, during this rage for fat Cattle, surely fed up to as great a weight & bulk as it was possible . . . but this was not enough – they were to be figured monstrously fat before the owners of them could be pleased'. Though to be fair, at least one such print details in the lower margin the actual dimensions of the animal and if these dimensions are scaled into three-dimensional form, then the reconstruction would certainly look ungainly to modern eyes.

To understand the needs of the 1800s breeders and their proud illustrations, one should recall that at that time fat was necessary for the production of tallow candles and of soap. Both products had to be made from animal fat and were being produced in ever-growing quantities as the population increased and industrial production of all kinds expanded. Moreover the northern miner believed (perhaps with good reason) that very fatty meat gave him his necessary energy. So the early breeders were merely seeking to satisfy both local and national needs and their cattle bred fatter and fatter!

Later in the nineteenth century, as demand changed, the Durham Shorthorn breeders took another direction which led them towards improved milk production. A continuing urban population growth required more milk, whilst tallow candles were being replaced by oil and gas lights and soap could be derived from other sources. Hence this change of direction and the gradual change of the breed's name to that of Dairy Shorthorn.

Now the breed is threatened with extinction, for in comparison with modern breeds its milk yield and other features are not able to compete and in truth it has perhaps become too 'fossilised'. Yet its genes may still be of future value and since it was at one time the most important breed in the country (and frequently exported to Argentina and Ireland etc), an active attempt to rescue it has been set up by the North of England Open Air Museum at Beamish where a herd is being assembled and frozen semen and embryos are being stored. This is still just possible, before the current range of blood lines is depleted and the herd book run down too far.

61

FARMSTEADS AND COTTAGES

A characteristic feature of farming in Northumberland in the early and mid nineteenth century was the large farmstead, more like a hamlet than the kind of farm to be seen further south. Several great examples may be seen in the Bamburgh area: examples which impressed early nineteenth century visitors to that region. And not far away, at Chollerton, the farm is an agricultural version of the contemporary colliery villages which were being constructed over to the south east. Ilderton near Wooler, in the foothills of the Cheviots has been described by Robert Newton as 'perhaps the best survival in Northumberland of a self-contained mediaeval farm settlement rebuilt in the eighteenth and nineteenth centuries: a village which is virtually one farm'. These and many other large farmsteads, with terraces of well-built workers' housing, are clearly the result of well-funded and prosperous estates.

Yet at the same time, many agricultural workers in that same county were living in almost indescribable conditions. An attempt to describe the cottage life of the Northumbrian hind in the 1840s was published in an obscure article by the Vicar of Norham. Writing under the title 'The Peasantry of the Border', the Reverend W.S. Gilly commented that 'while some are directing attention to the flora, the minerals or the romantic localities of this fine border district, and others to the better . . . construction of cow-byres, pig sties and sheep folds, and to the irrational animals that are to occupy them, I will beg a few minutes in thought on behalf of the cottager and the tenement which is prepared for him, and of the provision which ought to be made for the culture of his mind and the advancement of its comforts as a moral and immortal being'. In the next twenty pages he enlarged upon this theme, pointing out that because of the annual *hiring*, 'the Northumbrian cottager can scarcely be said to have a 'home' – he is obliged to 'flit' every year.' 'He has no fruit trees and no flowers in the garden because he is a hind, and may soon be flitting' was a remark he noted.

The Reverend Gilly stated that in his Parish of Norham, where there were 174 cottages held on the hinding system, 'seventeen families only, are to be found on the hearths around which they were sitting in the beginning of the year 1831'. (That is to say, ten years earlier.)

Gilly went on to describe the dilapidated 'cabins': 'They are built of rubble, or of unhewn stone, loosely cemented and from age or from the badness of the materials, the walls look as if they would scarcely hold together . . . The chimneys have lost half their original height, and lean on the roof with fearful gravitation. The rafters are evidently rotten and displaced and the thatch, yawning to admit the wind and wet in some parts, and in all parts utterly unfit for its original purpose . . . looks more like the top of a dunghill than of a cottage.'

He then described the interior: 'When the hind comes to take possession he finds it no better than a shed. The wet, if it happens to rain, is making

PLATE 23 A village smithy in lower Teesdale

PLATE 24 Bondagers near Alnwick in Northumberland, c. 1870

a puddle on the earth floor . . . window-frame there is none. There is neither oven, nor copper, nor grate, nor shelf, nor fixture of any kind; all these things he has to bring with him, besides his ordinary articles of furniture . . . The general character of the best of the old-fashioned hinds' cottages in this neighbourhood is bad at the best. They have to bring everything with them – partitions, window-frames, fixtures of all kinds, grates and substitutes for ceiling . . .They have no byre for their cow, no sheds for their pigs, no pumps or wells, nothing to promote cleanliness or comfort. The average size of these sheds is about twenty-four feet by sixteen. They are dark and unwholesome. The windows do not open and many of them are not larger than twenty inches by sixteen. And into this space are crowded eight, ten, or even twelve persons. The case is aggravated when there is a young woman to be lodged in this confined space, who is not a member of the family, but is hired to do the field-work, for which every hind is bound to provide a female.'

Later Gilly described a hind, about to quit: . . . 'a fine tall man of about forty-five – a fair specimen of the frank, sensible, well-spoken, well-informed Northumbrian peasantry . . . He told me his family – eleven in number – were to inhabit one of these cottages . . . and that the eleven would have only three beds to sleep in – he himself, his wife, a daughter of six, and a boy of four years old would sleep in one bed; a daughter of eighteen, a son of twelve, a son of ten, and a daughter of eight, would have a second bed; and a third could receive his three sons of the ages of twenty, sixteen and fourteen.'

'In justice to the hinds of the Border,' as he put it, Gilly then described the interior of a cottage 'when it is fairly "put to rights"'. We first find that a cow occupies part of the cottage; 'There is no partition-wall divides them, but a slight wainscotwork of his own contrivance . . .There are two beds placed within a framework, which takes up the whole of one side of the room.

In the centre of the framework, and between the two beds, is a door which opens into the space behind the beds, where many useful articles such as pails and tubs are stored away; and perhaps, if you look in, you will see another bed on the floor in the corner. The two bedsteads within the framework are so contrived as to close by a sliding panel.'

As to the rest of the furnishings: 'our eye rests on the dresser and shelves of pretty crockery-ware which cover the greater part of another side of the room . . . Then comes the handsome clock in its tall case, and the chest-of-drawers – sometimes of new wainscot, sometimes of antique carved-work, and which contains decent apparel for all the family. The barrel of meal and the barrel of herrings occupy their place. The rack above displays some goodly flitches of bacon. Whitebread loaves are seldom seen. The griddle-cake composed of bakery and pease, and the oaten porridge, and potatoes, are the usual substitute for wheaten flour.'

'Now as to the food for our peasant's mind. One book cannot escape our notice . . . (It is the Bible) . . . and the Prayer Book, some few other books of devotions, of history, or of useful knowledge, are ranged side by side of the Bible; and they all show that they have been frequently read.'

In conclusion the Reverend Gilly mused 'Oftentimes, when I see ornamental lodges, and pretty dairies . . . and gardeners' houses, decorated without and full of accommodation within, and dog-kennels, which may be called canine-palaces; and stables like sacred temples . . . I indulge in the ardent hope that the time will come, when the peasantry on a property will have as much taste and forethought expended on them . . .'

If further confirmation of the state of these Northumbrian agricultural workers' hovels were needed, it can be found in a note from the Reverend John Hodgson (whom we have previously met as a Northumbrian historian and author of a significant pamphlet on the 1812 colliery explosion at Felling). Around 1810 he wrote to his wife about some of his travels in Northumberland: 'At Wooler, Etal and Millfield the cottages are most miserable, especially at the two latter places. They are dirty thatched hovels, the walls built with mud and small round stones of whin or granite gathered from the fields'.

5
EXPANDING TOWNS

CIVIC PRIDE

Legislation

Many aspects of the work of today's Local Government are currently under review, but it is salutary to observe the enormous range of responsibilities which were put upon Local Government by Victorian legislators. Truly so much of our present way of life was established during the nineteenth century.

National Government itself underwent great changes, as inevitable forces prevailed, though as long as government was in the hands of a select few the pressures from a growing population, with an awakening awareness, could only slowly take effect. But beginning with the Reform Act the pattern of government in England changed fundamentally within a single decade. The 1832 Reform Act (from the 'Great Reform Bill' of 1831), passed under Earl Grey (who is still remembered in Newcastle by Grey's Monument, standing at the top of Grey Street), disenfranchised fifty six 'Rotten Boroughs', gave seats to many others and effectively gave the vote to a wider range of the middle classes. Prior to this there were only ten MPs for Northumberland and Durham: two for each county and two each for Newcastle, Morpeth and Durham City. Afterwards there were nearly twice as many voters and four MPs for Durham, four for Northumberland, and Sunderland, South Shields, Gateshead and Tynemouth elected MPs for the first time.

Following this, new municipal councils were established by the Municipal Corporations Act in 1835. This major Act marks the beginning of local government reform. A uniform system of councils, directly elected by the ratepayers was imposed on the old borough councils; mayors and aldermen were indirectly elected. The election of Justices of the Peace was abolished and the Police placed under watch committees. The new Poor Law Act of 1834 established Guardians of the Poor and the Police system was extended to counties in 1839.

The Highway Act of 1835 commenced major improvements of the road transport system by abolishing statutory labour, empowering the levy of a highway rate, providing for the unification of parishes into Highway districts and allowing the payment of a district surveyor.

Although the first Census had been made way back in 1801, and subsequently each ten years, it was not until the Municipal Corporations

Act of 1835 had produced reliable local officials in towns and the Act of 1836 had made provision for the civil registration of births, marriages and deaths, by appointing local registrars, that the work of enumeration could be carried out with reasonable accuracy.

This attention to basic facts, and the growing importance of statistical evidence, helped to make possible and indeed aided the great inquiries by Parliamentary Committees or Royal Commissions, which began to be set up following the Poor Law Commission of 1832.

A Factory Commission was established in 1833 to collect information about the employment of children in factories. Later in that same year (we rarely legislate so expeditiously today!), Lord Shaftesbury's Factory Act was passed. It applied primarily to textile mills, but after it no child under the age of 11 for the first year, under 12 for the second, or under 13 for the third, was to be employed for more than 48 hours a week. No person under 18 was to be employed for more than 69 hours per week. Above all the Act provided for inspection. Four full-time inspectors were appointed with wide powers; the new regulations had teeth in them.

The First Factory Inspectors very soon saw themselves not merely as observers, for they began at an early stage to inform industry of the best practices followed elsewhere. And their Inspector-General wrote that he saw this first Factory Act as a legislative step towards an eventual compulsory education 'for all classes'. These Factory Inspectors were followed by the Prison Inspectors and these by the Schools Inspectors, the Railway Inspectors, and the Mines Inspectors.

As the century wore on more and more legislation appeared, dealing with Education, Employment, Poor Law, Public Health, Transport (both road and rail), Utilities, Libraries and – by no means least – Drink. Much of this affected the urban areas and led to further expansion of the work of local Councils and their officials.

All this had its effect on the growth and development of urban areas and of the countryside, the freedom of movement of individuals, both locally and in terms of seeking work further afield and above all the material wealth and health of the country. So much of what we take for granted today both in the way we live and in our surroundings, stems from decisions taken in those early years of last century.

Town Halls

As urban legislation proliferated through the nineteenth century and the responsibilities of the Town and Borough Councils grew, the need for suitable administrative accommodation, not surprisingly associated with a growing civic pride, often resulted in the construction of ostentatious Town Halls: properly dignified symbols of authority. The proud phrases used when proposing many a town hall may be typified by the recommendations of the *Weekly Gazette* of Middlesbrough in 1881: 'We hope the Council . . . will have under consideration the wants of the borough for fully one hundred years to come . . . The building itself must be of an imposing character befitting a go-ahead community which proposes to have as much reverence for culture as for power'.

As befitted its place in the region, Newcastle had the first Town Hall in the North East, though this one was built long before the era of Victorian expansion. On the Sandhill down by the riverside, the mediaeval Guildhall, rebuilt in 1655–8 after a disastrous fire, was later extended in 1794 and again in 1826, this time by John Dobson. By now this building provided an unusual combination of functions, for as described in 1844 the Exchange News Room and Fish Market were at opposite ends of the ground floor. On the first floor were the Mayor's Chamber, the Guildhall and Merchants' Court and the principal offices for the Town Clerk. The Engineer, Town Surveyor and Revenue Committee also had offices here and there were several other offices on the upper storey.

Town Hall offices were later moved nearer the middle of the city when the Corn Exchange, originally built in 1839 between the Cloth Market and the Groat Market, was bought by the Corporation and practically rebuilt. This took place between 1858 and 1863. Sadly this well-sited building, just to the north of the Cathedral, was demolished in the mid 1970s. It had a classical front with columns and big arched windows, with side windows of Venetian style. Alas as so often happens – not only in the North – the building which replaced it has few if any calls to one's attention.

Much less ostentatious and relatively early, is the North Shields Town Hall in Saville Street, designed by Dobson and put up in 1844 in a vaguely Tudor style, originally for the North Shields Improvement Commissioners and taken over as Town Hall in 1849. Only two years later Middlesbrough – that rapidly growing 'infant Hercules' as Gladstone described it – had built its first Town Hall, now the 'Old Town Hall', designed by William Moffat of Doncaster. This simple and quite attractive front is somewhat unusually rendered and the groups of small windows on the ground floor are typically Early Victorian, with upper windows larger and arched. In 1881 Middlesbrough celebrated its Jubilee, though the celebrations were somewhat muted because of what the press called 'the death of a staple industry' (the decline of the iron rails industry). However in 1887, four years after the foundation stone had been laid, the new Town Hall was officially opened by the Prince of Wales. This impressive Gothic building – colourfully described as being 'in the style of the thirteenth century suffused with the feeling and spirit of the present time' – had a clock tower 170 feet high, a large assembly room and a Council Chamber embellished with full-length portraits of major industrialists: Joseph Pease, Bolckow, Vaughan and Bell (Plate 25).

Durham, the prime city of the region, but in fact by Victorian times completely scaled down in importance, built its Town Hall in the Market Place in 1851. After a period of worsening mid-twentieth century traffic chaos, this Market Place has now partially reverted to pedestrians and the buildings here can once more gain a little of their former dignity. Although Pevsner suggests that 'for a Victorian town hall this is nicely humble', it holds its own in the Market Place and has a fine gothic hall with 'hammer-beam' roof.

Much less can be kindly said of the Old Shire Hall built in Old Elvet just down the hill and across the river from the Market Place, in 1897–8. This was to be proud centre of the newer Durham County Council, created in 1888, though it has now been vacated by that authority and has served as the headquarters of the University since the later 1960s. Pevsner's description can hardly be bettered: 'A building with monumental intentions and disastrous effects on the surrounding Georgian architecture. Big, symmetrical ... and faced with that imperishable red Victorian brick, which is such crushing proof of technical efficiency and aesthetic dumbness.'

Darlington, the busy railway centre of the region, and proudly prosperous in the middle of the last century, took a different direction for its town hall and, in 1864, built a Market Place and Public Offices in yellow brick. A covered market with glass roof and outer iron colonnades separates the Public Offices from the tower which was clearly intended to be a focal point in the Market Place.

The last big authority in our region to construct its Victorian administrative centre was less successful in achieving architecture of note. The very name of Sunderland's 'Municipal Buildings' suggests a certain sense

PLATE 25 Middlesbrough Town Hall (Photo: Cleveland Planning Dept)

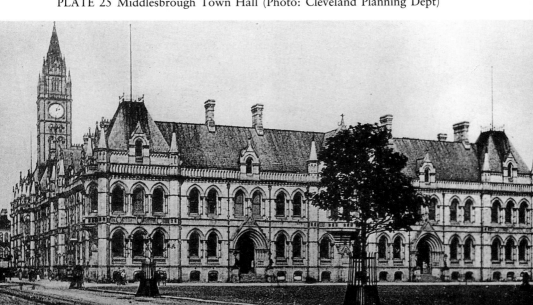

of inferiority and the 1890 construction which had little to its credit, has now been demolished. Before that, the still-standing 'Exchange' building (by Stokoe, 1812) served as administrative centre. The mid twentieth century 'Civic Centre' (of red brick and designed to a distressingly confusing hexagonal plan) replaced the earlier 'Buildings' but, one cannot help feeling, without adding to civic dignity. Though perhaps civic efficiency has been improved, and that after all is what really matters.

Public Libraries
By the middle of the century the Victorian concept of 'self-help', combined with an awareness of the need for a fuller life, began to evince itself in the growing pressure for a public library service.

The history of Newcastle's Public Library shows these early beginnings, though little in the way of beneficial results until late in the century. As far back as 1854 Dr William Newton, who had become a member of the Town Council in 1851, moved the appointment of a Committee to consider the establishing of a Free Library. This could have been done under the 1850 Public Library Act. Newton died in 1863, with the project still dormant and the idea was next taken up in 1870 by Newton's son Councillor Dr Henry Newton. After still more delays and public meetings, the idea of a Public Library was at last fully agreed and a temporary lending library housed on the ground floor of the Merchant's Institute was opened on 13th September 1880 by Joseph Cowen MP who took out the first book, J.S. Mill's *On Liberty*.

During the last years of the nineteenth and the early years of the twentieth century, an immense upsurge of spending on public libraries was encouraged by support from Andrew Carnegie, the Scottish-born American self-made steel magnate. His grants, ranging from £400 to £120,000 helped to finance 295 municipal libraries in the United Kingdom. In all, his grants amounted to 1¾ million pounds and they had financed in whole or in part more than half the total number of public libraries in existence in 1913.

North country libraries were far from being amongst the earliest in the country, but several authorities took advantage of Carnegie's generosity and obtained grants to help in the construction of their libraries. Most of these were based on the 'indicator' system. This system – now long forgotten – allowed readers only to check a series of panels of indicator boards from which they could learn whether a book was available or already in use. The serial number of each book was shown on these boards together with a card marked 'in' or 'out'. The books themselves were kept on shelves away from the public area and there was a printed catalogue of the library's stock from which readers could make their selection.

By 1905 the number of indicator panels in the Newcastle City Library had increased to the point where there was practically no room for further expansion: the indicator spread round the library, blocking out the light and being a great source of trouble to reader and librarian alike. Hence the more up to date method of card-issue was introduced in which a book card was placed in the reader's ticket and filed in a tray. By 1908 most of the indicator panels were removed.

However a further step beyond 'card-issuing' was that of 'open access' and the first example of this was only opened in Britain at Clerkenwell in London in 1893. It was so popular that others soon followed, and not long afterwards the eleventh edition of *Encyclopedia Britannica* (1911) was able to report that 'now over 100 cities and districts of all sizes in Britain have adopted the system'. The main features of the British system were then described as being 'an exact classification, the construction of automatic locking wickets to regulate entrance and exit of borrowers and the requirement that borrowers must be registered'. In America, it was reported, losses of books were sometimes enormous, but the British system was much superior and was quite rapidly adopted.

At this time too, the use of cards for classification was still sufficiently new for it to be described in full. It may be quite startling to a modern reader to realise that a card index – now itself on the way to being replaced by microfiche readers – only came into regular use less than a century ago. Indeed, before 1881 very little had been accomplished even in the way of scientific classification and that was the point when the Decimal system of Melvil Dewey was first adopted in British municipal libraries.

The rather daring 'open-access' system does not appear to have been completed at the Newcastle Central Library until the unbelievably late date of 1950, by which time Newcastle Central Library was the last major library in England to be so converted, and almost the last library anywhere in the country. Forty years earlier a Carnegie grant of £5,500 had enabled a branch library to be constructed at Benwell and this was opened in 1909; the grant having been promised as far back as 1904 before Benwell was incorporated into Newcastle.

Sunderland was aided by Carnegie to the extent of having three branch libraries: at Hendon, Monkwearmouth and West Branch. These were modest but useful buildings which still serve the same function today.

No Carnegie libraries seem to have been constructed in Northumberland, but County Durham has one: a good example at Annfield Plain in North West Durham, which was opened in 1908 (Plate 26). At the Hartlepools (where confusion can arise because the single name Hartlepool is now used for both old Hartlepool and the later West Hartlepool, but originally 'Hartlepool' meant the old settlement only) – a Public Library was built in West Hartlepool in 1895, whereas in (old) Hartlepool a Carnegie grant of £5,000 enabled a foundation stone to be laid in 1903

PLATE 26 A Carnegie-aided branch library, at Annfield Plain, County Durham, 1908

and the building opened in 1904. It was delightfully described as being 'lighted by electricity and having heating and ventilation on Longfield's patent moist air system'. Both these buildings are still in use, though plans are prepared for the replacement of the main library. The old Hartlepool (Carnegie) library is now known as the Northgate Branch Library.

A small library at Thornaby was begun in 1894 and enlarged with the aid of a Carnegie grant of £1,500 in 1903.

However the pride of place in the region for size of Carnegie grant, as well as for a somewhat shameful administrative brouhaha, must go to Middlesbrough. There a grant of £15,000 was agreed by Andrew Carnegie in 1908 and quite a striking building was erected by 1912. It was then found that there was an overspend of £1,380 and the Town Clerk seems to have written to Carnegie asking for more. The reply from Carnegie's Secretary was quoted in full in the local press, which described it as being written 'on the new spelling reform lines':

Dear Sir, – Mr Carnegie has yours of 16th November, but he does not see his way to advance further sums for the library bilding, as he considers that the amount promist was sufficient to have coverd the cost of library bilding needed, more especially as there has been expenditure on massiv pillars and masonary giving no return in accomodation and not unavoidable in architecture of taste. The bilding also appears to be unnecessarily high.

Aside from details, however, the fact is that £15,000 was promist, and if that amount was thot insufficient the question of an additional amount should have been settled before any expenditures whatever were entered into

Very truly yours,
J. A. S. BERTRAM
Secretary

The fuss went on well into 1913 before it was agreed to apply for a loan from the Local Government Board, in order to make good the default.

Public Museums
The present North East is well-supplied with museums, for the second half of the twentieth century has seen considerable expansion of museums and art galleries administered by local authorities. The Bowes Museum was rescued from near collapse by Durham County Council in 1956, the North of England Open Air Museum at Beamish was founded in 1970, the museums of Teesside were first brought together under the short-lived Teesside Borough, and then continued by successor Districts in the new Cleveland County, and the establishment of Tyne and Wear County Council made it possible to rescue and coordinate museums within that administrative area, with considerable improvements.

By contrast, the earlier history of museums in the North East is but slight, though probably the earliest public one was that of Sunderland which took over responsibility for the collections of the Sunderland Literary and Philosophical Society in 1846 (these collections having originated with the Natural History and Antiquarian Society of Sunderland in 1836). For some years these collections were housed, along with the Public Library, in the old Athenaeum Building in Fawcett Street. The present Central Library, Museum and Art Gallery building was opened in 1879, and extended not very many years ago. South Shields was another authority to have an early museum; it opened in 1876, though was occupying only one room as recently as the 1940s.

Both these Authorities probably took their powers from a long-forgotten Museums Act of 1845 which enabled town councils to found and maintain museums. It was the curiously-named Museums and Gymnasiums Act of 1891, however, which resulted in the creation of a greater number of municipal museums throughout the country, though less so in our region. This Act permitted a rate limit of a halfpenny and sanctioned 'museums for the reception of local antiquities and other objects of interest'. Such museums were to be 'open to the public not less than three days in every week free of charge'.

Middlesbrough's Dorman Memorial Museum was opened in 1904, presented by Sir A.J. Dorman Bt. in memory of his son who fell in

PLATE 27 Statue of Queen Victoria at Tynemouth by Alfred Gilbert, 1905

the South Africa War. And in that same year the Laing Art Gallery and Museum in Newcastle was opened to the public, the cost of the building having been defrayed by Mr Alexander Laing, a wealthy wine-merchant. This building which has, according to Pevsner, 'the typical neo-Baroque stone-domed tower of that date', was added on to the Public Library of the day, though the latter has now been demolished.

The two great North Eastern museums of Victorian times were the Bowes Museum at Barnard Castle and the Hancock Museum in New-castle. Though the former is now in public hands, neither began in that way, and their histories are accordingly described in Chapter 8.

NEWCASTLE AND MIDDLESBROUGH (An old town and a new one)

By comparing and contrasting the two towns of Newcastle upon Tyne and Middlesbrough, we shall be able to observe differing ways in which the Victorians both stimulated and reacted to population growth. It is difficult to compare the present-day populations of these two towns because recent administrative and boundary changes are confusing, but in the 1960s when each was a finite District Council, the population of Middlesbrough was around 160,000 and that of Newcastle around 270,000.

There has, for most of the present century, been a hidden tug-of-war between Tyneside and Teesside, headed by these two authorities lying at the northern and southern extremities of their region, and each undoubtedly influences its surrounding population and countryside. The lack of national influence by the North East may also owe something to the difficulty with which the north and south of the region co-operate. But for all these tensions, and apparent similarities both as river crossings and as growth-points, the two towns could hardly be more dissimilar.

Newcastle is sited on a steep south-facing bank, with origins going back to Roman and Norman times, with broad central streets, good public buildings and quality housing. Middlesbrough on the other hand stands on dismally flat land, and was non-existent in 1800. It was well-planned in 1830, but ended up with mean streets, few public buildings and acres of rapidly 'run-up' working-class housing.

Newcastle upon Tyne

The keep of the 'new castle' was built at the top of a steep bank running up from the River Tyne by Henry II in 1172–7 (for £911.10.9!): of the even earlier Roman fort of Pons Aelius very little remains to be seen. Thus Newcastle had an early start and its town walls, built in the time of Henry III, probably date from the middle of the 13th century. Even now, despite centuries of destruction or at best thoughtlessness, more remains of the walls than in any other English town except for Chester, Chichester, Southampton and York. That the walls and their towers have been so little known has been due as much to the dark colour of the weathered and soot-blackened stone as to the way in which the wall has been treated by adjoining buildings and roads. Happily things are changing here and there and stretches of the wall are once more appearing and being readily seen across patches of green.

Through four centuries the town thrived mostly within its mediaeval walls, for right up to the time of the Union of 1707 there were continuing wars with the Scots and as the major crossing point of the Tyne, Newcastle served an important protective function for north eastern England. Towards the end of this period, when Celia Fiennes visited it in 1698, she remarked that 'it most resembles London of any place in England, its

PLATE 28 The Side, Newcastle

buildings lofty and large of brick mostly or stone, the streets very broad and handsome'. Around 25 years later Daniel Defoe wrote 'Newcastle is a spacious, extended, infinitely populous place; 'tis seated upon the River Tyne...and ships of any reasonable burthen may come safely up to the very town'.

It was in the late 18th century that change began, gathering momentum within our period, in about 1825. Some indication of the need for building expansion can be gained from population figures:

Year	Population
1750	— 20,000
1801	— 28,000
1821	— 35,000
1851	— 88,000

Eldon Square (1824–6) and Leazes Terrace (1829) still stand at least in part, to demonstrate this early period. The latter was designed by Thomas Oliver: a man to whom we owe much early descriptive information and mapping of the old town; whilst John Dobson was responsible for Eldon Square (now two thirds destroyed by what one cannot but call twentieth century vandalism). Dobson owes his fame not so much to his ability as an architect – though he was indeed competent – as to his association with the speculative genius of Richard Grainger the builder and the administrative and financial abilities of John Clayton, land owner and Newcastle's Town Clerk.

If, for the purpose of this book, we concentrate upon the Victorian development of Newcastle, our view must nevertheless be placed in historical context and since this began with a brief sketch of pre-Victorian times, so we should glance forward to the present. For the twentieth century has been another period of rapid large-scale change. Important though Newcastle is within its region, it is far enough away from London, Birmingham and the Midlands to have escaped the notice of 'property developers' and in part owes its present state of relatively good preservation to this isolation and also to a state of inertia and reduced affluence in the middle of the present century. Thus whereas the centres of London and most larger towns and cities have suffered enormous destruction in the 50s, 60s and early 70s of this century, Newcastle has suffered less so. Gateshead, on the other hand, across the river and in one sense almost part of Newcastle, has suffered terribly at the hands of both minor developers and road-builders in the later twentieth century.

However Newcastle's very isolation has created its own problems. For if it is true that 'a prophet is . . . without honour in his own country', where can this be more so than in Newcastle, where so many of its twentieth century citizens have lived within its confines to such an extent that they have not fully realised its remarkable qualities. 'It is only perhaps relatively late in life that many Newcastle folk have become aware of why Newcastle looks and feels so "different" from any other provincial commercial city and – after being taken for granted for many years – appreciation begins to grow of the ornate stone pilasters and columns in Grey

PLATE 29 The River Tyne, with Swing Bridge open at Newcastle upon Tyne

PLATE 30 Grey Street, Newcastle upon Tyne (Photo: Newcastle upon Tyne City Libraries)

Street and Grainger Street and the graceful simplicities of Clayton Street West, Hood Street and St Mary's Place': so wrote two north easterners, Judge Lyall Wilkes and Gordon Dodds in 1964. It was as a result of non-appreciation in the immediate post-war Newcastle that a minor rape was permitted to take place, destroying most of Eldon Square and Pilgrim Street and driving an urban motorway through the eastern half of the city. Happily Grey Street was spared, though not for want of trying, for even that was threatened in 1963 and only saved by a development proposal being refused by a Ministry of Housing Inspector.

Yet our generation should not accept all the blame, for our Victorian forbears made similar dramatic slashes across the city they found. The railway line which destroyed the southern fortification of the Castle (thus making it impossible to see the Keep properly) and – later – the County Hall (1910) built over its Great Hall, are – at least to this writer – quite unforgiveable. On the other hand even more dramatic changes are accepted by us as vital improvements, notably the clearing away of Anderson Place (seat of Sir William Blackett) to make room for Clayton Street, Grainger Street and Grey Street in the 1830s. Thus each generation must be judged afresh by its own works and the foregoing paragraphs should not be construed as a plea for stagnation and mass-preservation.

Middlesbrough

Sadly it is difficult to say much that is complimentary about Middlesbrough and it is not surprising that Pevsner, though he tried hard, wrote in 1966 that 'the big-townish appearance only goes skin-deep. Everywhere, looking out at the few main streets, are the interminable rows of two-storeyed cottages'. A more positive, though more flowery, quotation comes from W.E. Gladstone on his visit to Middlesbrough in 1862: 'An Hercules, an infant Hercules no doubt, but an Hercules all the same', and it is true that long before the 1860s Middlesbrough had outgrown all early estimates. Today, a very large proportion of the old housing has been cleared and replaced by a shopping precinct, carparks and other developments.

Certainly there were cities outside Britain, in the United States or Australia, which grew from nothing even faster during the nineteenth century, but in Britain Middlesbrough was unique:

Year	Population		Year	Population
1801 –	25		1861 –	19,000
1829 –	40		1871 –	39,500
1831 –	154		1881 –	56,000
1841 –	5,463		1891 –	75,500
1851 –	7,500		1901 –	91,000

The period of 1831 to 1841 was that of initial planned development of a community, by the 'Middlesbrough Owners'. These Quaker gentlemen were following up the initial construction of the Stockton & Darlington Railway, from Witton Park to Stockton, with the intention of bringing coals rapidly to the riverside at Stockton for shipment down the coast, thus opening up a coalfield in South West Durham. However the river between Stockton and Teesmouth was narrow, winding and very difficult to manage by sailing ships. It is true that the Mandale and Portrack 'cuts' (of 1810 and 1829 respectively) had shortened the river journey by about three miles but the journey remained lengthy and expensive. To improve this the 'Middlesbrough Owners' decided to extend the railway by a further six miles to develop 'Port Darlington' on the edge of acres of bleak salt marshes, near the planned site of Middlesbrough.

It says much for the vision of Joseph Pease, 'father' of the Stockton & Darlington Railway and of Middlesbrough that he could write in 1828: 'Imagination here has very ample scope in fancying a coming day when the bare fields will be covered with a busy multitude and numerous vessels crowding to these banks denoting the busy seaport'.

Pease and his partners – all Quakers – bought the Middlesbrough estate in 1829 and set about developing a port which they determined would rival Sunderland or Newcastle. They talked, perhaps a little grandiloquently, of 'taking the lead of both Tyne and Wear'.

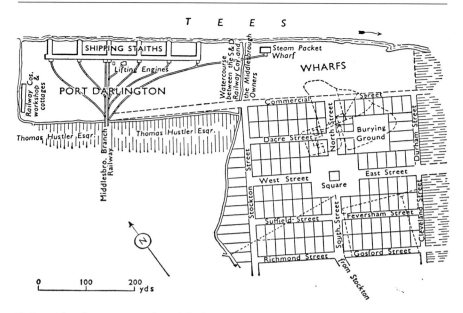

FIG 3 The beginnings of Middlesbrough. Based on the 1830 plan for Joseph Pease's new town, prepared by Richard Otley, Surveyor

Yet their optimism began to be justified for whereas Pease, in 1826, had modestly estimated that 10,000 tons of coal could be exported each year from Teesside, the actual figure in 1830–31, the first year after the Stockton & Darlington Railway had been extended to Middlesbrough, was over 150,000 tons. By 1840 total coal exports had risen to over one and a half million tons. Little, alas, remains visible of the original well-planned settlement, but Fig 3 indicates the initial 1830 plan, symmetrically set out with a central square and four main streets, not very imaginatively named North Street, South Street, East Street and West Street. The Quaker owners stated their intention 'to produce some uniformity and respectability' in the houses they built and generously provided land for the building of the Parish Church of St Hilda. £1,200 was subsequently raised by a grand bazaar and lottery. The church was eventually built (1838–40) to a design by John Green of Newcastle.

1840 was the beginning of urban institutions. A Wesleyan Methodist Chapel was opened in 1840 and Richmond Street Primitive Methodist Chapel in 1841. A Mechanics Institute was founded in 1840 and in 1843 the first new school buildings were erected by the British and Foreign School Society. In 1841 an Improvement Act put the government of the town in the hands of thirteen Commissioners who were given power to deal with Watch, Paving, Lighting, Cleansing and Drainage. These men were energetic, if a little rough and ready in their approach. They appointed a local solicitor as their Clerk and he also held the posts of Chief of Police, Surveyor and Collector of Rates: all this on a salary of £60 per year. In 1846 a Town Hall was built in the central square of the new town. A description at the time put it as 'a very unpretentious pile ... designed evidently with an eye to utility rather than ornament'; though Pevsner had been much kinder: 'simple, attractive Italianate front with typically early Victorian groups of small arched windows on the ground floor'. Later in the century this building served as a branch police station. In the late 1840s a fire engine was kept there – one which had been bought for £15 from another local authority. It was not until 1849 that the present Town Hall was opened, having a great hall with a double hammerbeam roof (of iron construction!) and a tall off-centre tower.

The relatively short history of Middlesbrough is very much linked with local personalities and two names – so closely associated almost as to seem a double name – were those of Bolckow and Vaughan. Henry Bolckow, who transformed both the economic and social life of Middlesbrough, was a Mecklenberger who arrived in Newcastle in 1827 at the age of 21. He settled in Middlesbrough in 1841 with a capital of £50,000 which he had made in Tyneside commerce. His partner John Vaughan had moved around Britain in a managerial capacity in the iron industry, before settling in Middlesbrough. The two formed a powerful partnership. Moreover they had married sisters and lived next door to each other. They were, it is reported, 'continually in each other's company, consulting, controlling, planning and advising'. Between 1841 and 1850 they established a

PLATE 31 Albert Road, Middlesbrough

small scale enterprise, collecting their ironstone from coastal places such as Whitby, sending it to blast furnaces in mid Durham and then working it at their Middlesbrough foundry. All this was changed when, in 1850, Vaughan discovered an important supply of ironstone in the nearby Cleveland hills. A first load of seven tons was transported within three weeks of the discovery and within a few months more than three thousand tons were being extracted daily. Their first blast furnace was built in 1851. By 1861 production of pig-iron had leapt to half a million tons per year and by 1867 nearly a million tons. By 1873 the North East Ironfield, with Middlesbrough as its capital, was producing over two million tons of pig-iron – about one third of the total British output. At this time, of course, iron was being required in ever growing quantities for railways, shipbuilding and heavy engineering and all this Victorian prosperity continued to push up the price of iron.

Another significant name in Middlesbrough's history was that of Pease. The family was linked with so many aspects of the town's prosperity: Joseph Pease and Partners dealt in coal, J.W. Pease & Co. in ironstone and limestone; J. & J.W. Pease in banking and Henry Pease & Co. in manufacturing.

Isaac Lowthian Bell and his two brothers were ironfounders and built the Port Clarence Furnaces. Lowthian Bell had a good scientific education and remained interested in science throughout his life. Apart from their industrial basis, these men played their part in the social and administrative growth of the town. Henry Bolckow, for example, became its first Mayor. He was also first President of the Chamber of Commerce when that chamber was formed in 1863 and he became first Member of Parliament for Middlesbrough when it became a parliamentary constituency in 1868. He also gave Middlesbrough its first public park in 1868 and always headed local subscription lists and left generous benefactions at his death. When he died the *North Eastern Gazette* appeared with black borders around its columns.

Cultural matters, never as successful as in Newcastle, began reasonably well. The Mechanics' Institution acquired a new building in 1860 and its work was supplemented by the Middlesbrough Athenaeum, 'a society for the cultivation of literature, science and the arts'. In 1875 the society changed its title to that of 'Literary and Philosophical Society'. An Orpheus Music Club prospered during the late 1860s, as did a Choral Society and a Philharmonic Society.

In 1870 a reading room and free library were opened under the Public Libraries Act. A working men's club was opened in 1873 by Bolckow, with a quarterly subscription of two shillings. The *Middlesbrough Chronicle* (monthly) started in 1853. In 1855 it became a weekly. It was a liberal paper as also was the *Weekly Gazette* which became the *Daily Gazette* in 1869. Gradually the great names of earlier years withdrew from active

PLATE 32 Linthorpe road, Middlesbrough

industrial and public life. Improvement, which had depended so long on the paternalism of the 'owners' and of the ironmasters, faded. Liberalism became less powerful.

Even chemistry was against the town. For when Henry Bessemer developed the steel converter in 1856, this required phosphorus-free iron and Sheffield became the centre for this new industry, whilst Middlesbrough, still with plentiful supplies of phosphoric ore, lagged behind. Due to the energy of Bolckow and Vaughan, however, the industry picked up again importing suitable raw materials and in 1879 a new process of steel-making was demonstrated by the company which permitted steel to be made from phosphoric iron ore.

Turning now to the housing of the people, we should note that in the earlier years of Middlesbrough's history, it was sometimes argued that Middlesbrough was 'new' and did not need excessive health legislation. A cry from the *Middlesbrough Weekly News* of 1859 has a modern ring about it: 'you cannot even build a pantry without submitting plans and specifications for the approval of an authorised architect'. Yet public baths and washhouses, commonly found in Newcastle, were not built in Middlesbrough until 1884.

Over the period 1871–3 the death rate was almost 24 per thousand of the population as a whole and far worse than this in the crowded

83

working-class districts. 40 per cent of the total recorded deaths over the same period were of children under the age of one year and deaths of children aged between 1 and 8 amounted to another 20 per cent.

In 1878 a petition by certain ratepayers requested the Council to cut its capital expenditure on such rates as water and drainage ... 'such an increase at a time of unprecedented commercial depression is neither expedient nor warrantable.'

A large railway station, completed in 1877 served both the old planned part of the town and the newer more sprawling development, so the town was finally linked to the rest of the region. Yet even today Middlesbrough does not always see itself as part of the region: too far away from the urban centres of Yorkshire to be part of that county, and not readily associated with the north eastern 'power centre' of Newcastle, against which it 'pulls' on many an occasion.

FINANCE AND COMMERCE

Matters of Finance
Centres of finance today lie, as often as not, outside one's own country, certainly outside this region, and the few financial firms still to be found in Newcastle are closely linked with London and of relatively little importance in their own right in the North.

Yet throughout the eighteenth century and much of the nineteenth century the North East saw not only a growth of industry with increasing production, but a parallel growth in commercial and financial activities, though there were a number of set backs which should not be glossed over.

For several centuries Newcastle had been a trading centre, dealing with a wide variety of commodities: coal, lead, grindstones, agricultural produce, glass and pottery and trading on this scale necessitated financial support in various forms such as banking and insurance. As the nineteenth century moved on the financial organisations became more sophisticated, and as funds increased a need developed for improved methods of investment. For example in 1841 there were only five stockbrokers recorded in Newcastle whereas in 1845 the number had risen to twenty and in that year the Newcastle Stock Exchange was created.

Similarly insurance services expanded to meet growing needs, but it is in banking that one can best see how the expanding economy produced additional financial resources.

For fifty years or more back in the eighteenth century there was an obvious need for smooth arrangements for the movement of funds. An apparently minor matter like a delay in the sailing of the collier fleet caused by bad weather could cause a shiver in financial circles, for the receipts from coal sales in London were now a significant item in the region's funding. An increase in trade and a wish to find profitable outlets

PLATE 33 High Street, Stockton-on-Tees

for increasing resources led also to a need for improved banking facilities.

The first local firm which can be seen as a bank was Bell, Cookson, Carr and Airey, set up in Newcastle around 1755 and probably the second oldest country bank in Britain. This was a profitable operation, for with its founding capital held by the four partners, in sums of £2,000 each, it produced annual profits in the 1770s of between £3,700 in 1771 and £5,712 in 1776. Not surprisingly other banks followed, both in Newcastle and also in Darlington, where the Backhouse bank became one of the most famous in the region. The Quaker families played a large part in these banking activities for not only were they already considerably involved in trading (linen and worsted manufacturing in Darlington, for example), but as a close-knit and co-operating group they could be depended upon to rally round in any difficult period.

The chief risk at this time lay in the unlimited liability which existed for partners and indeed for shareholders in joint stock banks, until legislation in 1862. Clearly it was difficult, for the best of managements, to maintain profitable application of funds, whilst retaining sufficient liquidity for any unforeseen eventuality. And a 'run' on a bank could be disastrous as the public's demand for immediate repayment of cash was triggered off by a rumour that the bank was in difficulties. A lively, if somewhat romantic, description of such an event can be read in *John Halifax, Gentleman* (1857) by Mrs Craik: a notable book in its day and is still readable today.

85

PLATE 34 King Street, South Shields

PLATE 35 South Shields Market

A history of regional banking during the second half of the nineteenth century becomes more specialised and complex as the century wears on. There were to be several examples of bad growth, of bad management and of hard lessons to be learned, as the regional banks gradually merged with the nationally based banks. This development, together with increasingly effective legislation helped the region's banking facilities to offer wider and more responsible services: a matter of importance at a time when there was an accelerating economic growth. No doubt the hard lessons of the first half of the century were of great help in the second.

Ladies' Shops and Shopping
Shopping is a modern leisure activity, though perhaps it always was for the leisured class. In common with much of the western world, the North East now has a number of 'Shopping Centres' and 'Shopping Malls' where the nationally-known as well as some regional shops throw themselves open by way of 'self-service'. Two of the most recent developments: 'Eldon Square' in Newcastle and 'Metro Centre' to the west of Gateshead, now attract enormous numbers of well-dressed shoppers, the latter especially, catering for an out of town car-borne clientele.

As for our Victorian forbears, their shopping took place in the town centres and much of what is to be described must of necessity have related mostly to the middle-class Victorian residents of some of the larger towns. Whilst the clothing of working people would be simple and often made of some long-lasting material such as fustian, the clothes of the middle-class and the gentry would be fashionable and hence changed frequently. Changes of fashionable dress for the middle-class is one of those factors which we may observe developing especially markedly during the nineteenth century.

It is particularly interesting to observe how certain items or activities 'change class' over a long period and the method of purchasing clothing and dress accessories is one such. Jane Austen, for example, purchased 'some Irish (linen) to make six shifts and four pairs of stockings' from a Scotchman in 1789: the Scotch Draper or Scotchman was an itinerant draper who would visit families living in the country with his wares, possibly with a horse and cart. Before the end of the nineteenth century the Scotch Draper would have found his customers changing and he would often be dealing, for example, with mining families who would be using his service as a kind of 'hire-purchase' method of buying their 'Sunday clothes'. Until the advent of cheap large sheets of glass, shop windows were of necessity glazed with small panes and hence unsuitable for striking displays, though before the end of the century we find illustrations in Trade Directories, on bill-heads and the like, of large-glazed windows then filled with crowded displays and surrounded by further hanging goods.

We would today find the interiors of these drapery shops oppressively gloomy and hung around with goods, whilst overhead might roll the 'cash balls', carrying cash or change. Lamson's Cash Balls were an ingenious invention of the early 1880s. Each comprised two hollow wooden hemispheres threaded to screw together, one with a spring-loaded plunger, so that the money and the bill could be gripped in the central hollow. They rolled along gently inclined tracks above the counters and thence to the Cashier's Office, and back. One such system has been installed in the re-erected and restored Co-operative Draper's Shop at Beamish, the regional open air museum, where it delights young and old.

Whereas London — and of course Paris — were the cities where one would expect to find the latest fashions, Newcastle was not far behind. An exceptionally elegant and exclusive establishment was opened there in 1882. This was the original shop, at 4 Northumberland Street, of Mr. J.J. Fenwick. Northumberland Street was then still mainly residential, Pilgrim Street being Newcastle's main shopping area. Two adjacent residences in Northumberland Street were owned by doctors and when they moved out Mr Fenwick bought these imposing stone-built houses and commissioned an eminent architect, W.H. Knowles, who designed much of Armstrong

Few people visit Newcastle, without being struck with the magnitude of its business establishments; few places will give you a better idea of these hives of industry than a visit to one of the establishments of Stewart, the tea dealer. You may form some conception of the business energy in this thriving concern, from the fact that upwards of sixty-three thousand pounds of tea were retailed during 1862. Such power has this spirited proprietor gained over the minds and tastes of the public, with his characteristic advertising, that you cannot pass 33, Grainger Street, or 27, Sandhill, without feeling an inclination to enter. Then memory links a chain of merry associations of home, and the joyful clatter of the evening meal, and remembering the words of the lady that obstinately insisted her husband was a model man, and assigned, as her reason, that he never went to Newcastle without bringing home a packet of Stewart's tea. You feel assured there is no gift more acceptable, and certainly none more easily carried. You yield to your instincts, pay for a packet, and go on your way rejoicing, thinking only how bright will be the smile of her that rules at home.

PLATE 36 The window of a Newcastle Tea Merchant, c. 1865

PLATE 37 Potato carts at Alston

College (now part of the University of Newcastle), to design the shop-front. This in itself caused a sensation, presenting as it did two large display windows with graceful supporting pillars with fluting picked out in gold leaf. Moreover the windows, projecting out beyond the building frontage, curved round the central entrance in which stood a metal statue supporting a large lamp.

Mr Fenwick was particularly insistent that his windows were not to be crowded with merchandise, such as commonly choked the windows of most drapery shops of the day. So determined was Mr Fenwick to keep this shop 'exclusive' that when later he required another shop to satisfy a growing demand for ready-made clothes, he bought premises on the other side of the road in order not to detract from his main premises.

Earlier than all this was the beginning of Bainbridge's also of Newcastle. As long ago as 1830 Emerson Muschamp Bainbridge was apprenticed, at the age of 13 to a Newcastle draper Robert Kidd, who had a wholesale and retail business on The Side. After completing his time, Bainbridge spent two years working in London and then returned to Newcastle, being taken into partnership by William Dunn in 1838. In 1841 he left to establish his own business and by 1845 Bainbridge's stock included dress and furnishing fabrics, fashion accessories, furs and family mourning as well as 'sewed muslin dresses': an early form of ready-made clothing. Perhaps the most significant change which Bainbridge instituted at this point was to abolish bargaining and all his goods were then marked at fixed prices. This resulted in a greater turnover enabling him to undercut other major

89

PLATE 38 Green Market, Newcastle upon Tyne

specialist shops and in 1856 he was able to advertise that Bainbridge's 'had no hesitation in stating that they will sell all goods in the Woollen Branch of their Business at Prices with which exclusively Woollen Houses cannot compete'. In 1865 Bainbridge bought a block of property running back from Market Street and Bigg Market and later rebuilt all of this to a height of four storeys. In 1883 the firm expanded into the manufacturing business, with a factory in Leeds for men's and boy's clothing and a little later took over a boot and shoe factory and then factories for women's clothes.

A detailed and illustrated article in *The Gentlemen's Journal and Gentlemen's Court Review* in 1912 describes the factory methods employed by Bainbridge Brothers at Leeds and Newcastle upon Tyne. Photographs show views in 'The Cloth Warehouse' and 'The Cutting Room' and very crowded scenes of hundreds of young women at work in 'The Jacket Machine Room' and 'The Cap Department'. These premises even had their own engine house 'where the electric light for over 1,600 lamps is also generated'. This laudatory article ends: 'A certain great authority has recently told us that certain British industries are dead and that others are dying, but so far as the Clothing Market Industry is concerned we saw every proof that, so far as Messrs BAINBRIDGE are concerned, it is very much alive and working. And no wonder, for clothing so artistically designed and carefully manufactured cannot fail to find a market, not merely at home but also in the Colonies, for it gives new life to the well-known phrase: "British and Best"'.

90

6
LIVING AND DYING
IN TOWNS

PUBLIC HEALTH

Cholera and the Drains

The building of great towns and cities was a typically Victorian activity: grandiose and with excellent detailing in places, but lacking in organisation such as we today would require of our planners. These towns present a mass of contradictions. It is difficult for us to understand how the authorities in Newcastle – with a centre so beautifully conceived and constructed by Dobson and Grainger – could still permit incredibly squalid housing down by the riverside, where cholera could be rampant and sanitary conditions indescribable. Of course we can hardly expect the Victorians to have set themselves the standards which we have come to expect ourselves, any more than we can think of them as being deprived because they did not have refrigerators or television sets. It is, however, the contrast between the best and the worst which we may note.

Maintenance of the well-being of an urban population is clearly more complex than that of a rural one where everything is on a smaller and more comprehensible scale. The farmyard pump or the 'netty' at the bottom of the garden, so ably illustrated by Thomas Bewick, the northern wood-engraver, (Fig 9) would be reasonably adequate even if the pig was not far away. But when towns expanded and accommodation (we can hardly call much of it 'housing') proliferated, problems rapidly multiplied. Where was the source of fresh water? And how was it to be brought to the houses; or at least near to them? Where were the privies to be built and how were they to be cleared?

It may be difficult for us, accustomed as we are today to controls and regulations, to imagine the chaotic way in which towns were allowed to expand without any real oversight. Indeed little note was taken until Edwin Chadwick produced his Report on *The Sanitary Condition of the Labouring Population of Great Britain* in 1842. This was followed by the Public Health Act of 1848 which set up Boards: in the Boroughs the Councils acted as Boards. From this date builders had to submit plans before commencing building and connection by drain to the public sewers became regularised. Where this was followed, then water-borne sewage became the norm. Unfortunately not every Borough adopted the Act, and the task of the small

91

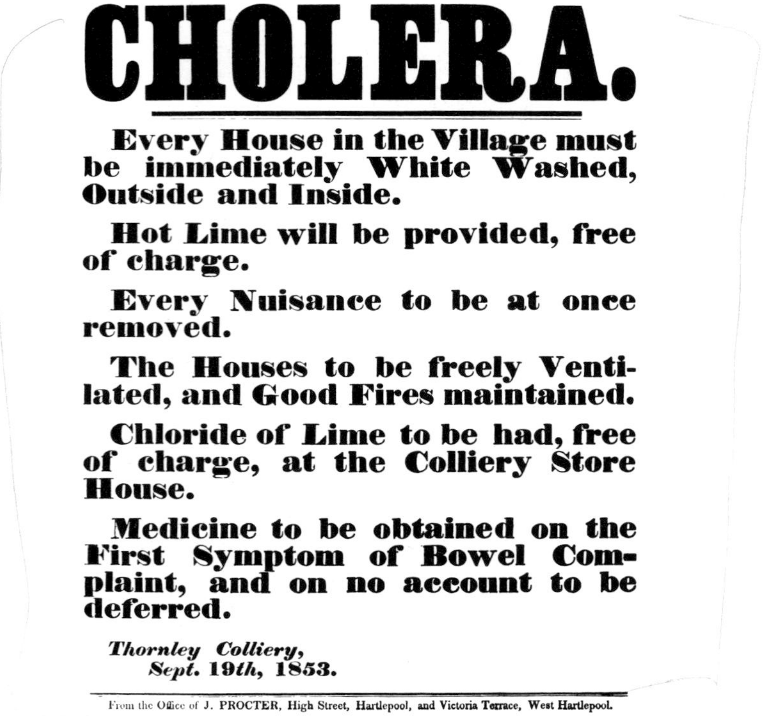

CHOLERA.

Every House in the Village must be immediately White Washed, Outside and Inside.

Hot Lime will be provided, free of charge.

Every Nuisance to be at once removed.

The Houses to be freely Ventilated, and Good Fires maintained.

Chloride of Lime to be had, free of charge, at the Colliery Store House.

Medicine to be obtained on the First Symptom of Bowel Complaint, and on no account to be deferred.

Thornley Colliery,
Sept. 19th, 1853.

From the Office of J. PROCTER, High Street, Hartlepool, and Victoria Terrace, West Hartlepool.

FIG 4 Cholera poster from County Durham, 1853

Inspectorate, set up by the Act, was a daunting one. As things improved, stand pipes or public water taps were erected, the water being conveyed by heavy lead pipes. Earth closets were supposedly better organised and regularly cleared; street drains led off to the main sewers; the widths of streets and back-roads were specified. In the poorer parts of most towns, where squalid cheap housing had been thrown up and subdivided into tenements, there were no such niceties, as will be realised in a moment, when we look at the inevitable disease which was nurtured by these inadequate systems. For too long a general desire for 'cheap government' had allowed these to continue.

An outstanding feature of the later Victorian town was the system of drains and sewers, eventually provided with what we would call water-seals and their designers called stench-traps. In Newcastle these drains tended to run into the denes or natural stream-beds flowing down to the river and eventually the denes themselves were piped and covered over. Today the

PLATE 39 Updated nineteenth century sewer, passing under the old 'High Bridge' in Newcastle upon Tyne (Photo: Newcastle City Engineer)

92

natural topography of mid-nineteenth century Newcastle is less easy to understand since the denes have been so deeply covered. New Bridge Street, for instance, is so-called because it originally led to the bridge constructed over Pandon Dene. That bridge lay roughly between Argyle Street to the east and the present route of the Central Motorway to the west. All the land around there has now been raised towards that bridge level, and the dene is only recalled by the name of Pandon Bank, which runs down to City Road. Northwards, upstream along the dene, the next bridge was Barras Bridge, again completely forgotten as a bridge except by name; but at one time in a rural setting. The bridge is still in part visible to the really intrepid traveller, in the shape of deserted stonework above the present main sewer. Similarly High Bridge can be traced as a stonework arch crossing another of Newcastle's old rivers, later to become another main sewer (Plate 39).

All these drains continued, as had the denes when they were clear streams, to flow into the River Tyne, and it is only in very recent years that a major new drain was cut parallel to the river to pick up all these sewers and carry their contents to a major sewage disposal system down river at Howdon.

Really to appreciate the dreadful conditions in a city such as Newcastle or a town such as Sunderland in the middle of last century, we need to read contemporary reports. The triggering of such reports was usually a traumatic experience which established a need for investigation and possible amelioration. Cholera provided just such an occasion. This disease is caused by a bacillus carried by faeces on food or in tainted drinking water, and the crowded and wholly unhygienic conditions of early Victorian towns made them completely susceptible to it. For some years it had been found across Asia, apparently having appeared in India in 1817. It spread across Eastern Europe and into Germany and in 1831 a sailor from Hamburg unwittingly brought it to Sunderland. Within a few weeks it was in London.

A factual description of one of the first Sunderland cases is recorded for us in *The Cholera of Sunderland* (1832) by none other than Dr W.R. Clanny, who has already been noted for his early work on a safety lamp for the coal mines:

A few doors off on the same quay lived a keelman named Sproat, aged sixty; he occupied a clean, well-ventilated room on the first-floor of a house in the most open part of the quay. He was in failing health, and had been troubled with diarrhoea for a week or ten days previous to the 19th October, on which day he had to give up work. Next day, a surgeon, who had been sent for found him vomiting and purging, but not at all collapsed, with no thirst, and in good spirits. He improved so much that on Friday he had toasted cheese for supper and on Saturday a mutton chop for dinner, after which he went out to his keel on the river for a few minutes. On his return he was seized with rigor, cramps, vomiting and purging. Medical aid was not sent for until seven on Sunday morning, when he

PLATE 40 A Dales funeral

was found in a sinking state, pulseless, speaking in a husky whisper, his face livid and pinched, his limbs cramped, the purgings like 'meal washings'. He continued like that for three days, and died on Wednesday, the 26th October, at noon.

The 1831 epidemic in the North eventually died out, but further outbreaks occurred in 1848–9, 1853–4, and 1866. After the second of these outbreaks a Cholera Inquiry Commission was set up and its report (published in 1854) on the sanitary conditions of Newcastle, Gateshead and Sunderland makes sombre reading.

Mr William Lee, CE (ie Civil Engineer – nothing to do with his religion!) a superintending inspector of the Board of Health, gave evidence of observations he had made in Newcastle in 1853, having – he said – been sent there by the General Board of Health to aid the local authorities:

In my examination of the town I have found in the seats of cholera large accumulations of dung, litter and ashes, mixed with vegetable and animal refuse. In all these decomposition is going on: some have pools of fluid and semi-fluid matter connected with them; and from others the liquid is oozing through walls and doors and trickling away along the surface gutters of the narrow ill-ventilated court-yards and alleys and even along the streets.

FIG 5 Part of a map of Gateshead, showing the effect of the cholera outbreak of 1853. (Each black dot indicates the site of a death: the total in the Borough was 433)

There are some public privies and urinals belonging to the corporation. I have examined some of them and think they are in a very objectionable and offensive condition. I would recommend a copious use of earth and lime to these, and a frequent examination and renewal of the treatment, if any stench should be found to exist. I was informed that the public privy under the lower bridge is used by about 1,000 men and boys every day. A man was attacked by cholera while in that privy and died, as I was informed, in a few hours. I could perceive the stench from the place at a distance of many yards.

Another matter is that there are several tripe boilers in the same infected district, and in parts of the town. The contents of the intestines and paunches were settling into the open joints of the boulder pavement, and the skin and hooves from the feet of sheep were sweltering upon the ash heaps. In a house contiguous to one of these places I found two persons dying of cholera.

White Board Entry is a very narrow abominable place, full of tenements and filth . . . In certain places where the old deans or watercourses (which are now only imperfect sewers) cross the streets, there are often untrapped gratings . . . persons all around the neighbourhood having no privies, bring their utensils and empty them in these gullies, until all the bars and the surface around are covered with human ordure.

I have not mentioned until now an occupation which I saw carried on in those parts of the Cholera districts of Newcastle having public sewers. I have already stated that the gully gratings are untrapped; and also that from the absence of privies, they are the general receptacles for the garbage and excrements of the inhabitants. There is a large population of rats in the sewers of Newcastle, especially in the Cholera localities, and the side drains from the open gully gratings appear to be their favourite feeding places. To these gratings boys from ten to fifteen years of age resort and combine amusement and profit by ratcatching . . . the young sportsmen kneel down over the poisonous effluvium and wait for their prey. I ascertained that one boy will take from four to seven or eight rats per day and sell them alive at 2d or 3d each, according to the size. They are bought by persons who resell them at about 6d each, to be worried by dogs.

Fig 5 is taken from the above 1854 Report and shows a map of the centre of Gateshead, each black dot indicating one cholera death.

However it was not only the major towns of the region which suffered epidemics on this scale. Barnard Castle, now a pleasant market town in south west Durham, with relatively unspoilt eighteenth century frontages to its main street, hides away its yards and alleys down which, early last century, were tucked scores of tiny hovels and tenemented larger houses. These, built to provide for the many workers who were drawn early last century to the

PLATE 41 Briggate or Bridgegate, Barnard Castle

flourishing manufacturing town – weavers, leather-workers, linen-thread makers, and iron-workers – proved to be a rich breeding ground for cholera. So despite its apparent isolation (16 miles from Darlington and a similar distance from Bishop Auckland) an epidemic reached and swept through the town. It is recalled today by a memorial in the churchyard noting that 143 inhabitants died here between August 16th and October 18th, 1849.

Hospitals
Perhaps it is imagination, but probably one is correct in sensing the acceptance of fate regarding personal health, when looking through a list of the kind of hospitals which served the Victorians. The list of hospitals in Newcastle, as detailed by Thomas Oliver in his 1844 *Plan of Newcastle upon Tyne and Gateshead* is shown below in date order of foundation or construction of existing buildings. Most of those dating from the nineteenth century relate to some special service or need:

1701   Keelman's Hospital
1752   Infirmary
1754   Blackett and Davison's Hospital
1777   Dispensary
1804   House of Recovery or Fever Hospital

1822 Eye Infirmary
1824 School of Medicine and Surgery
1825 Lying-In Hospital
1838 Asylum for the Blind
1839 Newcastle Asylum for the Deaf, Dumb and Blind

It was of course inescapable that most illnesses which would today be of relatively little concern, being dealt with by suitable drugs or treatment: septicaemia, tuberculosis and appendicitis for example, led almost inevitably to an early death. So hospitalisation, to use a modern concept, was inconceivable. Although the introduction of ether and chloroform as anaesthetics (1846 and 1847 respectively) permitted operations to take place under calmer conditions, unhastened by the pain of the patient, and Lister's use of antiseptic in 1865 (following Pasteur's theory of germs of 1861) made successful surgery more hopeful, yet the hospitals themselves were not fit to nurse the patients. Little was known or understood about how hospitals should be built and run.

It took the ceaseless efforts of Florence Nightingale, having made her discoveries and observations on hospital needs in the midst of war, to bring them painfully into effect in England. She came across abysmal ignorance of the first principles of how a hospital should be designed and tirelessly drafted papers on Hospital Construction. These were published in 1859 under the title *Notes on Hospitals* and other editions followed. The opening paragraph sets the scene.

It may seem a strange principle to enunciate as the very first requirement in a Hospital that it should do the sick no harm. It is quite necessary nevertheless to lay down such a principle, because the actual mortality in hospitals, especially those of large crowded cities, is very much higher than any calculation founded on the mortality of the same class of patient treated *out* of hospital would lead us to expect.

She startled her readers by postulating that the high rate of mortality – then apparently inevitable in large hospitals – could be prevented. The answer to hospital mortality, she suggested was 'neither prayer nor self-sacrifice, but better ventilation, greater cleanliness, better drainage and better food.

In *Notes on Hospitals*, Florence Nightingale paints a distressing picture of a contemporary hospital: walls streaming with damp and often covered with fungus, dirty floors, dirty beds, crowded wards, insufficient food and inadequate nursing. 'Hospital diseases' – so called – flourished in the wards: gangrene, fever, pyaemia and erysipelas.

So whatever she was able to achieve – and it was an incredible amount which she did – it was bound to be of some benefit, though there was a considerable lapse of time before many of these improvements were generally adopted.

PLATE 42 Lying-in Hospital by John Dobson (1826), New Bridge Street, Newcastle upon Tyne

As a footnote one may mention that the innovatory layout of a hospital ward not surprisingly became known as a Nightingale Ward. What is surprising is that in many hospitals today the same term is still used; it is only in the most recently constructed buildings that smaller wards have rendered the phrase out of date.

HOUSES

The stages of development of any area of a town can be traced using a series of early maps and street directories such as those of Kelly's and Ward's. A particularly fruitful area for such a study is that of Elswick, that heavily populated community to the west of Newcastle, which grew so rapidly as Armstrong's works developed and expanded.

For example in 1831, Oliver's map shows the only development to be the cemetery at the 'Big Lamp'; whereas Oliver's next map of 1844 shows several new terraces and streets and ten important sandstone quarries (Fig 10).

By 1857 another map by Oliver shows the area between St Paul's Church (built 1858/9) and Elswick Road to be built up and subsequent maps show how the area continued to extend westwards.

An interesting map of 1904 (Reid) shows the completion of much of the area. Around this time the details of various large buildings can be traced:

Co-operative Society, Benwell High Cross	1901
Canning Street School	1904
Methodist Church, Adelaide Terrace	1905
Benwell Library (Carnegie Trust)	1908
Benwell Grove Methodist Church, West Road	1908
(originally Primitive Methodist Assembly Hall)	

Another source of information is the series of Census Returns, from which occupations of householders can be traced. Thus at Rye Hill, Elswick, the following records suggest an exclusiveness of 'better classes' in 1861:

1861 Census

House number	Occupation of Householders
10	Ship & Insurance Broker
13	Manager of Lead Works
15	A Lady
21	Silk Mercer & Draper
22	Grocer
24	Importer (Exporter of grain & coal)
25	Presbyterian Minister
26	Merchant
28	Banker's Clerk
29	Flint Glass Manufacturer
30	Bank Manager
31	Shipbroker, General Merchant
32	Surveyor, Builder, Brick Manufacturer

Whereas Mill Lane, not far away, shows that a butcher, an ale-house keeper, a grocer, a plumber, a mechanic, a saddler and a cheesemonger inhabit its more humble dwellings.

On the other hand, at Wylam Road in 1880 there was a good deal of social mix: the first six houses were occupied by an engineer, a Bible Society agent, a commercial traveller, a gentleman of private income, a housewife, and one property was used as a lodging house.

Examining town-housing from a commercial point of view raises some interesting points, for houses are an unusual commodity: they are long-lived and when built by the traditional methods of the nineteenth century involve considerable labour and materials. All this, too, had its effect upon the likely rent to be charged.

North Shields provides some useful facts in this connection. In the nineteenth century it was a seaport town with an industrial base. Three townships make up what became known as a whole as 'North Shields': North Shields, Chirton and Tynemouth. A listing of their populations and numbers of dwellings (taken from Census returns) are informative. Note especially the average larger number of occupants per house in North Shields, compared with the better-class Tynemouth: rarely less than ten in North Shields, over the period 1851 – 1901, and rarely more than seven for Tynemouth.

	North Shields		Chirton		Tynemouth	
	Pop.	*Dwgs.*	*Pop.*	*Dwgs.*	*Pop.*	*Dwgs.*
1851	8,882	844	3,960	891	14,493	2,177
1861	9,595	891	5,544	1,047	16,560	2,589
1871	8,619	850	8,005	1,289	19,326	2,719
1881	7,250	794	11,248	1,667	22,548	3,230
1891	6,046	665	13,066	1,898	23,678	3,198
1901	5,737	484	15,668	1,996	24,881	3,448

Conditions in North Shields in 1845 were described by the 'Health of Towns Commission' in scathing terms. The old township was full of verminous tenements inhabited by potential transportees and surrounded by open sewers. At about this time attempts were made, by the Buildings Bill of 1841, to impose minimum national building standards, but these failed and it was not until the establishment of the Municipal Borough of Tynemouth in 1849 that local building regulations and sanitary controls were established and clearly these were becoming effective by the 1860s when the first of that regionally characteristic form of artisan housing – the Tyneside Flat – began to be built.

Tyneside Flats
Tyneside flats consist of one small terraced house divided into two flats: an upper and a lower one, with separate entrances and exits and a backyard each (or sometimes shared). Typically the upstairs flat has four rooms and the downstairs flat has three rooms, with a kitchen located in an offshoot at the back with w.c. at the end of the back yard. (Of course this latter would have been a privy at the time of construction.)

PLATE 43 Houses on Manor Road, Tynemouth

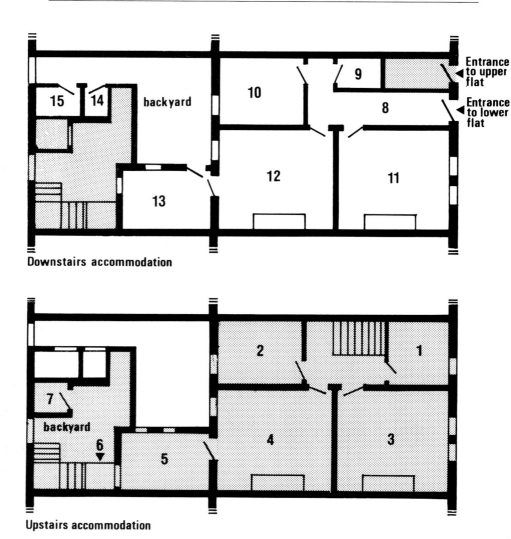

Downstairs accommodation

Upstairs accommodation

FIG 6 Plan (two floors) of Tyneside Flats in Park Terrace, Swallwell, c. 1890 (after Turnbull). Downstairs accommodation comprised: the passage (8); cupboard under the stairs (9); back bedroom (10); front bedroom (11); living room (12); kitchen (13); backyard (14); and the toilet (15). Upstairs accommodation consisted of: the front bedroom (1); back bedroom (2); main bedroom (3); living room (4); kitchen or scullery (5); and the backyard containing the coalhouse and scullery

PLATE 44 Tyneside flats, Beaconsfield Street, Newcastle upon Tyne; somewhat modernised

There is plenty of documentary evidence for these regional flats, as for example the First Report of the Royal Commission of Housing of the Working Classes (1885).

The raising of funds for this building-work takes us into another field of finance. A frequently-used method was to borrow, secured against a mortgage on the land and work in progress, often with a small local building society, of which the builder might himself be a director. Private mortgages were also important, though on a lesser scale. Mr Strachan, manager of the Newcastle Permanent Benefit Building Society (note the word 'Permanent') in giving evidence to the Friendly & Benefit Societies Commission in 1871, pointed out that the newer Building Societies were 'becoming mainly agents for the investment of capital rather than for enabling the industrious to provide dwellings for themselves'. There was a shift in control of the Building Societies from working men to the middle-classes, with an increasingly dominant role of solicitors who had money to lend.

By the end of the century, the permanent societies were taking over from the smaller societies originally set up by artisans and others, to help them build their houses. Here is a sample table of Building Society balances in 1894 in the Tynemouth and North Shields area:

Permanent Societies	Date founded	Value of Mortgages
North Shields Permanent	1875	£53,550
Tynemouth Permanent	1880	£33,820
General Permanent	1882	£62,341
Tynemouth Victoria Jubilee Permanent	1887	£10,290
Other Societies		
Borough of Tynemouth (62nd Starr-Barkett)	1862	£8,662
Shields, Whitley & District Model 20	1889	£3,094
North Shields, Tynemouth & District Perfect Thrift	1890	£1,366

In fact, in 1894, all the Permanent Societies in this area had mortgages totalling £209,346 – enough to buy 700 pairs of Tyneside Flats. Whilst the value of the other societies' mortgages were only £23,418 or 12 per cent of that of the permanent societies.

In the parliamentary papers of the 1860s and 70s there is frequent emphasis on the value of building societies as a stabilising device, by making artisans into property owners. But after 1870 the permanent building societies seem to have cut out the artisan home-owner and their funds then were being used for the more lucrative business of building artisans' dwellings to rent.

Certainly one plain advantage of the Tyneside Flat was that an owner could occupy one of the pair of flats and let the other, though it should be stated that this was not common practice in North Shields before the first world war. However, evidence given to the 1885 Commission referred to above, stated that 'most working men took out mortgages on four or five dwellings and lived in one themselves'. The old rate books for North Shields record this kind of ownership, but by the end of the century building society finance was readily available for larger-scale landlords.

The actual building costs of a pair of Tyneside flats do not seem to have varied widely between 1870 and 1910. In Trinity Street, North Shields, a pair of flats sold in 1869 for £325. Around this time pairs of flats in Gardner Street were sold for around £310 at auction. In 1884 evidence to the Commission recorded that the building costs of a pair was about £250, excluding the cost of the land. Rents were around 6s 6d per week, and in the 1890s a typical net rental for a pair of flats in North Shields was 6s 6d upstairs and 5s 6d downstairs, giving annual rent for the pair at £31.8s. The flats would be mortgaged for £380 the pair, at 4 per cent, giving the landlord a surplus over his interest of £16.4s. Clearly some of this went on repairs and management costs, and estate agents managed on the basis of 5 per cent of rents collected (ie £1.11s a year for such a house). But even so, the return was a handsome one for the owner, total yield after all costs had been met, being 6¼ per cent on his investment.

Front and Back Houses

If the Tyneside Flat (of one house *above* the other) is relatively well-known, at least within the region, another type only recently 're-discovered' around Darlington seems even more unusual. Houses of this type, constructed in the 1870s and 80s seem to have been called 'front house (or kitchen house) and back house'. Each house in each pair has both back and front doors and a long passage, the passage in one house leading to the living room, the other from the living room to the scullery (Fig 6). Accommodation in each consists of a living room (or kitchen), pantry under the stairs, and scullery, with two bedrooms over the living room. The land on which such houses typically stand in Darlington lies immediately west of the town centre, in an area which was laid out as new streets and building plots in the 1870s. This land was, at least in part, the former grounds and fields of the mansion 'Greenbank', built by the Darlington Quaker draper and botanist Edward Robson.

It must be stressed that these 'back and front houses' are not 'back to back houses', such as are frequently found in West Riding houses, for example in Leeds. Such houses had only one exit door. Nor, despite the similarity of twin doors and only one window on their street facade, are they the same as the 'Tyneside Flats', which – as described above – had one house above the other. On the original builders' applications and plans they are variously identified as 'houses', 'tenements', terraced houses' and 'cottages'. All had a living room ranging from 14 × 12ft to 16 × 13ft (approximately 4.25 × 3.7m to 4.9 × 4m). All seem to have had the same layout, with two sets of stairs running together and sideways across the centre, thus separating the two houses, although fireplaces varied in position on different builders' plans. The front doors of a pair might be together on the same side of the front house's living-room corridor, or one on each side of it.

It is of interest to note that these houses were 'discovered' in Darlington

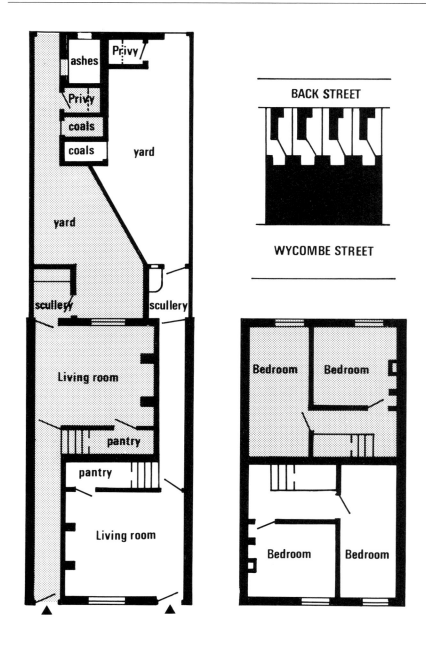

FIG 7 Plan of 'Front and Back Houses', 1877, Wycombe Street, Darlington (after Chapman)

in 1982 by a local historian, Mrs Vera Chapman, who remarks that she had often parked her car near them, before realising their oddity. (This leads one to wonder what else which may seem obvious to those accustomed to it, remains to be brought more widely into view.) There has been a subsequent suggestion that houses of this type may very occasionally have been constructed in Sunderland and Newcastle upon Tyne.

In Darlington, areas where these houses can be observed include Greenbank Road, Duke Street and Larchfield Street. They may also be observed in Outram Street and on the north side of Dodd's Street, off Greenbank Road, where there is a terrace of forty eight houses of this type. Builders include J.W. & M. McKenzie (builders and contractors), William E. Gent (joiner and builder), Haxby Dougill (builder) and Richard Bosomworth (builder and contractor). Francis Par, an architect, produced at least one set of plans. These various building applications and plans, submitted to Darlington Borough Council in the 1870s to 1890s, are preserved in the Darlington District Library.

The Sunderland Cottage
Another peculiarly local style of dwelling is the single-storey cottage typically found in street after street in and around Sunderland. Built of local brick, these cottages are only one room and a passage wide and usually three rooms long. The passage is therefore unlit and consequently there is a fanlight over the door, adding slightly to the decorative effect as seen from the front of the house.

When Building Regulations were first adopted in 1852, the width of the road was established as thirty feet, the back street eighteen feet wide and the length of the house and yard sixty feet. Whereas in Leeds a pair of 'back to back' houses would only measure thirty feet from one side to the other. It is reasonable to deduce from this that land must have been more readily available and cheaper than in Leeds.

These houses were built for artisans, not for the very poor, which were housed in 'courts' in East Sunderland. It is worth remarking that workers in the North East, and especially in the flourishing ship building area around Sunderland, generally had a high level of wages in the 1870s and 80s, comparable indeed with London. Thus it is not surprising to find that of these Sunderland cottages, many terraces were over 80 per cent owner-occupied, according to the 1871 census. The figures varied between 30 per cent and 100 per cent, in various terraces, compared with 3 per cent to 14 per cent in other parts of the region. But by 1914 the figure was much lower.

An important feature of these cottages was their privacy, and this was much appreciated. Each cottage had its own back yard and its own privy. Emphasis was put by builders on the good ventilation and the space, which was afforded by these cottages; for the past outbreaks of cholera were naturally still recalled.

PLATE 45 'Sunderland Cottages' at Alice Street, Sunderland

In a slightly more 'upmarket' version, terraces were built with a semi-attic first floor, with dormer windows. A very attractive terrace of this kind of housing is Alice Street, with good dormer gables and featured chimneys. It was designed by Pritchard of Darlington (Plate 45).

As an addendum on this section on housing, mention may be made of the use of boys as chimney sweeps. Everyone is familiar with *The Water Babies* written in 1863 by Charles Kingsley in which the chief character is the little 'climbing boy' or Chimney Sweep Tom. Kingsley was indeed describing something still practised and it was partly as a result of that book that in 1875, the year that Kingsley died, Shaftesbury eventually succeeded in pushing through Parliament an Act which forbade such employment.

EDUCATION FOR ALL

Looking at inscriptions on older school buildings in our region – and there are still a few left – one not only sees 'BOYS' and 'GIRLS AND INFANTS', but indications as to date of construction and even, occasionally, something of educational theory and signs of Victorian fervour.

Inevitably we shall find 'Board Schools' of the 1870s and 1880s. Of even earlier date we may find 'National Schools' and 'British Schools', some going back to the very early years of the nineteenth century. To whom are we indebted for these well-built and still useful monuments to the ideal of popular education? The most recent name, still being recalled by schools celebrating their centenaries, is that of William Edward Forster, author of the Elementary Education Act of 1870. This Act resulted in 'Board Schools' being constructed over the following two decades as free primary education for all was gradually implemented.

But before looking into the beginnings of Board Schools and finding what remains of them in this region, we should first seek the earlier educational origins. Two names to be found in the early history of British education are those of Andrew Bell and Joseph Lancaster. They each had a basically similar idea, namely that education should be made available generally to children of all classes of the population. Yet in detail they and their supporters differed bitterly and to a degree we may find difficult to understand today; their personalities and whole way of life too, were very different.

Andrew Bell (1753 – 1832) was born at St Andrews of a fairly well-to-do family. He graduated there, took holy orders and sailed for India where he became Superintendent of a male orphanage at Madras. Due to a scarcity of teachers he devised a system whereby the better pupils helped the others: 'mutual tuition' he called it, and in 1797 on his return to England he published a small pamphlet describing his theories.

Little notice was taken of this until Joseph Lancaster (1778–1838) came across it. Lancaster was the son of a Chelsea pensioner with few opportunities, but early in life he showed an aptitude for learning. As quite a young man he joined the Society of Friends (Quakers) and by the age of twenty he had begun to gather together a few poor children and given them simple lessons. Soon – and quite remarkably – a thousand children were assembled in Southwark and this came to the attention of the Duke of Bedford. As a result he was given the means to build a schoolroom and to furnish it. He based his method on that published by Bell, and improved on it in terms of scale and efficiency. Older children were called 'monitors' and by an elaborate system they were able to impart basic reading, writing and arithmetic to large numbers at the same time. Little equipment was needed: scraps of paper, slates and a desk spread with sand on which the children wrote with their fingers.

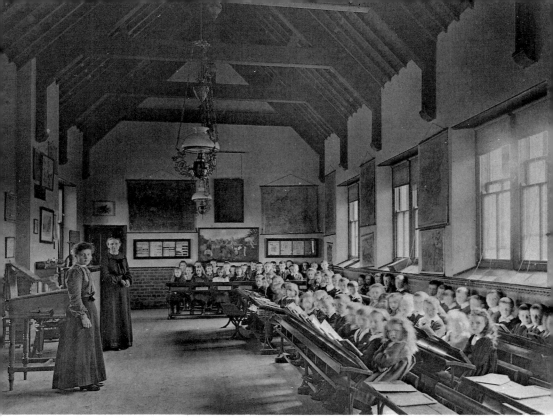

PLATE 46 Cambo School (Northumberland) in class, c. 1900

A description of Lancaster's work states 'The order and cheerfulness of the school and the military precision of the children's movements attracted much public observation'. This was at a time when the education of the poor was almost entirely neglected.

In a memorable interview with George III, Lancaster was encouraged by the king's wish that every poor child should be taught to read the Bible. Unfortunately Royal patronage and succeeding fame rather went to his head: he became vain, reckless and extravagant. In 1808 a group of enthusiastic people paid his debts and founded a Society at first called the *Royal Lancaster Institution* but afterwards, because of Lancaster's excesses, its name was changed to the *British and Foreign Schools Society*. This is not the whole story, however, for religion also has to be considered. Lancaster faced pupils drawn from a variety of religious beliefs. Hence he conceived a national system of popular education, on a voluntary basis, based on a common doctrine which would be acceptable to all the orthodox denominations of the day.

Meanwhile, members of the Church of England, alarmed at educational patronage being in the hands of dissenters, decided to set up schools of their own. Andrew Bell was pressed to organise a system of schools along these lines. The disagreements between Church and dissenters came to a head in 1807 when a Whig statesman, Mr Whitbread, made a remarkable attempt at legislation. His Parochial Schools Bill proposed to make it compulsory on 'parochial vestries' to levy rates for the support of schools, which would then teach what we still talk of as the 'Three R's': reading, writing and arithmetic. But when this Bill came before the House of Commons, the compulsory provisions had to be dropped, and the Bill was later rejected by the Lords.

So everything was back to voluntary effort, and the race was on between the dissenters with their *British and Foreign Schools Society* and the Established clergy and members of the Church of England who set up the *National Society for the Education of the Poor in the Principles of the Established Church*, of which Bell became Superintendent in 1811.

Both Societies went on to do good work, though the National Society met with greater success and was reported in 1831 to have 13,000 schools connected with the church, of which 6,470 were both day and Sunday schools, and having a total attendance of 409,000.

The one common factor, which assisted both societies, was that of the monitorial plan of teaching. We have to realise of course, that this was not based on good educational theory (though it may have seemed so at the time), but simply a makeshift rough-and-ready expedient, to get over the practical difficulty of a lack of competent teachers. However, it was important as the precursor of the pupil-teacher system which so long formed the basis of the English elementary system.

'National Schools' and 'British Schools' still stand as monuments to these pioneers. Since religion played such a part in these institutions it is not surprising to find, for example, a range of buildings labelled as 'British Schools, 1866' at Crook, a mining area in County Durham; for here, as in so many mining areas, the Established Church made little impression against the nonconformists (Plate 47). Equally predictably a 'National School: 1844' adjoins the churchyard in the small market town of Barnard Castle. This large and well-built school includes, at its rear, a covered playground facing south towards the River Tees (Plate 48).

The foregoing is by way of an explanation as to why several early school buildings – some of them still in use – came to be established and can still be found in the region. The main contribution towards education for all young children, however, was the Elementary Education Bill of 1870, introduced by W.E. Forster with the words 'What is our purpose in this Bill? Briefly to bring elementary education within the reach of every English home, aye, and within the reach of those children who have no homes . . . Upon this speedy provision of elementary education depends our industrial prosperity'. The Liberal party, coming to power in 1868 with a majority of a hundred, had entrusted Forster, MP for Bradford, with the difficult task of drafting the Education Bill and guiding it through Parliament.

PLATE 47 'British Schools: 1866' at Crook, Co. Durham

PLATE 48 'National Schools: 1844' at Barnard Castle

Although the Act of 1870 did not create a national, or a completely compulsory or indeed a free system of education, nevertheless it brought about a fundamental change in the attitude of the ruling classes towards the education of poorer people. No longer was education to be a charity: it was to be the right of every child.

Earlier in the century, in addition to the two national schemes already described, industrialists had played a part in the provision of schools. The London Lead Company and the Beaumont Company built or subscribed the schools in the Wear and Tees Valleys and in the coalfields the miners looked to the coal-owners to provide schools for their children. In the North East, by 1860, the Marchioness of Londonderry had established schools at Penshaw, Rainton, Pittington, Seaham and Thorpe Thewles (Plate 49). For the urchins of the larger towns there were the Ragged Schools, supported by subscriptions. Durham City had one such in Milburngate. The wives of the parish clergy usually took an active part in running such institutions.

However, far outnumbering all these free schools were the private schools, varying in size from the small Dame School to the large academies. These schools relied entirely on fees and were frequently poorly-staffed. In 1846 Durham City had fifteen such schools within its boundaries. The old Yorkshire boarding schools, attacked by Dickens in his novel *Nicholas Nickleby* (1838) filled rather a different role: 'These Yorkshire

PLATE 49 The Marchioness of Londonderry's School, Seaham Harbour, 1858

115

PLATE 50 'Board Schools: 1877' at Helmington Row, near Crook, Co. Durham

schoolmasters were the lowest and most rotten rung in the whole ladder. Traders in the avarice, indifference, or imbecility of parents, and the helplessness of children; ignorant, sordid, brutal men, to whom few considerate persons would have entrusted the board and lodging of a horse or dog'. Though by way of balance, one should see this as an exaggerated fictional description, certainly over-generalised.

The aim of the 1870 Act was to provide enough schools to 'fill the gaps' in school provision throughout the country. The Voluntary Bodies were given six months grace to comply with the requirements of the Act and failing this a School Board was to be elected by the ratepayers. These elections were not unnaturally fought with great bitterness, yet the School Boards introduced local control into education for the first time. A surprising number of 'Board Schools' are to be found remaining in the region, several of them still in educational use (Plate 50).

By 1900 education was beginning to mean more than just the three R's and the next great achievement was to be the provision of secondary education. Elementary schooling was virtually free following the 1891 Free

Schooling Act. By 1918 the system whereby children were allowed to go to work on a part-time basis was finally abandoned and the school-leaving age was raised to fourteen years. It was not until 1947 that it was again raised, to fifteen years, and then to sixteen years in 1972.

Two notable early foundations, providing secondary education to a fee-paying clientele, are still to be found partly with nineteenth-century buildings in use: Barnard Castle School (or 'Northern Counties School' as it used to be titled) and Durham School in the city of Durham. In Newcastle very early foundations include the Royal Grammar School and Dame Allen's Schools. All these establishments have provided free places for able children, but have suffered at the hands of politicians in recent years, as has education generally. There are times when one wonders whether Forster's words of 1870 are still understood in political circles: 'upon . . . education depends our industrial prosperity'.

PUBLIC SERVICES

Modern North East is indebted to its Victorian forbears in terms of its public services as in so much else. For the networks of sewers and supplies of water, gas and even electricity: all took their early form during last century.

Probably the most essential public service for an urban area is a safe and thorough sewerage system and we have already seen how this need was identified and acted upon, in terms of the demands of public health. Close after that came the need for an adequate supply of fresh drinking water, though as we shall see shortly, a piped water supply was often first installed with fire precautions in mind rather than the supply of good drinking water.

Other public services which followed as they became technically available were gas, in the first half of the 19th century, and electricity in the final quarter of the century. Both were initially used for public lighting and then for domestic lighting, but electricity quickly began to be used also as a source of power and heat, though gas continued to be used for cooking after ceasing to be used for lighting.

Water Supply

A plentiful supply of fresh drinking water was essential for any population and there was an early provision of *pants* or public water taps, supplied by heavy lead pipes, in all the towns. A report in 1848 on the water supply of Newcastle and Gateshead refers to these and mentions that Newcastle had some 15,000 houses and Gateshead around 3,500. Of these 1,350 and 110 respectively were directly supplied with water and the rest had to resort to public pants and standpipes. There were 32 public pants provided by the local Subscription Water Company and a further 20 were owned by the Corporation of Newcastle. In Gateshead there were only 6.

Complaints were made that the poor had to pay a farthing for a tub or large pailful of water, which was 4 or 5 times the rate charged to the richer inhabitants who had their water piped directly into their houses. It was noted that extra labour was required to supervise the pants, which did not operate every day of the week.

The author of this Report, Dr Robert Reid (one of the major early Victorian sanitary engineers), found conditions on Tyneside much the same as those in other major industrial areas; although the houses of the wealthier inhabitants were above criticism, 'in lanes, courts and alleys frequented by the poorer part of the population, the condition of their

PLATE 51 Reservoir-Keeper's house, by John Dobson (c. 1850), Whittle Dene reservoirs, Northumberland

habitations indicates the accumulated influence of evils that must have been progressively increasing for a long period and augmenting with the density of the population'. The town of Newcastle was considered, in this report, to be severely overcrowded in the poorer areas, the normal rate of occupancy being one family per room and the number per family ranging from four to twelve. Combined with overcrowding, Reid found the streets narrow, some being little more than three feet wide although the average was seven or eight feet.

Much of the water supply at the time was pumped from the River Tyne. Somewhat surprisingly, in view of the way that all drains poured into the river, this water was described as the only trustworthy supply for most of the inhabitants. Domestic filters were referred to, though it seems that these were recommended for freeing rainwater from soot, rather than purifying the rainwater. A major requirement of piped water within Newcastle was in connection with fire-fighting and it was a local insurance company, the Newcastle Fire Office, which provided some of the earliest water supply points in order to have within its own power the means of extinguishing fires. The fire office obtained much of its water from flooded colliery workings in the Coxlodge area, the water being pumped out by a windmill and run via a brick conduit to a reservoir on the Town Moor. The Newcastle Subscription Water Company was established in 1834 and in 1836 it merged with the fire office. Better-planned proposals led to the Whittle Dene Water Company being established in 1845 and this in turn purchased the Subscription Company. Reservoirs were planned at Whittle Dene above the village of Ovingham. They are clearly seen today as one drives along the old 'Military Road', some twelve miles to the west of Newcastle. These reservoirs, completed in 1848, at last gave Newcastle and Gateshead a steady, clean and regular supply of water. The directors of this company were working towards an ever improving service and establishing traditions, apparently followed by so many companies, of providing buildings and structures of the best quality: even the reservoir keeper's house at Whittle Dene was designed by John Dobson (Plate 51) and built at a price of £549. At this point the major works of the new company were completed and later described as 'the greatest step with reference to the hydraulic supply of a Town that has been taken in the Kingdom'.

Following those early beginnings the Newcastle and Gateshead Water Company came into being, gradually extending its area of supply and increasing its supply points. The position in Sunderland was not dissimilar. At the beginning of the 19th century the whole town was supplied by the springs, the best known of which was 'Bodle Well'. Fordyce, the Durham historian, writing in the 1850's records that it was usual for the inhabitants of Wearmouth Walk, and even further westward, to send their servants every evening, as a regular part of their work, to the Bodle Well, for a skeelful of water. A few houses in Bishopwearmouth had the advantage of private wells.

(Wright's *Dialect Dictionary* identifies a *skeel* as a wooden bucket or pail.) Fordyce goes on to quote an 1820 advertisement:

The inhabitants of Bishopwearmouth are respectfully informed that they may now be supplied with excellent water, at the Improved Patent Ropery, in South Street, at a farthing a skeel on the spot, and by a watercart in a few days at a halfpenny a skeel, at their own homes. N.B. This water is found to make excellent tea water, and answers well for washing.

A public meeting was held on 31 August 1824, to consider the practicability of supplying the town of Bishopwearmouth with water, and it was resolved to raise £5,000 in 200 shares of £25 each. Two steam engines were built, of 40 and 20 horse power respectively and from these two reservoirs each holding 100,000 gallons (456,000 litres) supplied the town until new works were built in 1850. The scale of technical improvement (as well as the growing needs of the town) may be seen by the description of the 1850 improvements, constructed at Humbleton Hill, two miles from Bishopwearmouth. A condensing engine of 130 horse power was constructed and a reservoir holding 1 million gallons:

The engine is capable of working 10 strokes per minute and delivers 105 gallons per stroke or 1,050 gallons per minute, 63,000 per hour, 756,000 in 12, and 1,512,000 in 24 hours. The water is always on day and night, in every part of the borough. The reservoir is 100 feet above the level of the road at Bishopwearmouth church gates, which gives a sufficient pressure to throw the water over the top of the highest house without the aid of fire engines. Pipes are laid in every street and lane in the town ... The main pipe to the entrance of the town is 19 inches diameter; that down the High Street is 14 and 12 inches to Bridge Street, and 10, 9, 8, 7 and 6 inches to the docks ... About 8,000 tenants are supplied with water, at charges varying from 5s. to 30s. per annum, according to the rental.

In 1851 the South Shields Water Works was purchased and the name of the company changed to 'The Sunderland and South Shields Water Company', by which it is still known.

Gas Supply

Some idea of the scale of Victorian endeavour can be gained from the many miles of lead pipe (about ½ inch diameter: 12mm) which were

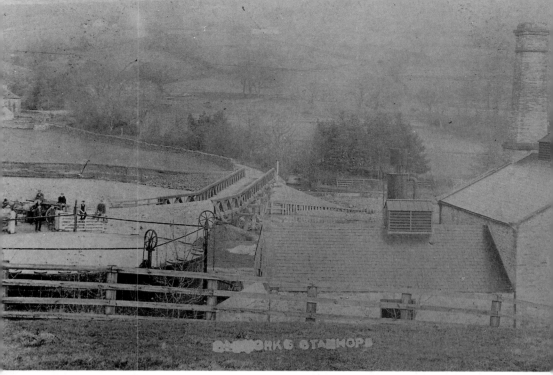

PLATE 52 Small Gas Works at Stanhope, Weardale, next to Gas House Bridge
(now demolished)

laid under the floorboards and in the plastered walls of many thousands
of houses built in the region's towns. These, terminating at wooden pat-
tens and elaborate brass brackets with porcelain nozzles and glass shades,
brought relatively cheap light into the urban environment. It is difficult for
us today, accustomed to light our room at the flick of a switch, to realise that some sleight of hand was required to apply a lighted taper near
the fragile mantle, whilst turning on the gas. A 'pop' and the room would
be seen by a warm yellowish light associated with a slight characteristic
odour. Still more difficult is it to realise how grateful the Victorian householders must have been not to be dependent upon firelight and flickering
candles, or the smoky flame of the open paraffin lamp, or – for a relatively short time – the pressure paraffin lamp. Whilst these earlier methods
persisted in many country areas until only a few years ago, gas provided
urban lighting over several decades and was only replaced by electricity
in the twenties and thirties of the present century.

Yet it was for public street lighting that gas was first produced commercially, and in the early years of the 19th century many towns were
beginning to have their own supplies for this purpose. This gas was produced by heating small coals in horizontally-placed iron tubes, or retorts,
about twelve inches in diameter (35cm) and several feet long. These retorts,
in banks of five or seven, were heated by a coke fire beneath and the gas
was pumped up and away from the retorts. Gas was then treated by various

processes to remove such materials as sulphurous compounds, tar and so on, which would make it too smoky and smelly, when used – as most of it was – for lighting. Gas prepared and treated in this way was then held in water-sealed tanks known as 'gasometers', which gave pressure to the supply.

We are fortunate in having several contemporary descriptions of these early systems, such as, for example, that at Sunderland. According to William Fordyce, the Sunderland Gaslight Company had been established in 1823, in shares of £25 each, and the town was first lit by gas on 9 March 1824, the cost of the works being about £8,000. These were bought in 1831 by the Sunderland Subscription Gas Company and enlarged in 1837.

Later in 1846 an Act of Parliament was passed whereby the Corporation Gas Company was established. New works were put in hand and

> beds for 80 retorts were built, capable of producing 280,000 cubic feet per diem. The hydraulic main is 20 inches in diameter . . . The station meter . . . is capable of registering 30,000 cubic feet per hour. Two gasholders, 60 feet in diameter and 18 feet deep, contain together 100,000 cubic feet . . . The gas is daily submitted to careful chemical tests, and is free from sulphuretted hydrogen and ammonia. Its price is 4s. per 1,000 cubic feet . . . The consumption of gas in the borough . . . is upwards of forty million cubic feet per annum.

The Coal Gas Works in Newcastle were situated, in the 1820's, in Manor Place and the lights were first exhibited on 10 June 1818. Parson and White in their *Gazetteer of Durham and Newcastle* of 1827 wrote:

> Besides the two gasometers in Manor Place, there are two others in Forth Street, which altogether are capable of containing from 50 to 60,000 cubic feet of gas (1,700 cu metres). In addition to these it is (1827) in contemplation to erect another of similar capacity for the exclusive use of the lower part of town. The street lamps are supplied with gas from these works, and a great number of shopkeepers, and the inhabitants avail themselves of this brilliant and economic luminary, which, calculating the quantity of light evolved, is supposed to cost about one-third the price of candles. The consumers are supplied either at the rate of 10s. per 1,000 cubic feet (50p per 28 cu metres) or, by a scale of charges, which is considerably lower than those of any other works in the kingdom.

Electricity

One of the more significant 'firsts' to take place in the north east was Joseph Swan's demonstration of his electric 'lamp'. On 18 December 1878 Swan, an almost self-taught scientist, demonstrated his first electric bulb to the Newcastle Chemical Society, though it burnt out after a few minutes. Less than two years later (20 October 1880) came a famous occasion when he was lecturing to the Literary and Philosophical Society of Newcastle, addressing a galaxy of Northern intellectual, commercial and social elite. He made a deep impression by having seventy gas jets turned down and their job taken up instantaneously by twenty electric bulbs.

Simultaneously with these developments Thomas Edison had also been experimenting to find a suitable filament for an electric bulb and very happily both came together, benefitting incidentally from the invention of the evacuating pump which could remove air from glass bulbs, allowing the filament to glow but not burn. They set up a joint company, The Edison and Swan United Electric Light Company, and their lamps became known by the trade name 'Ediswan'. Swan lit his own home in Gateshead and that of his friend Sir William Armstrong, at Cragside, with these new bulbs. It was for a time only the rich who could afford this form of lighting: bulbs cost twenty five shillings each (£1.25) – perhaps more than the equivalent of a working man's weekly wage – and current was about one shilling per unit (5p). And of course it was necessary to have one's own generating set. In a letter to *The Times* a Mr Octavius Coope calculated that gas plant was cheaper to install in his home (£1,333 compared with £1,430 for electricity), but that electric running costs were half those of gas and he had 'no nuisance of lime or of tar and other refuse; no leakage of gas, no smell . . . or damage to my garden'.

Swan founded the Swan Electric Light Company, with a small factory at Benwell near Newcastle. German glass-blowers had to be encouraged to move there from Thuringia due to a lack of such skills locally. After his liaison with Edison this became the Edison & Swan United Electric Light Company (1882). By 1883 they were producing ten thousand lamps per week and the unit cost fell rapidly.

Soon after this, one of the first examples of the great 'drift' to the South took place, when Swan decided to transfer his works to Bromley in Kent, in a market-orientated move, for already more electricity was being generated in London, with a consequent and growing demand for bulbs there.

For a time innovations continued in the north and the first shop to use electric light, for the purposes of publicity, was Swan's own: Mawson and Swan in Mosley Street, Newcastle.

Whilst electric power was used from the beginning for lighting, it was not long before it also began to turn electric motors, driving trams, powering cinema projectors and then heating ovens and radiators.

Over most of the country the generation of electric power was an irregular affair. As late as 1917, for example, it was reported that 'in Greater London 70 authorities supplied electricity to the public, and owned some 70 generating stations, with 50 different types of system, 10 different frequencies and 20 different voltages'.

In contrast the North East was remarkably uniform, with a relatively integrated power network operating over Northumberland, Durham and Tyneside. This was not so much due to regional planning as to the vision and tenacity of the electric-entrepreneurs, the Merz family. Charles Merz for example started three-phase industrial power and erected the first real central power station with integrated control in Great Britain.

In the early days two companies had begun to supply power in the Tyneside area: the Newcastle and District Electric Lighting Company (1889) and the Newcastle upon Tyne Electric Supply Company (NESCO, also 1889). South of the Tyne British Electric Traction held sway (through its County of Durham Electric Power Distribution Company). Around the turn of the century the power struggle came to a head, with a furious war in Parliament. NESCO won, partly because of its competent management and partly because it called several first-class witnesses including Lord Kelvin. Kelvin opined that NESCO could not only manage the North bank quite comfortably but that it could put a cable under the Tyne, in order to serve the South side too. The 'war' came to a sudden end and British Electric Traction ceased to fight, having indeed had problems of supplying traction in Gateshead as well as lighting.

Later NESCO bought out two other British Electric Traction stations in County Durham and, a little later, the ailing Cleveland and Darlington County Electric Power Company, which had served most of the Durham coalfield and parts of Teesside.

And so, until complete nationalisation throughout the country brought everywhere else into line, the North East was relatively well organised electrically, thanks in large part to Charles Merz, a gifted eccentric who was also a strict and peaceful Quaker and efficient entrepreneur.

CHURCH AND CHAPEL-GOING

It is generally acknowledged that Methodism was the dominant religious force in County Durham, but quite remarkably we can adduce quite a precise figure to support this, for the mid-century: 76,642 worshippers or 21 per cent of the population.

The reason for this precision was that a Sunday in 1851 had been selected by the Registrar General, George Graham, on which to hold the first ever (and, as it happened, the last) Census of Worship in this country. He had decided to take the opportunity of the general census of 1851 to procure, at the same time, statistical evidence upon the state of the country's religious institutions, by recording the accommodation of places of worship and attendance at them.

PLATE 53 Tramcar of the Tynemouth and District Electric Tractor Co. Ltd, at the New Quay terminus

At that time, as the introduction to the Report indicated:

For many reasons the religion of a nation must be a matter of extreme solicitude to many minds. Whether we regard people merely in their secular capacity, as partners in a great association for promoting the stability . . . of a state; or view these . . . as subjects of a higher kingdom . . .; in either aspect the degree and direction of religious sentiment in a community are subjects of the weightiest import.

The date selected for the Census was Sunday 30 March 1851, the day before the civil census was to begin. Unlike the latter, the Census of Worship was unenforceable and therefore entirely voluntary. However it seems to have been carried out with great thoroughness. On the appointed day, ministers or responsible officers in all churches, chapels, meeting houses, mission halls and synagogues, were invited to complete a form giving details of their place of worship, stating its capacity and the total numbers of worshippers who attended at all services that day.

The population of Durham was recorded – in round terms – as 370,000 and that of Northumberland as 301,000. 621 places of worship were recorded in County Durham, divided thus:

Church of England	169
Older Dissenting bodies (Presbyterians, Independents, Quakers, Baptists & Unitarians)	72
Methodists (Wesleyans 192 & Primitive Methodists 113)	351
Roman Catholics	20
Jews	2
Mormons	2
Isolated Congregations	5

The Methodists were the dominant religious force in County Durham. In all the 351 Methodist Chapels there was accommodation for 76,642 worshippers, or 21 per cent of the population. The Church of England's accommodation, on the other hand, totalled 66,319 or 17.6 per cent of the population of the county, the figure which gave the Church of England in County Durham the lowest such percentage for any English County. The next lowest was Northumberland with a percentage of 18.1 per cent. These two counties formed, at that time, the diocese of Durham and demonstrated the need for the subsequent great work of Bishop Baring over the next two decades, who engaged in building churches and founding new parishes, to make good the deficiency in the Church of England in his diocese.

PLATE 54 Scotch Church, 1811, by John Dobson, Howard Street, North Shields

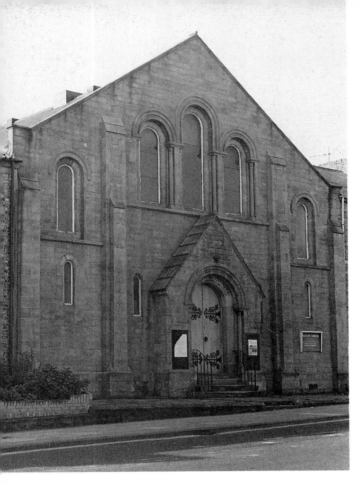

PLATE 55 Baptist Church, 1811, by John Dobson, Howard Street, North Shields

PLATE 56 A Church of England church in a pit village: Holy Trinity, Pelton, County Durham; by John Green, in 'Early English' style, 1842

PLATE 57 Presbyterian Church, 1850–57 by John Dobson, Northumberland Square, North Shields

This deficiency, though of longstanding, had been exacerbated by the growth of population, particularly in County Durham between 1801 and 1851. In that period the Methodists, less encumbered by the legal procedures dogging the Established Church, had been busily building chapels and of their 351 places of worship referred to in the Report, 311 had been built or acquired between 1801 and 1851.

Much more can be gained from this remarkable Census for, despite its many omissions, imprecisions and weaknesses, it enables us to assess, with some accuracy the church-going habits of our Victorian forbears in 1851.

A thought on the country's religion comes from *The Making of Victorian England* by G. Kitson Clark, 'It might not be too extravagant to say (he writes) that probably in no other century, except the 17th or perhaps the 12th, did the claim of religion occupy so large a part in the nation's life ... The century opens with a great agitation about slavery, nationwide, highly emotional, magnificently organised, which was largely responsible for one of the most drastic changes in the world's policy there has ever been: the abolition of the age-old institution of chattel-slavery.' Kitson Clark goes on to point out that this action was taken as a model for many other agitations and indeed so effective was it that the agitation against Corn Laws consciously followed this form, though actually launched by secular politicians.

7
INCREASING MOBILITY

O ne of the fine sights that lifts the heart of many a Geordie, returning to
his native land, is to be seen at that moment when his train crosses the
River Tyne, with its clustered sequence of bridges and the skyline ahead
dominated by the Keep, the spire of St Nicholas and the industrial and
commercial buildings along the Quayside. Much of the landscape is owed
to the Victorians, though to be precise the bridge from which we are looking is probably the 'Edward VII', opened by the King in 1906. Alongside is
the fine High Level Bridge of 1844–9 designed by John Dobson and built
by Robert Stephenson. As our screaming '125' enters Newcastle Station,
look around: for (apart from the unfortunate central 1980s 'feature') the
station is almost as Dobson designed it, and as opened by Queen Victoria on 27 August 1850.

In the formative years of the British railway system the North East
played a significant role: the Stephensons and George Hudson in the
early phase and the heavy locomotive and wagon works in later years,
at Newcastle, Gateshead, Shildon and Darlington. Thousands of families
owed their livelihood to 'the railways': whole communities in some areas.
Around the region were important railway buildings now all gone: goods
sheds, and cattle marts adjoining many rural stations, and loco sheds such
as the big circular one at Hartlepool and the attractive station groupings
on many of the lesser lines such as that of the NER Cornhill Branch. On
this, opened in 1887, still stand for example the fine station buildings of
Whittingham and Glanton.

Of all the subjects touched upon in this book, the railway system is
certainly the one which still retains a number of significant buildings of
Victorian origin, for apart from Newcastle Central Station and its linked
bridges, there are several other passenger station buildings of note, including Darlington and Durham and smaller ones like Hexham: all still in
use, unlike Whittingham and Glanton, which are privately occupied but
preserved. A further glimpse is to be seen at Beamish (the Open Air
Museum), where the village station of Rowley (1867) has been moved
from the Stanhope to Consett line and restored, together with two early
footbridges and a signal box from Consett.

The North East may therefore be seen to be proud of its railway history and indeed it is not overly fanciful to describe North East England

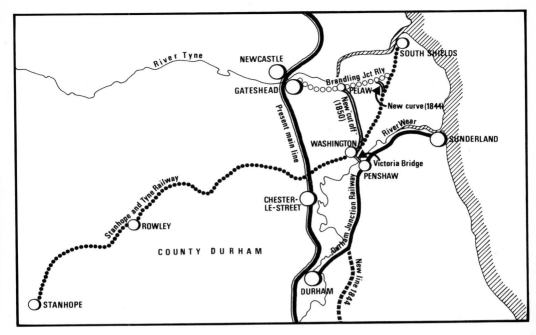

FIG 8 Sketch map of railways in County Durham, 1844–1850, showing how Hudson constructed his Darlington to Gateshead route of 1844 (after Rolt)

as the birthplace of the railways of the world, on two quite separate counts.

In the early eighteenth century wagonways, often known as 'Newcastle roads' began to be constructed, at first of simple wooden and later of iron rails, as a means of facilitating the transport of coal from the Northumberland and Durham coalmines to the banks of the nearest river. From here *keels* would carry the coal downstream to deeper stretches where the sea-going *colliers* could be loaded. The popular name of these simple trackways demonstrates the early origins of railway systems.

A century or so later George Stephenson, builder of early locomotives (including 'Locomotion' of 1825 to which reference has already been made) was almost certainly responsible for the present gauge, or width, of so much of the world's rail-track, of 4ft 8½ins. This he probably based on farm-track ruts made by generations of horse-drawn wooden-wheeled carts and wagons. The axle-length of these wooden carts, by the way, was controlled by the spacing of the shafts fixed either side of the horse and the positioning of these in turn resulted from the broad haunches of the average cart-horse. So we may reasonably suggest that our rail tracks were determined by a Victorian north country cart horse!

Stephenson, moreover, was able to establish the world's first locomotive-drawn, public passenger-carrying railway system, when he persuaded Joseph Pease that what we now know as the Stockton and Darlington Railway would be better constructed as it eventually was, in preference to a canal

131

system which had been the previous proposal. Canals at that time were still fashionable and – in modern jargon – Stephenson broke the mould and established a new fashion: that of the steam-hauled railway system.

A self made man and entirely empirical in all his work, he gave his son Robert a somewhat better education and lived to see Robert establish a locomotive-works and become a notable man in the railway world in the middle of the nineteenth century.

Another name in northern railway lore is that of George Hudson who took advantage of 'railway mania' in the 1830s and 40s. In fact he was probably more responsible for that 'mania' than affected by it. Born – as so many of the entrepreneurs of his day were – of humble stock (his father was a yeoman farmer in East Yorkshire), he rose to become a millionaire and known as the 'Railway King'. He gambled heavily on the creation of rail companies and lines, particularly trying to create a line linking the east coast ports. He was quite capable of paying dividends from newly floated capital, but for several years kept himself and his companies on an upward trend. He created the Midland Railway and most of the lines which later formed the North Eastern Railway, with headquarters in his own stronghold of York, were built at his inspiration.

In 1834, having received an unexpected legacy and become a joint-stock banker, Hudson had become involved in the newly popular railway speculation, and met George Stephenson at Whitby. The two rough and ready northerners took a liking to each other and Hudson took advantage of Stephenson's reputation as an engineer and surveyor. Stephenson talked of his dream of an east-coast route to Newcastle and beyond and Hudson spoke of his plans to make York a great railway centre. Thus Stephenson was persuaded to make York, and not Leeds, the pivot of his northern route.

As the plans for this system moved further north, young Robert Stephenson suffered an unfortunate financial blow, which curiously links with this story. He had carried out some consultancy work for the proprietors of the Stanhope and Tyne Railway Company and unwisely accepted shares in lieu of fee. A little later that Company came near to collapse and Stephenson was horrified to realise that, since the Company was not incorporated, there was no limit to the sums which individual shareholders might be called upon to meet. Suddenly, having just won through to success and prosperity, he found himself facing utter ruin.

Taking the only possible step he could, he called together the shareholders of the Stanhope and Tyne and formed a new Company to take over the old Company's property and debts and to apply to Parliament for incorporation. He desperately raised a large personal sum of money

PLATE 58 Statue of George Stephenson, 1862, by John Lough. Lower Westgate Road, Newcastle upon Tyne

by selling to his father half of his interest in his locomotive company and then set about to build up this new Company.

This is where we find a link between Robert Stephenson and George Hudson, for Darlington had been linked to London in 1841 and the next extension, to Gateshead, was being planned. It so happened that the old Stanhope and Tyne Company had a holding in a small railway company in north Durham: the Durham Junction, which could be linked with the Pontop and South Shields and the Brandling Junction Railways. Hudson used this rather circuitous route as the Newcastle and Durham Junction Railway, thus speeding up his route to Gateshead. It entailed constructing a splendid stone viaduct at Penshaw, across the Wear (known at the time as the Victoria Bridge because the last stone was laid on the day of Queen Victoria's coronation, 28 June 1838) to link up to the Durham Junction Railway with the eastern stretch of the Stanhope and Tyne Railway. Hudson's Darlington to Gateshead line in 1844 thus completed his dream; Tyne and Thames were united by rail. Six years later a 'cut-off' from Washington to Pelaw shortened the route and of course the present main route through Chester le Street is much more logical, but this earlier route was not only expedient and economical, but it had the especial advantage of saving Robert Stephenson and his fellow shareholders from all future anxiety. At this time, too, through Hudson's influence, Robert was appointed Engineer in Chief of this last link and hence became responsible for the High Level Bridge over the Tyne (Fig 8).

To complete the story we have to record that Hudson finally met his downfall in 1849, when a group of Liverpool shareholders, who had never forgiven him for an over-subtle stroke of some years earlier, took their opportunity and brought his meteoric flight to an end. This pricked the railway bubble and the resulting slump took some years to recover. But the north eastern system was soundly based and as we shall now see, went on to serve the region for many more years.

The North Eastern Railway Company

The history of the railway industry is littered with multiple names of companies, but two, found in North East England, are surely redolent of their period: *The Stockton and Darlington Railway Company* and *The North Eastern Railway Company*.

The former has already been mentioned, having originated as a coal transport system, but incorporated with an early passenger carrying facility. The Stockton and Darlington Railway continued as a separate entity from its inception in 1825 until 1863 when it became part of the growing North Eastern Railway Company.

The North Eastern Railway Company was created in 1854, as a result of amalgamation of the York and North Midland, the Leeds Northern

PLATE 59 Snowbound train at Rowley Station, Co. Durham, January 1910

and the York, Newcastle and Berwick Railway Companies. This resulted in a total mileage of 720, giving the new undertaking control over a larger empire than that possessed by any other railway of the time. The area served by the North Eastern comprised pretty well the whole of Northumberland, all of County Durham and most of Yorkshire to the north and east of Leeds.

By the time of this amalgamation the through-route to Scotland had been completed, facilitated especially by the construction of the High Level Bridge over the Tyne, in 1844–9. But although passenger movement was of importance, it was the movement of goods which produced the greater finance. For the several heavy industries: iron (and later steel), coal-mining, shipbuilding and heavy engineering, resulted in considerable traffic, and a large part of income came from carrying both raw and finished materials such as timber, coal, iron ore, pig iron and rails. It is known that around the middle of the century about half the railway revenue of the country was derived from passenger traffic. But at that time the North Eastern took less than 40 per cent of its gross income from this source, and it was accordingly particularly susceptible to trade fluctuations.

At the time of the original 1854 amalgamation which established the North Eastern Railway, several other companies continued to operate within the region, notably the Stockton and Darlington, the Newcastle and Carlisle and the West Hartlepool Harbour and Railway Companies. In the '50s and early '60s another event of significance was the opening up and development of the Cleveland ironstone district which also gave such a fillip to the growth of Middlesbrough. This resulted in intense

135

competition between the major railway companies in the region and went so far as to encourage invasion of the North Eastern's 'territory' by outside companies anxious to take a share in the regional traffic. As a result of these struggles, a realignment of the local companies led to their eventual absorption. The Newcastle and Carlisle (1862), the Stockton and Darlington (1863) and the West Hartlepool (1865) gradually found themselves part of the North Eastern Railway and so efficient was this process that the 1866 *Report of the Select Committee on Railway Companies Amalgamations* acknowledged the Company to be 'the most complete monopoly in the United Kingdom'.

It would be wrong, however, in taking such a broad view of regional railway development, to give the impression that the construction of new lines and services was simple, straightforward or indeed logical. And the history of just one line – that of the Darlington and Barnard Castle Railway – is worth giving in a little detail as an indication of how landowners could delay extensions and damage trade.

After the Stockton and Darlington Railway had demonstrated the success of a local line the inhabitants of Barnard Castle showed a desire to be linked up with Darlington and the first meeting to consider this was held at the Rose and Crown in Barnard Castle on Thursday 1 November 1832. The good offices of Mr Joseph Pease were sought and an outline route was agreed. He in turn encouraged the promoters but suggested a variation in the route which would help to keep clear of most of the Duke of Cleveland's land, he having opposed the Stockton and Darlington Railway in its early stages.

For a time the fear of facing wealthy opposition and consequently expensive Parliamentary law suits, caused a postponement of plans. But it soon became clear that Barnard Castle was being left as a back-water and trade was suffering, so an attempt was made to get the Duke's consent, and another public meeting was held on 7 November 1839. Mr Witham of Barnard Castle presided and agreed to see His Grace, but met with a positive refusal and again the project was halted.

On the death of the first Duke in 1842, there was hope that the second Duke might be more amenable. Moreover various industries such as thread-making and carpet-making, were being disadvantaged through lack of railway transport and some degree of urgency was felt. A meeting was therefore held with the Duke, this time at Raby, on 17 October 1844 and a deputation from the town included Mr Joseph Pease, who is recorded as having explained the advantages of railways and the disadvantages suffered by towns deprived of such a facility. However the second Duke was of like mind to his father and 'could not see the necessity of these branch lines, although through lines might be alright'. Indeed, he believed, 'if a place was within twenty miles of a railway, it was all that could be wished'. He had, he stated 'often hoped that one of these horrid railways would never be brought through this paradise of a county, the beautiful Vale of the Tees . . . He was determined to oppose the railway to the utmost of his power'. Once more the inhabitants of Barnard Castle were frustrated and disappointed.

Then came a calamity which took their thoughts elsewhere, for an outbreak of cholera in Barnard Castle in 1849 led to 143 deaths, causing some panic and a subsequent series of works for providing a good supply of water and a proper system of sewerage.

So it was not until 1852, after a period of considerable depression, that the townspeople again pressed for a railway, this time with renewed vigour, for otherwise the town might have no future at all.

A carpet manufacturer, Mr J.C. Monkhouse, called a meeting, in the 'Witham Testimonial' – now known as Witham Hall (Plate 26), on 31 August 1852 and a different route was discussed. Mr Watson of Spring Lodge presided at the meeting and was deputed, with others, to meet the Duke. However he happened also to be the Duke's Solicitor, and seems to have taken no steps to press the matter.

Eventually Mr Pease took matters into his own hands and wrote to the Duke on 7 October 1852, stressing the advantages and urgency and giving details of yet another scheme. Another public meeting was called for Wednesday 3 November 1852, presided over by the Reverend Thomas Witham. Things seemed set fair for Parliamentary sanction, when various tenant farmers, perhaps inspired by the Duke, began to oppose the line. In a letter dated 15 March 1853 the Duke was urged to withdraw his opposition, and it was shown how every attempt had been made to meet his objections and the hope was entertained 'that Your Grace will not subject us to the harassing procedure and expense of a contest . . . for a project which, while it will not prejudice Your Grace's comforts, will greatly benefit multitudes whose only resources lie in the trade and commerce of the district'.

The Duke, however responded with a long letter dated 17 March, expressing his surprise that they should persist in going on with the Bill. He made reference to the many donations he had made to the town's activities and went on to indicate pride in having helped to throw out other railway Bills for branch lines, when they were put before the House of Lords Committee.

The promoters, by now heavily committed, went ahead with a Bill which was fought the whole way. The hearing lasted nearly a fortnight and all seemed to be going well, when five words lost the Bill. A query had been made as to the width of the 'formation base' which was set at fifteen feet. The objectors stated that a nineteen foot wide base was required and would cost more than anticipated. Mr Robert Stephenson, the railway engineer, was called and said that 'Fifteen feet was safe, *if the ballast be good*'. These words seriously damaged the promoters' cause and the Bill was lost.

It was then decided by the persistent and somewhat desperate towns-people, to try once more, but this time to keep their plans from the knowledge of the Duke until they were ready to go to Parliament. Another survey was begun, under a guise of sappers and miners, but not surprisingly this was detected. A meeting, with proffered apologies between the Engineer and the Duke was unexpectedly successful and His Grace said that pro-vided the line were kept out of Selaby Park, he would not oppose the scheme.

So all was well, after all and the Bill became law on 3 July 1854. The first sod was cut on 20 July and in just under two years the line was com-pleted. Great festivities took place at the opening on 8 July 1856 and it is interesting to observe that the Duke accepted an invitation to be pres-ent at the celebratory dinner.

To bring the story up to date, little more than a century after that hard-won railway opened, it was closed as part of the 'Beeching Axe'. The town, which has surprisingly remained with a constant population of around five thousand for almost two centuries, now depends upon a modern road system and does not appear to suffer from the lack of that much-sought railway.

Finally, it would be wrong to imply that the development of the rail-way system created no damage except that to the cherished environment of the landowners. For the railway developers could be quite ruthless in driving their routes through urban centres. Whilst the approach to the City of Durham provides a marvellous, and indeed unparalleled, view of the Castle and Cathedral and a superb viaduct across the Tees provides a fine backdrop to the little market-town of Yarm, the southern parts of Newcastle were – by our standards – shamefully treated. The Norman Keep for instance was left isolated by the line cutting close by and, as can be seen in Richardson's painting *Excavations for the High Level Bridge* (Plate 61), the mediaeval heart of Newcastle was ruthlessly hacked about. On the oth-er hand Dobson's Central Station (although not quite what he planned), certainly adds to the dignity of the lower part of the present-day city.

PORTS AND SHIPPING

The ports of the North East are today but a shadow of what they were last century. Many of the smaller ones such as Alnmouth or Amble have disappeared or have become small marinas for leisure sailing. The lower reaches of the banks of the Tyne have lost many of their riverside indus-tries; shipbuilding is still diminishing and current riverside development leans towards leisure rather than heavy industry or port facilities. Sun-derland has suffered similarly and Teesside has dramatically changed too.

If one views these coastal regions with a philosophical long-term eye,

PLATE 60 Witham Hall, Barnard Castle, c. 1848

they are still changing in a continuum which began several centuries ago when they began to develop from what, to us, would have seemed pleasing rural riversides to busy industrial heartlands, and they now seem to be regressing once more.

As for how it all began, with the Cheviot Hills to the north, the Pennines to the west, and the Cleveland Hills to the south it is not surprising that the people of Northumberland and Durham turned to the sea for the transport of their exports and imports. So in the eighteenth century coal – a profitable but bulky commodity – was carried by horse and cart down to the main riverside staithes, primarily on the banks of the Tyne and the Wear. Even in the great days of canal-building, such waterways were never constructed in the region and only a few ever planned here, for the topography was far from suitable and coastal traffic was easier.

Thus when the nineteenth century dawned and rapid expansion took place in so many fields, one cannot be surprised to find the old horse-drawn wagonways encouraging the development of steam-powered railways and the common use of river and sea promoting boat-building and the growth of ports both natural and man-made.

As the shipping of coal by sea increased, so did the number of sea-going vessels returning in ballast and what had at one time been a waste product, dumped wherever possible (as the name Sandhill down by Newcastle's quayside indicates), now began to acquire a use as new industries found it possible to obtain their raw materials cheaply. The glass and pottery industries, in particular, needed special but bulky materials such as sand, flint and ball clay, which were entirely suitable and available as ballast. The presence of cheap fuel was the other attraction and the resultant products, again relatively bulky, led to further maritime transport.

The growing need for shipping resulted in an expansion of ship building and this in turn sponsored still further ancillary industries such as rope-making, sail-making, chain-making and anchor-making. Ports were enlarged and improved as the century drew on and an entirely new port was created, that of Seaham Harbour.

Even the railway system, as it developed, encouraged rather than diminished the function of the ports and – as we have seen – that great northern railway entrepreneur George Hudson favoured an east coast route linking with all the main ports.

Ports and Port Facilities
Naturally not all the north eastern ports concentrated upon the export of coal. Berwick upon Tweed, for example, had a flourishing export trade supplying London with salmon fished from the Tweed, as well as the more unusual export of eggs, since hens seem to have been kept in the hinterland on a quite unusual scale for the period.

140

PLATE 61 *Excavations for the High Level Bridge*. Oil painting by T.M. Richardson (Photo: Tyne & Wear Museums)

Seahouses and Beadnell are two small natural harbours which have, of course, supported local fishing vessels but which also, on account of their proximity to local limestone, were involved in the export of lime. Both ports still have the remains of lime kilns which probably began work in the eighteenth century, but continued well into last century. Until the invention of Portland cement in 1824 the common building material was quicklime, and for many years afterwards lime continued to be so used. Hence the need for this local export trade.

From Craster whinstone was exported from a local quarry convenient-ly near the tiny port. It is today better known for kippers, a local delicacy which is, of course, not now exported by sea.

Alnmouth is rather a sad place today. As far back as the fifteenth century it was a port for Alnwick and last century it flourished upon the import of guano and export of grain. At that time the eastern lowland of Northum-berland was good corn-growing land, needing guano and with food crops to export. Now Alnmouth is a small holiday resort with crumbling ware-houses, traces of a silted-up harbour and ruins of a guano store.

Amble is another shrunken port, once with a good coal-export trade but now, with a shrinking coalfield and good road services, the port is no longer needed.

Blyth is nearer to the present coalfield and has suffered less than Amble but, further south, Seaton Sluice is at best a place for modern holiday craft. Yet in the first half of the last century its port facilities, established in the preceding century, were flourishing and nearby was a large glassworks exporting enormous numbers of glass bottles and requiring ashes and pot-clay which could be brought in as ballast. Changes in the coal industry and Seaton Sluice's deficiencies as a port for larger ships had become obvi-ous by the middle of the century and its final blow came with the terrible New Hartley Colliery tragedy of 1862 when more than two hundred men and boys lost their lives, and shortly afterwards the port ceased to operate.

Not much further south the Tyne offered all the facilities that could be required by much of the region, with coal handling staithes along both banks and a broad river navigable well upstream of Newcastle. By the middle of the nineteenth century the administrative hold on river trade which had been jealously kept by Newcastle from mediaeval times, had been lost and South Shields, Jarrow, Hebburn, Felling and Gateshead on the south and Tynemouth along the north bank each had their own indus-tries, exports and imports. The old saying about Newcastle that 'the world over, you'll find a Scot, a flea and a Newcastle grindstone' reminds us of a now-forgotten export which once required heavy handling facilities at both Newcastle Quay and Gateshead. Grindstones and even larger 'pulp-stones' used in the crushing of sugar cane, were brought from Springwell Fell near Gateshead where the stone is still quarried, though now for lit-tle more than decorative fireplaces and the like.

Bill Lowther was a quarryman in the Wrekenton area south of Gateshead whom we have already met in connection with quarry work. His recollections help to remind us of a skill and a trade now completely lost. His quarrying memories have already been quoted but it is worth recalling here how this bulky product was transported to the quayside in the early years of the present century. After describing how stone was quarried at Eighton Banks and Springwell, and then laboriously cut into huge circular grindstones or even larger 'pulp-stones', he went on to say,

> They used to take the grindstones down to the Felling Shore – Peacocks of Wrekenton had horses – and a rolley – a flat cart – and you always had a trace horse for the banks – you used to come away from the quarry and two horses couldn't get up the bank without a trace one – to help them up. Sometimes they used to take them on to Newcastle Quay – and load them on to the boats – and then they'd go all over the world – grindstones!

He also recalled that the 'pulpstones' were used in paper mills for crushing wood pulp and that they used to be sent to Japan, early in the first war (1914–18), but he said, 'all that fizzled out and we started to send them to Norway – used to ship them out to Bergen'. And before all that, they had been shipped out during the nineteenth century to sugar-growing countries where they were used to crush sugar cane.

Coal was, of course, the largest export from the Tyne for over a century and it was brought to the riverside at many points on both banks, by wagonways worked by a variety of forces. Some wagons would come running down by gravity, others would be lowered by cable whilst hauling back under their weight a series of returning empty wagons, and some would be hauled along level tracks by horses. At the riverside they generally arrived at a relatively high level, due to the steep-sided river bank, and the coal then had to be lowered or shot down to the waiting boats. Since nineteenth century coal was so frequently – and quite literally – handled, every endeavour was made to maintain larger pieces of coal, and 'small coals' were looked upon as waste. For this reason the *coal-drop* was developed, as a means of lowering a whole truck (or 'black wagon') down to the boat, thus reducing coal breakage. This process cannot be better described than in the colourful text (entirely of his period) of William Howitt, an observant traveller, who wrote *Visits to Remarkable Places* in 1856:

> . . . As you advance over the plain, you see a whole train of wagons loaded with coal, careering by themselves, without horse, without steam-engine, without man, except there sits one behind who, instead of endeavouring to propel these mad wagons on their way, seems labouring hopelessly by his weight to detain them. But what is your amazement when you come into sight of the river Tyne, to see these wagons still

careering to the very brink of the water. To see a railway carried from the high bank, and supported on tall piles, horizontally above the surface of the river, and to some distance into it, as if to allow those vagabond trains of wagons to run right off, and dash themselves down into the river. There they go, all mad together! Another moment, and they will shoot over the end of the lofty railway, and go headlong into the Tyne, helter-skelter! But behold! The creatures are not so mad as you imagine. They are instinct with sense! They have a principle of self-preservation, as well as of speed, in them. See! as they draw near the river – they pause! They stop! One by one they detach themselves, and as one devoted wagon runs on, like a victim given up for the salvation of the rest, to perform a wild summerset into the water below – what do we see? It is caught! A pair of gigantic arms separate themselves from the end of the railway! They catch the wagon! They hold it suspended in the air! They let it softly and gently descend, ay, softly and gently as an angel dropping to earth on some heavenly message – and whither? Into the water? No! we see now that a ship already lies below the end of the railway. The wagon descends to it; a man, standing there, strikes a bolt – the bottom falls, and the coals which it contains are nicely deposited in the hold of the vessel! Up again soars the wagon in that pair of gigantic arms. It reaches the railway! It glides, like a black swan into its native lake, upon it, and away it goes as of its own accord, to a distance to await its brethren, who successively perform the same exploit, and then joining it – all scamper back over the plain to the distant pit again.

All this, which to those who never saw these things may seem extravagant nonsense, is but the plainest truth, and is performed by means of the most ingenious and simple machinery. A railway, on which these wagons are propelled by a stationary engine at a distance, with a machine called a Drop, acting by a proper adjustment of balance, does all the business, while it conveys the coal carefully and unbroken into the ships, and fills the stranger with the utmost astonishment. Formerly, the coals on reaching the river were shot down inclined planes into the vessels, or into the staiths, or coal-sheds and were much dashed to pieces, and deteriorated in value; these simple and ingenious drops, while they present objects of great wonder and interest to those who for the first time sail on the Tyne, convey the coal, very little broken, into the holds of the ships.

Only a few miles south of the mouth of the Tyne lies Wearside, a fierce competitor. Smaller than the Tyne and more tortuous inland, the Wear nevertheless provided a basis for good port facilities near its mouth and the town of Sunderland, placed close to the coast undoubtedly had an advantage over Newcastle sited twelve or thirteen miles inland, where the first river crossing was constructed.

For the larger part of the nineteenth century shipping was the largest employer in Sunderland. For example the 1861 census, when the industry was at its peak, showed it to employ almost one in four of all males over the age of twenty. And this despite the fact that so many seamen would be at sea on the enumeration night. (It has been estimated that over 60 per cent of all seamen might be at sea at this time.)

The risks of going to sea in the early years of the nineteenth century were high, when steam equipment could so easily fail. It was this weakness which led to the wrecking of the steamship *Forfarshire* whose boilers failed in a storm off Bamburgh in 1838. Grace Darling, daughter of the local lighthouse keeper, helped her father row a cable out to rescue the nine crew and passengers and so became a legend in her lifetime.

Lighthouses are an obvious safety feature needed along a coast and the harbour facilities at Sunderland were no exception in requiring a suitable structure. What makes a particularly interesting and quite typically Victorian story, however, was the complete transfer of a stone-built lighthouse from one site to another. A system of flags and 'lanthorns' had been raised on a flagstaff on a wooden structure from as early as 1767. Then in 1802 Jonathon Pickernell, the River Wear Commissioner's Engineer, built a very fine octagonal masonry lighthouse at the end of the new North Pier, lit by oil and later by gas and with nine huge reflector plates from Boulton and Watt. In 1841 the pier was extended and John Murray performed a remarkable feat of engineering by moving the whole lighthouse intact to its new position. The building which was estimated to weigh three hundred tons, had been cradled and supported on a hundred and forty four wheels running on eight parallel lines of rails and was drawn more than thirty feet each day, by a team of forty men working screw-winches. In all it was moved about five hundred feet, (152m), up a total rise of 7ft 7in (2.54m) above its original base position. A lead pipe, carrying gas from the gas works on the pier was extended each day so that the light 'was exhibited nightly as usual', during the course of the move. Plate 62 *Off Sunderland Harbour* by Carmichael shows Pickernell's 1802 lighthouse in its original position, but the extension of the North Pier along which it was moved is shown under construction, hence the scene is about 1839–40, though the painting is signed and dated 1864.

From Sunderland south to Hartlepool the coast does not lend itself to natural harbours but a large and successful one was constructed and known as Seaham Harbour, by the Marquis of Londonderry early in the nineteenth century. No port had ever existed here; there was no natural harbour of any sort. Credit for the idea of a coal-shipping port goes to Sir Ralph Noel who, in 1820, instructed an engineer named William Chapman to prepare a plan, incorporating some of the inlets on the coast and with piers built on the rocks. Shortly afterwards the Marquis of London-

PLATE 62 *Off Sunderland Harbour* Oil painting by J.W. Carmichael, 1864 (Photo: Tyne & Wear Museums: Sunderland Museum and Art Gallery)

derry, who had served under Wellington and was invalided out in 1812, bought the estates and instructed Mr Chapman to prepare an even more ambitious design. Lord Londonderry was seeking an outlet for his collieries south of Sunderland and at that time the port of Sunderland was too small for such large shipments and also charged heavy dues. On 28 November 1828 the Marquis performed a stone-laying ceremony at the north pier and later that day his son, the young Viscount Seaham who was almost eight years old, laid the foundation stone for the first house of the new town-to-be of Seaham. The town had been designed by John Dobson (responsible for so many fine buildings in Newcastle) and was an ambitious project. Although the plan was by no means fully implemented, the harbour and town prospered and seem to have continued to attract the attention of the Marchioness of Londonderry, as we have seen from the school she had built there in the 1850s.

A contemporary description (by Fordyce), of around 1850, gives a vivid and clear picture of a prosperous little community, developing commercially and aided by the Londonderry family which created it:

The town of Seaham Harbour, soon after its erection, began to exhibit some of that spirit and enterprise which have since been more extensively displayed. As the trade of the port increased, various branches of manufactures and trade have been commenced or extended. Amongst these may be named the works of Messrs R. Wight and Sons, anchor manufacturers, brass founders and finishers, iron founders, engineers &c. Seaham Harbour Bottle Works were commenced upon the co-operative system, and were opened in April, 1852; so successful were the company that it was found necessary to extend the works in the same year. They are now carried on by R. Fenwick and Co. of Sunderland. The Londonderry Bottle Works belong to John Candlish and Co. Seaham Harbour Pottery belongs to Mr John Hedley Walker. There are three ship-building yards; with sail makers, ship chandlers, ship smiths, block and mast makers, &c. Four ship and insurance brokers and eight coal fitters attend to the business of the port. Two fire and life insurance companies have offices at Seaham Harbour. There are fourteen inns and public houses, three breweries, an ale and porter merchant, two printing offices, and most of those trades and professions necessary in a rising town. A large steam flour mill is situated in the dene to the north; and public baths have been erected near the coast. The gas works, belonging to Mr Henry Wall Smith, are in Dawdon Dene: the price is 3s. 4d. per 1,000 cubic feet. A joint stock water company, with a capital of £2,500, in shares of £5 each, was established in the early part of 1851: and after some difficulties, the capital was paid up, and the works for the supply of the town and harbour were completed in the summer of 1853. A branch of the Union Bank was opened, about a year ago, in the North Terrace, and a savings bank has recently been commenced in connection with it. The Custom House is situated in the same row. The rural police have a station in John Street.

Seaham Harbour is about to participate in the advantages derived from the iron trade. It has been stated that the Marchioness of Londonderry intends investing a capital of £100,000 in the establishment of iron works at this place, which now possesses remarkable facilities for such a purpose.

Seaham Harbour Infirmary was built in 1844 by the Marchioness of Londonderry; her ladyship dedicating to this object the proceeds derived from the sale of a volume published by her in 1843, entitled, *A Three Months' Tour in Portugal, Spain and Africa*. It is a handsome Gothic building of stone, in an enclosed space of ground at the end of North Terrace. It contains, at present, a dispensary or surgery, five wards with twelve beds, and matron's apartments; but the building is about to be considerably extended. The infirmary is under the care of a house surgeon, and a visiting staff, consisting of a physician and three surgeons. It is managed by a committee of twelve, elected annually by the subscribers; the Marchioness of Londonderry being patroness.

At this time Seaham Harbour had a church, opened in 1840, a Wesleyan Methodist chapel begun in 1833, a Primitive Methodist chapel of 1846,

147

a Wesleyan Association chapel of 1837 and a Congregationalist chapel, founded in 1835. There were two boarding schools for young ladies and several day schools. National schools for boys and girls were in Church Street (Plate 49).

A public news and reading room (known by 1860 as the *Mechanics' Institute*) had opened in 1846, towards which the Marquis and Marchioness of Londonderry each subscribed one guinea annually and Mr H.W. Smith gave the gas to light the room.

The Londonderry Literary Institute had been founded in 1853. The Marquis of Londonderry had offered a plot of ground, together with lime for building and the foundation stone was laid in 1853. The building was completed a year later, aided by a bazaar held by the Marchioness and her family, to a design by Mr Thomas Oliver junior. It was opened in 1855. The subscription method, as described by Fordyce is interesting:

> Subscribers of one guinea per annum are considered full members, and entitled to the use of the library, news room, and free admission to ordinary lectures. Subscribers of 10s per annum are entitled to the use of either the library or news room, but not both, and admission to lectures. Labourers and mechanics are admitted to the use of the library or reading room on payment of 6s per annum, and to full membership, embracing both, together with free admission to ordinary lectures, on payment of 10s. The establishment of classes and delivery of lectures are parts of the system. The library contains about 350 volumes, and there are at present 45 members.

Hartlepool lies around a large bay, the older settlement being extended by the newer West Hartlepool, though both are together now known as Hartlepool. In 1832 the Hartlepool Dock and Railway Company obtained powers to build a railway from the ancient harbour into adjacent colliery districts and by 1841 this railway was carrying more coal than any other line in the north; indeed 27 per cent of all the coal shipped from the ports of the North East passed along its tracks. The effect on local communities was immediate: the population of the old borough of Hartlepool shot up from 1,330 in 1831 to 5,256 in 1841 and of course populations in the adjacent colliery districts also grew. A further line from Stockton to Hartlepool a few years later diverted coal from the Tees, to the new dock at Hartlepool, and led to friction between the proprietors of the two lines. Consequently 'poaching' by the Tees proprietors resulted in a new dock, Hartlepool West Harbour, being constructed as a coal-handling installation in 1847, and within a decade this had led to the new town of West Hartlepool. As for the Tees, we have already looked at Middlesbrough and its growth from a tiny hamlet to a prospering industrial town with considerable port facilities, so we shall now leave the ports and turn to the associated industry of shipbuilding.

Shipbuilding
Two notable vessels built on the Tyne: *John Bowes* and *Turbinia* have
already been mentioned as highlights in shipbuilding, but an overall glance
at this riverside industry will help to adjust our perspective. As early as
1804, it has been calculated that almost one sixth of all the shipwrights
employed in merchant ship yards worked in Durham, at a time when only
1.4 per cent of the people of Britain lived in that County. And this leading
position persisted through the next fifty years or more. However, over a
similar period, the Tyne struggled to maintain its importance relative to
the Wear as can be seen from the following figures. In 1804 the south
bank of the Tyne accounted for 706 shipwrights, compared with 658
on Wearside, while in 1841 there were 432 adult shipwrights at South
Shields, compared with 968 at Sunderland.

Ships were being built on the banks of the River Wear under often
surprising conditions, and a skilled shipwright could build a vessel with
only limited help from a few other men or sturdy lads. Even backyards
were used and an empty strip of beach was enough for a site. We come
across the Engineer of the Wear Commissioners giving notice in 1811 to
'Thomas Mordey . . . that if he builds ships on the common ground south
of the South Pier he will be proceeded against'. Yet Mordey launched a
211 ton vessel that year, so perhaps his actions were overlooked after all.

Many shipbuilders were also engaged in other business activities such
as timber merchants, coal-fitters or even owners of lime works. So that
when a builder came upon difficult times, he could offset his losses in
other directions.

Robert Thompson's career, as recorded in a memoir by another member of his family, is one worth following briefly. He was born the son of
a sea captain in 1797 and apprenticed to a shipyard in 1813. Perhaps he
never completed his seven year term because he married in 1818 and soon
afterwards began to build in a berth below the Lambton coal drops. Then
'he bought two keels and worked these for a time'. During 1820–21 he
'built with some other men a vessel of 10–12 keels (160–190 tonnes) on
North Sands'. For several years he worked for other men, being a manager at Jarrow in 1832. Later he returned to Wearside and in the boom
of 1838–40 he built at Washington Staithes where 'an inn tap room near
the yard served as a designing office'. In 1846 he founded what was later to become the world renowned Thompson shipyard, though in its first
year he only took 30s. (£1.50) per week and his three sons took around
25s. each (£1.25). They worked with four employees to build the 240 ton
brig *Pearl* in eleven weeks and made a profit of £200.

The two main changes in shipbuilding throughout the century were the
use of iron instead of wood for the construction of the hull and steam
instead of sail. Both were only slowly assimilated and until the middle of
the century the main products of the time were carried in wooden ships

driven by sail. The change to iron took place gradually, and on Tyneside a small iron boat was built as early as 1822 and *Star* was launched in 1839 at South Shields. The steam collier *John Bowes* was launched by Palmers of Jarrow in 1852, who could well be said with this to have launched a new era. Yet it was not until 1868 that iron shipbuilding tonnage on the Wear exceeded that in wood, though this point had been passed nationally six years earlier.

Needless to say the capital outlay for iron-shipbuilding was greater than that for wood and a much more diverse workforce was required: in addition to the variety of metal workers, there was still substantial work for woodworkers and also the problems associated with the installation of steam engines. Hence most builders in wood were discouraged from changing to iron and their work lingered longer than might have been anticipated. For example new wood shipbuilding yards were still being opened on the Wear as late as 1865. However before that time Charles Palmer was boasting to the British Association, at its 1863 meeting, of the success of iron screw-driven colliers and showing how the Tyne was again well in the lead:

Tonnage of Iron Ships launched in 1862

Tyne	32,175 tons
Wear	15,608 tons
Tees	9,660 tons

Palmer's Jarrow Yard alone produced 17,096 tons of iron ships in 1863, practically as much as the whole of Wearside, though by 1872 iron output on the Wear exceeded that of Tyneside.

It can now be seen that shipbuilding at any rate on Wearside, remained essentially a craft industry until the 1860s, though it was the forty or fifty years after that time which were to be the period of world domination of ship building on the North East coast.

North Eastern River and Coastal Craft
Before coming to the little craft of river and coast, it is worth mentioning, though strictly outside our period, an important contribution made to lifesaving in the form of the first successful *lifeboat*. It was as far back as 1790 that the first such boat put to sea, resulting from a competition held at South Shields stimulated by a local tragedy when the entire crew of the *Adventure* of Newcastle was lost within sight of the shore. A prize had been offered for the best model of a lifeboat and of the many plans put forward, those of William Wouldhave, a painter, and Henry Greathead, a boatbuilder, were selected. The committee awarded the prize to the latter, and, combining the good points of both designs, gave an order to Greathead for the construction of the boat. The names of these two men

PLATE 63 Sailing ships at Hartlepool

were inscribed on a memorial erected at South Shields on the occasion of the 1890 centenary.

The North Eastern *coble* is found up and down the coast with various minor differences. On the Tweed, for example, this boat is used by fishermen for salmon fishing. Smaller examples are to be found up-river and larger ones nearer the mouth. They are flat-bottomed, square-sterned, clinker-built open boats approximately 16–22 feet in length, with a pronounced sheer forward. The salmon coble has well-rounded bows and very sharply rounded bilges with sides nearly parallel. The free-board is low, particularly the aft, where there is an open space for storing the nets. These boats are generally tarred outside and used with oars, double banked.

The *foyboat* was larger than the coble, equipped with a sail and used as a workaday vessel on the Tyne and the Wear in connection with coal-shipping.

Throughout the age of sail the foyboatmen's main task was to tow or kedge-haul sailing vessels in or out of the river estuaries during periods of calm or contrary winds. Kedge-hauling was an arduous and sometimes dangerous job. A light anchor, the kedge anchor, was carried in the foyboat ahead of the collier and then dropped into the water, at which point the sailors on board the vessel would haul on the anchor chain and so pull the ship up to the position of the anchor. The fees, or 'foys' for this work were anything from 2s. 6d. to 5s. 0d. in the early 1800s: quite generous for the time and reflecting something of the danger and hard work of the job. One boat of this kind has been preserved by the Tyne & Wear Museum Service.

A vessel which is surely for ever associated with the north east is the *keel*, a small boat built to carry coal from the up-river coal staithes down to the deeper-draughted sea-going colliers. The keel would carry about twenty tons of coal (eight Newcastle cauldrons) and was crewed by four men, three at a large oar and one at a smaller oar for steerage. A single mast with a square sail was sometimes used and the keels normally made use of the tide for a loaded journey.

These Tyneside keels were carvel-built (ie with their planks fitted flush), double ended craft built almost without sheer (ie very little upward slope towards bow and stern). They were somewhat oval in shape and six or eight paces in length, with rounded bottoms and almost no freeboard when loaded.

No example of a keel has been saved on the Tyne or the Wear, though there must always be the faint hope that a wreck may one day be discovered in sufficiently good condition to justify rescue.

The keel was finally ousted by down-river coal drops and chutes which cut out the need for the intermediate transport by these small craft. However as these changing methods caused the decline of the keel, so the expansion of nineteenth century industry created the need for a more versatile general purpose vessel to carry both raw materials and finished goods along the river. 'Lighters' were also needed to ferry materials to and from visiting ships. Thus the Tyne *wherries* were developed to serve these two needs. At first they were propelled, like the keels, by the tide or by long sweeps or oars or by simple sails. Strings of wherries could also be towed by paddle-tug and before the end of the nineteenth century many were being fitted with small vertical boilers and steam engines placed aft to drive a screw propellor.

Typically a wherry would be up to fifty feet in length and twenty feet across the beam, weighing thirty to forty tons. They were shell-clinker built and their 'Viking' ancestry could be imagined in the similarly pointed stems and sterns and the shapely curves of their nail-fastened overlapping planks. Indeed the simple tools which the shipwrights used to build them could well have been recognised by their Viking predecessors.

PLATE 64 'The Master Mariners' Asylum', Tynemouth by J & B Green, 1837

ROADS, BRIDGES AND VEHICLES

Roads

Our modern roads, smooth, wide, well-drained and well-engineered are accepted without question and we may readily forget that no more than a century ago many were muddy tracks in winter, dry and dusty in summer, inadequately surfaced and frequently following field boundaries and natural features. Towards the latter part of the seventeenth century English roads were even worse: in as bad a state as they had ever been. Usage was gradually increasing, but methods of surfacing and repairing them were quite inadequate. The chief cause, however, was probably not so much technical as legal, for each parish was supposed to maintain its own roads by statute labour, yet the subsequent establishment of turnpike Trusts and the maintenance of roads from the funds obtained from tolls does not seem to have effected as much improvement as one might have expected.

From the early eighteenth century local companies, acting as turnpike trusts, were given control over short stretches of road by private Acts of Parliament, and these trusts increased rapidly between about 1750 and 1770. They were more readily set up after 1743 by a General Turnpike Act which was passed to facilitate their establishment. So that by 1790 quite reasonable improvements had been made and faster coach travel was possible. From 1888 county councils took over responsibility for main roads and the turnpike trusts were wound up between 1865 and 1895.

It was, however, the work of Telford (1757–1834) and McAdam (1756–1836), which helped to build the good road systems of the early nineteenth century, and which became so much better developed through that century. These two men brought scientific principles and regular systems to the construction and repair of roads. Perhaps oversimplifying a little one might remark that Telford was primarily concerned with the construction of new routes, whereas McAdam was particularly involved in the repair of existing roads and their two systems of work were therefore not so mutually exclusive as might appear.

The name of Telford is associated with a pitched foundation and he paid particular attention to a solid foundation, whereas McAdam ignored this, maintaining that the subsoil – however bad – would carry the weight if made dry by drainage.

Both were agreed as to the importance of gradients and it is interesting to examine contemporary observations upon which gradients were based.

On a level macadamised road in ordinary repair the force which a horse has to put forth to draw a load may be taken as one-thirtieth of the load. But in going uphill the horse has also to lift the load, and the

154

additional force to be put forth on this account is very nearly equal to the load drawn, divided by the rate of gradient. Thus on a gradient of 1 in 30, the force spent in lifting is one thirtieth of the load, and in ascending a horse has to exert twice the force required to draw the load on a level . . . These considerations have led to 1 in 30 being generally considered as the ruling gradient to be aimed at on first-class roads.

It may be difficult for us today to appreciate that the very much improved surface provided by McAdam was due not to any waterproofing or binding material, but to the practical observation that six or ten inches of broken stone, ideally of roughly cubic pieces (not exceeding 1¼in on any side) would — when rolled and consolidated — provide a good surface. Indeed, unlike Telford, who covered the broken stone of his new roads with one and a half inches of gravel, to act as a binding material, McAdam absolutely forbade the use of any binding material: he required the surface of broken stone to 'work in and unite by its own angles under the traffic'.

Before the end of the nineteenth century 'tar macadam' was found suitable as a surface for suburban roads: broken stone, mixed with bitumen, provided a smooth surface reasonably free from noise and dust. For dust had been the great disadvantage of McAdam's roads and in towns the water-cart, used to spray a little water on the surface in hot dry weather, was necessary for the maintenance of reasonable conditions.

Cobblestones, and the better quality 'setts' provided by whinstone cut into blocks, made a far superior surface for urban use in later Victorian times and can still be observed from time to time covered over by a layer of tarmacadam to give the appearance and most of the advantages of a still more modern surface.

Wood pavements are now rarely seen, though a close watch on road repairs in older areas may just discover a stretch. They were first introduced in England in 1839, made of hexagonal blocks of fir embedded in gravel, but these tended to work loose and the 'improved wood surface' was first laid in London in 1871 and by 1877 wood was being attached by tar onto a cement foundation. Such a surface was often laid past a hospital, to try and reduce the high level of noise of that period, caused by iron wheel-tyres and iron-shod hooves.

Where urban surfaces were still 'macadamised' it is not surprising that they were thick with mud in winter, helped by the enormous amount of horse-dung which must have fallen on them. An enlightening comment of around the end of the nineteenth century came from an English traveller to Venice who remarked that the most striking thing he noticed was the lack of the smell of horse-dung, though doubtless the canals had their own characteristic odour on a hot day.

155

Bridges

Bridges have already been mentioned, from the standpoint of engineering, and many were the magnificent structures built in the region over the nineteenth century. The Scotswood Bridge, originally constructed in 1829–31 was reputedly by Sir Samuel Brown and John Green. It had two good sturdy stone pylons, with enormous chains running through channels near the tops of the pylons. In later years a new suspension system replaced the original and now one of the most inelegant bridges of its type ever constructed spoils the Tyne at this point.

A very fine example of Brown's work is the Union Bridge across the Tweed near Loan End, of 1820: the earliest suspension bridge erected in Britain, calculated for the passage of laden carriages. It was based upon an improved method of manufacturing links for chain cables, invented by Captain Sir Samuel Brown, RN (1776–1852). By very good fortune it lies at a point where modern traffic is slight and it has not been necessary to 'improve' or 'upgrade' it.

The High Level Bridge at Newcastle by Stephenson and Dobson (1845/9) must of course be mentioned again, as must the Swing Bridge of 1876 which replaced the old Tyne bridge at that point. This was swung by hydraulic engines provided by Armstrong.

Whilst the eighteenth century bridge builders took the opportunity to

PLATE 65 The High Level Bridge over the Tyne, by Robert Stephenson, 1849

replace so many bridges following the disastrous floods of 1771 which destroyed so many buildings of the day, they did so in their own medium, namely stone. Similarly, when new bridges were required in the nineteenth century, or – as in the case of the Swing Bridge they had to be improved to assist the growing river traffic – the latest materials of iron and steel were used.

Tramcars

The tramway system so typical of most later Victorian towns and cities had a relatively short life, partly due to restrictive legislation, partly perhaps due to fashion. But however the systems ended, their beginnings were fairly slow.

The oldest passenger-carrying tramway cars seem first to have been used in the USA, in 1832, between New York and Harlem. These cars seated thirty people and were built in rather the same way as the earliest railway coaches: as an apparent combination of several horse-drawn carriages attached end to end, each with their own side-doors.

And it was an American, Mr G.F. Train, who brought the idea to this country and was responsible for a line being installed at Birkenhead in 1860. Only a year later Darlington – that pioneer railway town – had a horse-drawn tramcar service along Northgate, but this only seems to have worked for two years. Perhaps it was before its time. Further developments had to wait until the passing of the Tramways Act of 1870 which laid down the general structure of tramway operations and how they were to be regulated. One clause in particular, which may at first sight seem fairly harmless, was probably responsible in the end for the demise of so many systems. It was stipulated that the surface of the highway for 1ft 6in (0.46m) on either side of the track (as well as that between the tracks) was to be maintained by the tramway operator. The purpose of this was to safeguard the highway authority against wear and tear from the hooves of the tramway horses, but it remained in force to the end and obviously increased the maintenance costs to a considerable degree, long after horses had ceased to wear the cobbles!

Another damaging clause made it possible for the Local Authority, if it so desired, to purchase a tramway in its area compulsorily, after twenty one years. And as if that were not a sufficient threat to hold over the tramway operators, the option continued to be available every seven years thereafter. The effect of this upon capital expenditure may be imagined. Of course eventually many of the tramways came to be operated by local authorities.

The rate of expansion of British tramways may be judged from the following figures. In 1836 there were 136 miles of tramway in the whole country. By 1886 this had grown to 779 miles. Only ten years after that,

157

there were more than 2,500 miles in the USA. The electric street car was hampered in Britain by the legislators who, with a marked lack of imagination, could not visualise beyond the horse-drawn car. So even by the end of the century there were only just over a thousand miles of track in this country and this track was still mostly worked by horse or steam.

It has to be stated that by 1907 the number had rapidly increased to around 2,232 miles as the benefits of the electric tramcar belatedly came to be recognised, and by the time war broke out in 1914 there were more than 2,500 miles of track. However this was to be the peak of tramway development, for the war brought great improvements to the internal combustion engine and the advent of the motor bus was the death knell to the more restricted and capital-intensive route-construction required by the tramcar. Moreover the motor bus was not held responsible for the maintenance of the highway surface whereas, as we have seen, the tramway system was held responsible for a large proportion of the surface.

In terms of social history perhaps the most remarkable feature of the British urban tramways was the cheap transport systems which they made available to working people.

Motor Cars

Moving now to the newer styles of vehicles which began to invade the late Victorian roads, we may observe a kind of 'chicken and egg' situation: were road surfaces rapidly being upgraded because of the traffic, which was beginning to be generated by the internal combustion engine, or was motor traffic encouraged by the improved road surfaces?

In our own region whilst de Dion and other foreign makes of car were beginning to appear, it was not until 1902 that a locally-produced two-cylinder paraffin-powered van could be seen. This came from Sir William Armstrong Whitworth and Company Limited; the merged company which had grown from Armstrong's Elswick works. Whilst battleships, hydraulic machinery and armaments are the products most readily associated with this company, it nevertheless found itself suffering a shortage of warlike orders after the Boer War and diversified into motor cars and commercial vehicles.

By 1906, after producing small vans at the rate of one per week, the company turned to private cars and within a year production had risen to 300 private cars and 200 commercial vehicles. The cars gained a reputation for sound construction and reliability, but it was the onset of the 'Great War' that halted production, never to be recommenced after the war.

In the early years of the twentieth century Armstrong-Whitworth could offer ten body styles for their cars, of which the 'Eshott' was one of the cheaper ones and retailed at £125. Fixed seating for two was provided, with two folding seats in a locker behind the front seats. An electric lighting set was an 'optional extra', acetylene lighting being standard.

Of the total output of Armstrong-Whitworth cars only five are known to survive; three in Britain and two in Australia.

Bicycles
Only the fairly well-to-do could run a motor car but a bicycle gradually came within reach of almost any young man and some young ladies too. In the 1850s some intrepid designers built their own machines and Tommy Sanderson, well known in later years as Sunderland's Town-crier, built his own tricycle in the 1850s. A recollection, written thirty years or so later, describes it as 'after the fashion of a scissor-grinder's machine . . . To work it was no joke, for it was heavy and cumbersome . . . and also a vicious machine which had a most erratic way of its own in coming down a bank'.

William Sawyer of Dover began building 'velocipedes' on a commercial basis and in the later 1860s a Sunderland shipbroker, Mr H.F. Wilcox, bought one. He was delighted with it and wrote 'in my Sawyer I have climbed all the steepest hills in this neighbourhood except the celebrated Houghton Bank'. These machines had four wheels, and were considered preferable to those with two wheels (known as ordinaries) on account of their stability.

The first Ordinaries appeared about 1870 and gradually become popular with young men of the middle classes. The invention of the pneumatic tyre in 1888 finally made riding comfortable and gave encouragement to other improvements in springing and general design.

A problem of the day, especially for young ladies, was how and where to learn to ride this novel machine and in 1896 the Rudge-Whitworth depot in Newcastle advertised what they claimed was 'the First Ladies Riding School established in the North of England'. There was a large riding area and 'twelve skilled attendants to help'.

Meanwhile a regional manufacturer had begun to produce cycles: the Elswick Cycle Company, established by William Newton in 1880. 'Elswicks' it was written in *The Wheeler* March 1893, 'are famed for speed and strength and these beautiful machines catch the eye at once'.

It was inevitable that cycle-riding should lead to cycle-racing and a young professional rider called George Walker, in 1879, won the 'Long Distance Championship of the World'. Though only in his early twenties, Walker became an established hero and in 1880 bought a piece of land at Dalton Street, Byker, and built his own Bicycle and Recreation Grounds, with a cinder track for racing. He even went so far as to buy an enormous tent about 200 yards long (183m) and 80 yards wide (73m) with a demountable wooden track 150 yards (137m) in circumference. With this he toured the area with a group of fellow professionals, setting up six-day races at such places as Bishop Auckland, North Shields and Sunderland.

159

It was equally inescapable that Cycling Clubs should be established and no town was complete without one. The men wore rather military-style uniforms with a peaked cap. Military discipline was also called for, and the captain rode in front, followed by the rest in order of seniority, with the sub-captain bringing up the rear. There might even be a club bugler to give orders such as 'mount', 'dismount' etc. Since most people worked on Saturdays, and Sundays were naturally not acceptable, most runs took place in the evenings. The Sunderland Cycling Club's first run was, not surprisingly, to Penshaw.

Around the end of the century it became popular to attend the North East Cyclists' Meet at Barnard Castle. This, held at Whitsuntide, is still a popular event, though cycling does not now hold the attraction it did almost a century earlier.

Clubs such as that at Sunderland were concerned about the state of their roads and it is recorded that the Sunderland Borough Surveyor was on one occasion advised that his drain-gratings by the roadside were dangerous for cycle wheels and he agreed in all future castings to have the grids set diagonally. A Road Mender's Prize Fund was established for the whole of Northumberland and Durham, in 1892, and prizes were awarded to roadmenders who kept their own stretches of road in particularly good repair!

Gradually, as the new century began, and particularly after the Great War, cycles spread to ordinary folk, cycle clubs became tamer and perhaps more plebeian, and began to be seen as a way of getting out of the towns into the countryside, and the bicycle offered a cheap and acceptable form of short-distance travel.

8
PHILANTHROPY, PLEASURE AND PROPERTY

A way from the hurly burly of industrial life and the squalor of working-class housing, a leisured class pursued cultural values and established much more than ephemeral matters of the day. So many public buildings in the centre of Newcastle (noticeably more than anywhere else in the region) belong to the early years of the nineteenth century, when Newcastle was the hub of a near-metropolitan way of life. As a centre for commercial activity, social life, and many industries, it was doubtless an exciting place to live if you were comfortably well-to-do. So if, in some respects, life in the early part of the nineteenth century appears to us to have been nasty, brutish and short for many, we should balance this by considering the boldness, the optimism, the hopes and the ambitions of the middle-class of the day.

Consider for example the societies and organisations which sprang up at that time. Whilst the Newcastle Literary and Philosophical Society dates back to 1793, the Newcastle Society of Antiquaries was established in 1813, the Northumberland Institution for the Promotion of Fine Arts in 1822, the Mechanics Institution in 1824, the Natural History Society in 1829 and the College of Medicine in 1834. Humanitarian tendencies of the age gave rise to the Benevolent Society in 1807 and the Lying-In Hospital in 1826.

The Literary and Philosophical Society had considerable influence in the nineteenth century. Within its rooms George Stephenson demonstrated his new Safety Lamp, Lord Armstrong (then a young solicitor) enthused about the power of water pressure in moving machinery, namely his new hydraulic equipment, Hugh Lee Pattinson described his 'world-famous' process for the separation of silver from lead by crystallisation and Sir Joseph Swan fascinated his audience with the brilliance of his new lamp, powered by the new force of electricity. In 1868 Robert Spence Watson made a bold proposal to the Society . . . 'I advocate neither more nor less than the establishment amongst us of a college, where instruction of a high and liberal kind, in every branch of learning should be given to all who can and will avail themselves of it.' He pointed out that

Newcastle had already had the Society's Library and Lecture Room, the Natural History Society with its unrivalled Hancock Collection of Birds, the Medical College, the Art School and the Mining Institute. All these, and the many Societies, were part of the intellectual and scientific environment that could be found in Newcastle at that time.

As for interesting people who might have been found in Newcastle's Victorian streets it is worth comparing them with the people we might find in modern Newcastle.

It is just possible that a history of the North East written a hundred years hence will produce a string of names of influential men and women whose lives and actions will be seen to have moulded the life of the city and its environs, and who will have left behind them tangible remains of their noteworthiness. Perhaps.

There can however be no doubt that of last century, and particularly of its second half, many noteworthy names can readily be recalled. Names like Armstrong, Parsons, Stephenson, Dobson, Grainger and Clayton have already been mentioned: men who left their mark by their mechanical or design or building or administrative abilities. Others have left a less substantial but nevertheless tangible mark, like Spence Watson or Thomas Bewick or William Wailes.

Robert Spence Watson, born in Gateshead in 1837 the son of a solicitor and himself a successful solicitor, was a notable Victorian Novocastrian. As a staunch Liberal he was made President of the National Liberal Federation in 1890. He had long been known as an arbitrator in industrial disputes and his fairness was so well recognised by the Trade Union movement that he was chosen as President of the Trade Union Congress, held in Newcastle in 1876. In later years it was remarked that of some fifty arbitration awards made by Watson, not one had been disputed.

One of his most noteworthy actions already mentioned, was to press for a college of science for the North East. This college was established in 1871. In 1904 the college adopted the name of Armstrong College in memory of Lord Armstrong, and in 1910 it was formally recognised as one of the three constituent units of the University of Durham (ie along with the Newcastle College of Medicine). It is an indication of Spence Watson's activities that he was then appointed President of the reconstituted Armstrong College. Newcastle University is, of course, now a full university it its own right.

A very human side of Watson was recorded by him in connection with his care for the impoverished population in parts of Newcastle. He

PLATE 66 Statue of Lord Armstrong (1810–1900), below the Hancock Museum, Newcastle upon Tyne

PLATE 67 Cragside, home of Lord Armstrong, by Norman Shaw, 1870 and 1880–82 (Photo: National Trust)

describes how he and Detective Elliott (later Superintendent of Gateshead Police) would set out at midnight to find vagrant boys, ill-clothed, ill-fed, sleeping against the warm gas-house wall in the Manors district of Newcastle . . . 'We put them in a bath, then we cut their hair. We had a pair of shears and one of us held the hair with tongs while the other sheared it as close to the skin as could possibly be taken. We had a uniform for them and a comfortable pair of boots. When we began there were 103 boys on the Newcastle streets known to the police as thieves. Before we had been in operation 12 months, there was not one.'

Noted for a love of literature and art, Watson was closely linked with the Newcastle Literary and Philosophical Society for half a century, being successively Secretary, Vice President and President.

Parallel with all these moral and human issues, Watson was a keen businessman and in 1881 he took part, along with Armstrong, J.T. Merz and the inventor Joseph Wilson Swan, in forming Swan's Electric Light Company. The Company opened a factory in South Benwell and claimed to be the first in Europe to manufacture the electric lamp.

A final insight into Watson's character can be gained by mentioning a few of his many friends and acquaintances who visited his Gateshead home: Nansen, the explorer, Joseph Chamberlain, Froude, the historian, Tom Hughes, author of *Tom Brown's Schooldays*, Earl Spencer, Banzow Futimoto, the first Japanese to come to Newcastle, as well as Stepniak, author of *Underground Russia*, John Bright the reformer, Garibaldi, Louis Kossuth, leader of the Hungarian revolution, and Felice Orsini, the Italian who was guillotined in 1858 for attempting to assassinate Napoleon III.

A surprising list of visitors to a Gateshead home!

Truly north eastern, if not quite Novocastrian, we should mention a notable nineteenth century archaeologist. Perhaps he would be recalled by archaeologists of today as much for his trail of destruction as for discoveries and recording, but if he is to be judged by his time then Canon William Greenwell brought archaeology to the notice of the public and published his observations in *British Barrows of the North of England*. A newspaper report of his 90th birthday in 1910 also recalled that 'he has all his life been a devoted angler, and is the inventor of two well-known and very alluring flies.' At least one of these flies, a trout fly which is known as 'Greenwell's Glory', is still familiar to today's anglers. His archaeological collections are now preserved in the British Museum, where they form the core of its prehistoric material. Quite recently a scholarly appreciation of the Greenwell Collection has been published by the British Museum.

The Greenwell family were farmers in North West Durham (many of them are buried at Lanchester) and the Canon held his first appointment as Vicar of Ovingham in Northumberland, living in the same Vicarage as that where Thomas Bewick had gone to school nearly a century earlier.

In later years he became Canon of Durham Cathedral.

Another Reverend gentleman whose life touches on many points relevant to this book, was John Hodgson (1779–1845). He was the eldest of ten children born to Isaac Hodgson, a stonemason from near Shap and after schooling at Bampton he became a teacher and was eventually ordained at Durham in 1805. He became curate at Esh near Lanchester and was appointed to the living of Heworth and Jarrow in 1808. Here he met and married Jane Kell, daughter of a local stone merchant. In 1812, as we have already observed, a terrible explosion occurred at Felling Colliery, killing ninety-two men and boys. Hodgson conducted the funeral services and had his funeral sermon printed together with a plan and information about the colliery. As a result the *Society for the Prevention of Accidents in Mines* was founded and Sir Humphry Davy was encouraged to investigate the problems of lighting in mines, resulting in the design of the 'Safety Lamp'.

Hodgson was also a founder member of the Newcastle Society of Antiquaries and later prepared and published several important volumes on the History of Northumberland. No mere reader of documents, he carried out archaeological field work too, and is noted for his excavations at Housesteads, a Roman fort on Hadrian's Wall, where he uncovered the granaries. His historical work was so highly regarded that the full *History of Northumberland*, begun in 1893 and finished in 1940 with the fifteenth volume, did not include those areas which he had already covered. Hodgson's life was clearly one for which we should be grateful, at several levels of significance.

Northern Art-Collectors
Many Victorian art-collectors were solidly middle-class and middle-brow and perhaps there were so few of these in the north-east because those who had the money were too busy to trouble themselves with collecting. A notable exception was James Leathart (1820–1895), born at Alston in Cumberland, where his father was a mining engineer. In his later years Leathart became managing director of the lead works at St Anthony's and also a director of a shipping company and a shipbuilders'. At one stage he was Mayor of Gateshead. Though shrewd in matters of business he seems to have been somewhat shy and retiring and had a real interest in the arts. He acted as Secretary for the Art School in Newcastle and this brought him in contact with William Bell Scott, the first master of the school in 1844. Scott had a marked influence on James Leathart's collecting, and when he retired in 1864 and moved to London, he acted as a scout for Leathart. Most collectors preferred to buy off the Academy wall, but James Leathart bought Pre-Raphaelites while they were still unfashionable.

With a family of fourteen children, though one died shortly after birth, in 1864 he moved into a large house at Low Fell, 'Bracken Dene', and had a playroom built at the end of the garden, so that he could enjoy his pictures in peace. Unfortunately, on his death it was discovered that his considerable income had mostly been spent on collecting and his wife and children found it necessary to sell the majority of his pictures. In 1968 The Laing Art Gallery staged an interesting exhibition with the ambitious aim of re-creating part of the Leathart Collection, by borrowing works scattered as far afield as New York and Philadelphia. With the help of the collector's grandson, Dr Gilbert Leathart, more than seventy works were brought together, representing such artists as William Blake, Ford Madox Brown, Burne-Jones, William Etty, Holman Hunt, Millais and Rossetti. The list of lenders alone gives some idea of the importance of the original collection, including as it does, The Ashmolean Museum, Oxford, Birmingham City Art Gallery, The British Museum, Fitzwilliam Museum, Cambridge, Victoria and Albert Museum etc.

However, the greatest art collector of the North East was, without any doubt, John Bowes, whose museum at Barnard Castle has already

PLATE 68 The Bowes Museum, Barnard Castle by Jules Pellechet (commenced 1869) for John Bowes

PLATE 69 The Hancock Museum, Newcastle upon Tyne, 1878, by John Wardle
(Photo: The Hancock Museum)

been mentioned. He was indeed one of the great collectors of the nineteenth century. Possibly his background, as natural son of the 10th Earl
of Strathmore was responsible for his shyness and it is said that he was
once warned off his own horse by his jockey who did not recognise him
at the races. Certainly he spent much of his life in France and eventually
married a French actress Josephine Coffin-Chevalier, and this must have
strengthened his partiality for all things French.

Together John and Josephine built up a truly enormous collection of
French furniture, porcelain and paintings and Spanish paintings including 'St Peter' by El Greco and two important works by Goya. In several
respects John Bowes' life may be compared to that of the Marquess of
Hertford, who built up the Wallace Collection now in London, and the
two collections have much in common.

It is fortunate for the region that, unlike Leathart, Bowes still had
funds available for building despite amassing his collections, and The
Bowes Museum at Barnard Castle is the magnificent result. True it was
not built steadily, but rather spasmodically according to the price of coal
whence Bowes obtained his income. Nevertheless built it was and today it
stands incongruously French in its Dales surroundings, as a 'treasurehouse
of the North'.

Before leaving this subject of a privately-funded museum, mention
must be made of the Hancock Museum: quite different from the Bowes
Museum, though also typical of its period. Its collections which initially were almost entirely restricted to natural history, were commenced by

Marmaduke Tunstall about 1770. They were purchased by the Literary and Philosophical Society of Newcastle in 1822. In 1829 the Natural History Society of Northumberland, Durham and Newcastle was formed, and one of its objects was the administration and development of these collections. In 1884 the present building was erected, mainly through the efforts of John Hancock and the generosity of the Armstrong and Joicey families. In later years King's College (now University of Newcastle) accepted partial responsibility. Pevsner says of this building, designed in 1878 by John Wardle: 'It is almost unbelievably Dobsonian for that date: Dobson's Doric pilasters, Dobson's heavy attic and even having the sanserif capital letters of the pre-Victorian nineteenth century' (Plate 69).

Northern Artists
It cannot be claimed that the North East has produced many great artists, though there is one northern man who must be given a national accolade: Thomas Bewick. Born in 1753, son of a small farmer and colliery owner, Bewick spent his childhood at Cherryburn on the southern bank of the River Tyne. Early in life he showed promise (though it was not at first appreciated by his parents), by chalking pictures on the flagstones around the kitchen fireplace.

He was later apprenticed to Ralph Beilby, noted in Newcastle for engraving of all kinds, and found he had a flair for wood-engraving. His skills developed so well that within a year of 'coming-out' of his apprenticeship he was offered a partnership in the Beilby business. This outspoken Northumbrian worked a short time in London, but swore he would never go there again and retreated to the homely north for the rest of his life.

Several significant books which he illustrated and for the most part wrote still appear from time to time as new editions, the early editions treasured by collectors: *General History of Quadrupeds* (1790), *History of British Birds* (Land Birds, 1797 and Water Birds, 1804), *Fables of Aesop* (1818).

Though well known for these illustrations of animals, birds, fables and so on, he earned his everyday living from such mundane things as bill-heads, banknotes, newspaper advertisements and miscellaneous book illustrations. Occasionally he was involved in straightforward cuts based on the drawings of others, for example *A New Family Herbal* by Robert John Thornton, MD, 'the plants drawn from nature by Henderson and engraved on wood by Thomas Bewick', 1810.

He seems to have enjoyed himself, and brought his talents to perfection, in the little vignettes or 'talepieces' which he cut to fill blank half-pages, for example in *Quadrupeds* and *Birds*. These depict the countryside as Bewick knew it, with his racy down-to-earth humour to the fore. Each illustration is in fact a little 'tale'. This humour, of rather eighteenth century character, was deplored later in Victorian times by his daughters,

FIG 9 A woodcut by Thomas Bewick of a 'netty' (or privy) and a pig (enlarged)

who would doubtless have banned some of the illustrations, could they have done so. An amusing example of this concerns the 'netty' and the pig, illustrated in Fig 9. The original watercolour on which the engraving was based is preserved in The Hancock Museum and shows the seated man's bare bottom. At the special request of his daughters, Bewick added two diagonal planks as a measure of decency, when he completed the engraving.

Bewick's birthplace has now been established as a museum to commemorate this fine artist. It is fortunate that the Northumbrian countryside adjoining the Cherryburn cottage is still surprisingly unspoilt and consequently visitors are able to gain some impression of Bewick's view of country life and thus better able to appreciate how and why he produced his illustrations of his countryside.

It cannot be denied that most Victorian painters in the north east had a tendency to follow the realistic school led by the Pre-Raphaelites rather than the Impressionist school. None of them painted in the least like Constable or Whistler and perhaps therefore it is not surprising that Ruskin's name is found from time to time in reference to northern painters. Doubtless most of them would have agreed with Ruskin rather than Whistler in the famous trial over 'the pot of paint flying in the public's face', which was Ruskin's critical observation regarding Whistler's paintings 'Nocturnes in Blue and Silver'. It was over this comment that Whistler not unnaturally took Ruskin to court, though he won only to the tune of one penny damages.

PLATE 70 *Hexham Station*, 1835 with 'Comet', a locomotive built by R & W Hawthorn, on the occasion of the opening of the first part of the Newcastle and Carlisle Railway. An engraving by J. Archer from a drawing by J.W. Carmichael

Nevertheless, though few if any artists from the nineteenth century North East would be recognised nationally with the notable exception of Bewick, we should look at some of these regionally significant artists and may do so from the point of view of their favourite subjects.

Ships: a north eastern subject certainly, were painted on a grand scale by John Wilson Carmichael (1800–1868), though he was also responsible for many landscapes and architectural studies and particularly interesting is a drawing he made of Hexham Station in 1835, engraved by J. Archer (Plate 70).

Collieries and colliery landscapes were a particularly favourite subject for Thomas Hair, working in the middle of the century. A fine set of his watercolours is held by the Department of Mining of Newcastle University and he published 'Sketches of the Coal Mines in Northumberland and Durham' in 1839, which is based on these (Plate 3). A few equally strong and dramatic oil paintings of local topographical subjects are also known to be by him, though surprisingly little is known of his life.

Local subjects, especially of activities which vividly illustrate aspects of social history, were a favourite topic for Ralph Hedley (1848–1913). Born at Richmond, North Yorkshire, he was apprenticed to a wood carver in Newcastle and then studied at the Government School of Art under William Bell Scott. His paintings can be evocative of their period and are carefully observed in detail (Plate 71).

In topographical terms Thomas Miles Richardson (1784–1848) is one of the most highly regarded painters in watercolours produced by the North of England. To him we are indebted for some exciting and convincing early nineteenth century views of Newcastle (Plate 61). With Perlee Parker he established the *Northumberland Institute for the Promotion of Fine Arts* in 1822, and with John Dobson, he helped to set up, in 1831, the Northern Society of Painters in Watercolours. This became a meeting place for the region's growing number of talented watercolourists, many of them benefitting from Richardson's advice.

Topographical subjects are also to be found among the works of Henry Perlee Parker (1795–1873) who, although not born or even mostly domiciled in the region, spent twenty odd years in Newcastle and became one of the area's best known artists of his day. Primarily a portrait painter, some of his best-known oil paintings, classed by the art critics as *genre*, can be used by the social historian as probably presenting an authentic view of dress and scenery of the day.

PLATE 71 *The Wedding Quilt*: a painting by Ralph Hedley of a typical cottage scene, 1883

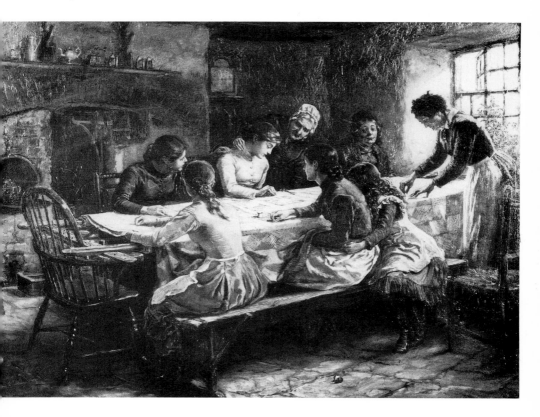

PLATE 72 *The Ouseburn Viaduct*: Watercolour by T.M. Richardson (Photo: Tyne & Wear Museums)

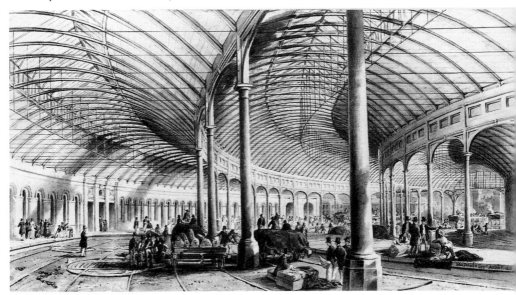

PLATE 73 *Interior of the Central Station, Newcastle upon Tyne* (1850). Watercolour by John Dobson and J.W. Carmichael (Photo: Tyne & Wear Museums)

Animals were the favourite subject of Joseph Crawhall The Third (1861–1913). His grandfather, of the same name, was a ropemaker in Newcastle but very able with watercolours, and also studied under Aloys Senefelder the discoverer of lithography. Joseph Crawhall The Second (1821–1896) produced large numbers of humorous drawings, many of which were used in *Punch*. He was a close friend of the descendants of Thomas Bewick and one of the executors of the will of Isabella Bewick, the last surviving daughter of Thomas. It was he, therefore, who was responsible for hundreds of Bewick's watercolours going to the Natural History Society of Northumberland, Durham and Newcastle (now housed at the Hancock Museum). Joseph Crawhall The Third, although born at Morpeth and educated in Newcastle, eventually studied abroad and spent much of his later life in Tangier, later moving to Yorkshire. He was buried at Morpeth.

Not all the region's watercolourists spent most of their days in this medium, for several were better known as architects, though often talented with the brush. John Dobson, one of the architects to make such a mark on the regional scene, was a capable and prolific watercolourist. He studied under John Varley but did not like London and returned to Newcastle to make his mark as an architect. Sometimes he would invite another artist, Carmichael, to colour his drawings and to add figures. Among the works in which they so successfully collaborated is 'Central Station Interior Newcastle' (Plate 73), wherein Dobson's superb mastery of perspective and Carmichael's flair for convincing animation, are seen to perfection.

John Green (1787–1852) designed the original Scotswood Suspension Bridge, opened in 1831 and now alas destroyed, and another of his bridges which survives, as a suspension bridge complete with toll-house is at Whorlton near Barnard Castle. He was also responsible for the introduction to this country of laminated timber construction and the viaducts for the Newcastle and North Shields Railway were so built, though later rebuilt in wrought iron whilst still retaining their original timber-built form. His watercolours were attractive in their own right, as for example one which was shown at the Royal Academy in 1837: 'A View of Scotswood Bridge.'

John's son, Benjamin Green (1808–1858) was another architect who was able to produce competent watercolours of his architectural work. He produced designs for the Theatre Royal and for Grey's Monument, Newcastle.

William Bell Scott has already been mentioned elsewhere. As the Master of the Government School of Design in Newcastle, he was in a particularly influential position in the region. Ruskin admired his work and recommended him to the Trevelyan family who were engaged in the 1850s in work at Wallington, where John Dobson was architect.

PLATE 74 *Iron and Coal*: one of eight paintings at Wallington, 1855, by William Bell Scott (Photo: National Trust)

Scott was commissioned in 1855 to provide paintings on the walls of a roofed-in courtyard, where they remain, well-preserved and attractive. As a convinced follower of the Pre-Raphaelites, he painted a lively series, but his most successful of the eight pictures is 'Iron and Coal', depicting the industrial life of Victorian Tyneside (Plate 74).

Another painter encouraged by Ruskin was Lady Waterford who became widowed at an early age in 1859. She then built a model village at Ford in Northumberland, with a memorial to her husband and a School (dated 1860), in which she painted a large series of biblical scenes suitable for children such as the Finding of Moses, David the Shepherd etc. Lady Waterford began this series in 1861 and completed it in 1881. Her models of the figures were mostly village people and the style as a whole is 'rather Michaelangelesque' (as Pevsner puts it). She did not particularly admire Ruskin ('He is the reverse of the man I like') but she respected his views. Ruskin, however, was dissatisfied with his pupil's work and, never one to mince his words, wrote 'I expected you would have done something better'.

Moving back from the aristocratic gifted amateur to the down-to-earth practising craftsman/artist, mention must be made of William Wailes, who was born at Westgarth, Newcastle in 1808. In his youth he visited Munich, where he studied stained glass and by 1840 he had established a Stained Glass Works on Grey Street, near the Grey Column. A year later he moved his works to Bath Lane where they remained for the next sixty years. Wailes himself died in 1881.

Particularly interesting is an eye-witness account of the studios, written in 1843 by William Bell Scott, then Master of the Government School of Design in the city ' . . . Here I found all the stages of art-education from the limited mechanic to the accomplished artist who drew out the cartoons . . . The master of this establishment, William Wailes, was the last man one would have expected to organise and succeed in this, then entirely new, species of art. He had been in trade and was successful, his general knowledge of art was nil . . . As to my object in visiting him, he wanted no more education among his workmen than they had. He had got his artists, and did not find workmen with art knowledge desirable. His ground object was to make his pot-metal pictures like the old ones, comparatively rude in execution. He knew what his customers wanted: restoration was the order of the day. Modern art . . . was his abomination.'

Scott goes on to say 'It was very trying to find the only branch of art-industry followed in the place repudiating my aid, and yet I was very much interested in Mr Wailes's workshop.'

By 1851 the staff at Bath Lane consisted of 61 men, 11 boys, 3 women and 1 girl. About eight years later Wailes purchased an estate in Gateshead, where he built Saltwell: an elaborate mansion in Gothic style,

intended to rival the nearby Ravensworth Castle. This was enriched with wood carving by another local artist, Gerrard Robinson. In 1876 Wailes sold the whole estate and mansion to Gateshead Corporation, for use as a public park, stipulating only that he be allowed to rent the mansion for the remainder of his life. Sadly in recent years the 'Towers' has been allowed to deteriorate terribly, though the park is still very well used.

As to Wailes's glass, many examples remain in churches in the region, as recorded by Pevsner. Notable windows in County Durham are at Darlington, Durham (St Mary the Less, South Bailey: most of the glass in this 1846 church is by Wailes) and at Shotley Bridge. In Northumberland, his work is to be seen at Morpeth, Newcastle: Cathedral (chancel south window), All Saints, St Andrew (including a memorial to four Wailes children) and St John. In the Cleveland area, with its rapidly expanding population, one is not surprised to find nineteenth century churches with Wailes's glass; for example at Baldersby (1856–8), Barton (1840–41) and Ormesby (1875). Catterick (of 1412) has a 'Last Supper' by Wailes over all five lights of the eastern window (1862).

Finally let us refer to John Graham Lough (1789–1876), particularly noted for his statue of Admiral Collingwood, at Tynemouth. This remarkable statue constructed in 1847, is 23ft (7 metres) high on a very broad base and a very high pedestal 50ft (15 metres) tall. It is one of the sights which any Geordie looks out for if he comes home to the Tyne by boat. Lough also sculpted another important regional figure, namely his statue of George Stephenson (1862) standing near Newcastle Central Station and comprising a large standing bronze figure with four seated bronze figures below. On a somewhat smaller scale, in terms of actual size, but of a remarkable number, are his sculpted figures in the gardens of Blagdon, the seat of Viscount Ridley, in south Northumberland: a good example of aristocratic patronage of an artist of the region. Here at Blagdon are marble bas-reliefs in the courtyard to the south of the house, well-sculpted marble standing figures at each end of the massive stone bridge of 1860, an interesting marble group in a woodland grove nearby, heads of members of the Ridley family on the white-painted iron bridge of 1881 and a fine bronze group: 'Milo fighting the Wolf', now sited in a circular pool at the end of a striking canal designed by Lutyens in 1938. Perhaps in view of this praise one should add that the Blagdon gardens are not normally open to the public, though they are generally opened once or twice a year in aid of the Red Cross.

PLATE 75 Saltwell Towers, Gateshead (1860); home of William Wailes, stained-glass maker

THE COMMON PLEASURE

Until the prosperity of the nineteenth century provided leisure time for the middle classes and – later in the century – for the 'Artisan' class, leisure was largely the prerogative of the very well-to-do: in fact the 'leisured class'. Gradually, however, free or non-working time extended until for many, life was not entirely occupied by work and the enforced rest of exhaustion. Yet an elderly Durham coal miner recalling his youthful years of work around the end of the nineteenth century said 'It was hard work, tedious work – I've come home many a time, and I've got washed and bathed and I've gone upstairs and changed and got on the bed . . . and I've been there when I've had to get up to go to work next morning . . . Aye, many a time . . . It was terrible hard work.' (This comes from a tape-recorded recollection by seventy seven year old John Kell of Leasingthorne, near Bishop Auckland, made in 1964.) So even a suggestion of growing leisure-time in the nineteenth century must be qualified.

It is difficult for us today, accustomed to an average thirty seven hour week (which even within the writer's memory has shrunk from a forty four hour week), to understand the arguments which were propounded by the 'Nine Hour Movement' of the early 1870s. This was a concerted effort by engineers to reduce the working day by an hour, thus cutting the number of working hours in a week from sixty to fifty four. Sir William Armstrong, as he then was, bitterly fought this move amongst his men, but caved in after a long strike and in 1872 *The Shipping World* commented 'It is to the Tyneside engineers that the skilled workers of the United Kingdom are indebted for establishing the day's work at nine hours'.

Another factor in improving living conditions, if not in extending leisure time, has already been referred to: namely the advent of the electric tramcar as a means of providing cheap transport, allowing workmen to travel further to work and so encouraging the growth of suburbia.

As to the use of leisure hours, the working man has long been castigated for his simple and brutish sports and pastimes, often associated with his 'pub'. Most of these had a strong gambling element from cock-fighting, coin-tossing, wrestling, quoits and the ball-alley to larger-scale observer sports such as rowing and football.

A sport that preceded Association football as a focus of popular attention was competitive rowing along the Tyne. Its great era was in the 1850s and '60s, but reports in local newspapers of the 1840s demonstrate a wide popular following and this grew over the next three decades. During the 1850s there were great matches between the champions of the Tyne, the Mersey and the Thames, and the riverbanks were frequently crowded by supporters. Naturally large sums of money changed hands as gambling grew with the sport. Among the first North Eastern oarsmen to attract attention was Harry Clasper and his seven keel-men brothers, and in his heyday Clasper claimed to be the champion sculler of the world. When he died at the Tunnel Inn, Ouseburn in 1870, aged fifty eight years, his funeral was a great scene of popular grief attended – as the *Newcastle Chronicle* reported – by upwards of a hundred thousand mourners. He was buried at Whickham and a large memorial bears witness to the respect such a sportsman was accorded. It is recorded that 'This monument was reared to his memory, by the ardent affection of friends and admirers from every class and from all parts of the Kingdom' (Plate 76). Only two years earlier 'Honest Bob Chambers' had died. Chambers had won the sculling championship of the world against Green on the Tyne in 1863, having been initially trained by Clasper, but after these two deaths sculling lost its major attraction and swimming grew steadily in favour.

This led to public swimming baths being provided at five of the seven public baths and wash houses which were established by Newcastle Corporation in Gallowgate, Scotswood Road, Newbridge Street and other parts of the town.

Football on the other hand, which began nationally with the Football Association being formed in 1863, did not become popular in the North East until a northern club first won the Challenge Cup in 1882. Then its popularity spread with astonishing rapidity. Newcastle United, originally playing as Newcastle East End on a ground at Heaton junction, amalgamated with Newcastle West End in 1895 and acquired the ground – an intake of the Town Moor – which is known to the football world of today as St James Park.

Another nationally known sports area is the Gosforth Park Race Course to which race meetings were moved from the Town Moor in 1882. It was around this time that an annual Temperance Festival was inaugurated in Race Week to serve as a counter attraction and over the years this has amusingly changed in character to become the 'Town Hoppings', one of the largest and best known fairs and amusement pitches in the country.

As to indoor entertainment Music Halls had been a particularly British phenomenon, especially of the nineteenth century, and probably began in the 1830s. Admission was often in the form of a 'Refreshment Check' or 'Wet Money', so called because it was returnable by drink to the value of the check. Singers, comedians or other entertainers were engaged by the landlords of various inns, to entertain and draw clients into the 'Singing Room' Not surprisingly in time the singing room or 'Music Hall' might become more important than the inn or the pub to which it was originally attached.

Recollections of north country Music Halls have been brought together by an enthusiast, Geoff Mellor, in *The Northern Music Hall* which includes mention of several famous Halls, such as the Canterbury at Middlesbrough where in the 1860s whisky retailed at 16s. a gallon. The old Free Chapel on High Street in Gateshead became a 'Theatre Royal' in about 1860.

179

PLATE 76 Monument to the famous Tyne oarsman, Henry Clasper, 1870, in Whickham Churchyard, County Durham

It was later run as 'The Royal Theatre of Varieties' and known by other names too such as 'The Queens'. Still later it went over to films, as did so many other music halls, and ended its career as a Woolworths store.

Yet before so many of these popular amusements of the common people began, Richard Grainger had built a rather more sophisticated 'Music Hall' – indeed of a very different kind – on Nelson Street in 1838. Upstairs was the Hall itself (40 × 80ft) and beneath was the Lecture Room with platform and nine tiers of seats. The Hall was in constant demand for concerts, bazaars and public dinners. It was particularly well used when – in 1838 – the eighth meeting of the British Association for the Advancement of Science was held in Newcastle and an elaborate programme was devised for the visitors. In 1861 Dickens gave a reading here, but in 1879 it became The New Tyne Concert Hall, marking a change of character and by 1884 it had completely lost its sophistication and become The Gaiety Variety Theatre, part of the Moss empire. It was so successful in this role as to be described as 'The Eldorado of the North', but was quickly found to be too small, for the 'naughty nineties' were here: the golden age of the Music Hall.

One of the big names in Northern Music Halls towards the end of the century was Tom Barrasford of Jarrow, son of a Newcastle publican, who pioneered the 'Two Houses a Night' system and set up a tour of fourteen halls, thereby simplifying his bookings and building up a more economical operation. He began, in 1895, in a wooden circus on a pit heap in Jarrow which he called 'The Jarrow Palace of Variety'.

A more famous Music Hall on Tyneside was The Old Wheatsheaf in Cloth Market, Newcastle, originally a public house with a built-on singing-room. It was here in 1862 that George Ridley, a crippled ex-pitman, first sang the immortal north eastern ballad he had just written: 'Blaydon Races'. The proprietor of The Wheatsheaf at that time was called Balmbra and his name is perpetuated in the song:

Aw went to Blaydon Races, twas on the 9th of Joon,
Eighteen hundred and sixty two, on a Summer's efternoon;
Aw teeuk the bus fra' Balmbra's, and she was heavy laden,
Away we went alang Collingwood Street – that's on the way ti
Blaydon . . .

This singing room became the 'Oxford Music Hall' in 1865 and seems to have been known as 'The Vaudeville' at the end of the century. However on the anniversary of the Blaydon Races in June 1962 it was used again as 'Balmbra's Music Hall' and in this resuscitated version it lasted several more years.

Around the same time as George Ridley, another music hall performer and song-writer was also drafting songs with a lilt. For Joe Wilson will go down in history as the writer of 'Keep your Feet Still Geordie

PLATE 77 Sword-dance team from Winlaton, County Durham

Hinny', an intrinsically sad yet lively song. He also died in his thirties of that dreaded disease of the day: tuberculosis. Tommy Armstrong, on the other hand, was a pitman who lived into his seventies and did his singing in the local pubs rather than the music hall. He kept himself in drink by writing popular ballads and selling these as broadsheets at a penny a time.

Perhaps less a leisure activity and more a curious historical remnant, is the Northern sword dance: an elaborate formalised performance by five men holding 'swords' which form an integral part of the dance. The sword dance has been recorded at many points throughout England and is generally acknowledged to have been saved from oblivion by Cecil Sharp, founder of the English Folk Dance and Song Society, who recorded and published these dances around the beginning of the present century, just as they began to disappear. Sharp travelled widely and devised his own notation for recording the complex steps which conclude with the triumphant production of a 'knot of interwoven swords held high by the leader' (Plate 77). The dance may be linked with the other 'folk' performances of an Easter play variously referred to as the 'St George's play' or the 'Plough Stots' in which latter case a wooden plough was included as part of the performance. However the most northern of the dances recorded by Sharp are of the short-sword or 'rapper' variety. The rapper, made of a flexible steel strip some 24in (600mm) by just over 1in (28mm) wide, has a rotating handle at one end and a block of wood fixed at the other. Its origin is unclear, though it has been suggested that it might be derived from a metal strip used to scrape down sweating pit-ponies. Sharp published five of these dances: from Swalwell, Earsdon, Beadnell, Winlaton and North Walbottle. Each of them had five dancers and a musician, together with a 'Bessy' or 'Betty' – a male dancer dressed in woman's clothes who carried a box and collected the money. These dances certainly pre-date the Victorian period and indeed may have pagan origins, but they seem to have flowered during the nineteenth century and several can still be seen today, rather self-consciously performed by serious young men. Women too, as one would expect in the late twentieth century, have now made their way into what undoubtedly was – as a pagan festival – purely a men's activity.

Spas and Holidays

The fashionable way of holidaying has quite naturally varied over the centuries and the attractions of the spa, now long out of fashion, were quite remarkable in their day. Even the Romans bathed in the mineral waters of Bath and the medicinal properties of chalybeate (iron-bearing) spring water and other equally peculiar-tasting waters were lauded in the eighteenth and nineteenth centuries. As the fashion for attending the spa increased, so did the added value of sea-drinking and sea-bathing, particularly after the Prince of Wales had popularised Brighton as a resort.

PLATE 78 Bathing and bathing machines at Seaton Sands

From being places of pilgrimage for health, the spas became places of amusement and then models for resorts of a new kind, the sea-side watering places. As for the North East, the coast of County Durham was too spoiled by shipping or by nearby coal mining to provide good sea-side resorts, but in Northumberland to the north and the North Riding of Yorkshire to the south, one could find respectively Whitley Bay and Redcar. Further south, and outside our area was the more notable Scarborough.

We can, however, trace several spas within our region in the early years of Victoria's reign and some tiny remains are still there to be sought for even today. Our guide might be a readable little book *The Spas of England and Principal Sea-Bathing Places* by A.B. Granville published in 1841 and reprinted a few years ago.

From Dr Granville we learn of two spas near the River Tees, at Croft and Dinsdale. His contemporary description incidentally is charmingly informative:

I hastened towards Croft . . .passed Northallerton, and alighted at the 'Spa Hotel', in full time to examine the various parts of this comparatively modern watering-place. The road, before reaching Croft, passes under one of the arches of the great rail-road now constructing from York to Darlington, which is projected across the valley and forms part of the great north of England rail-road. John Emerson the very civil and obliging landlord of the 'Spa Hotel', in manners far superior to persons of his class, escorted me to the springs, at about a quarter of a mile from the hotel, in a field near the roadside.'

184

Granville goes on to describe the actual spring, kept covered by a flag-stone and the adjoining cistern for public use. Inside the adjoining cottage or 'spa-house' was a cold plunging-bath 'six and a half feet long and four feet wide, sunk four feet into the ground. Five stone steps lead down to the bottom, which is paved with large flagstones'. So far Granville has been describing the Old Spa. He then goes on to describe the 'New Well' which had been sunk twenty six fathoms to find a much more strongly impregnated sulphur water.

In front of this well (sunk in 1827) Sir William Chaytor of Witton Castle had erected a suite of baths, with a 50 × 70ft pump room. During the season of 1837, we are told, there had been as many as eight hundred bathers here. Of this fine building, little now remains.

Not far away, the Dinsdale Spa seems to have had even more reason for popularity, for a local surgeon Mr Walker pronounced its water efficacious in dealing with 'hepatic disorders, Dyspepsia, Hypochondriasis and Diabetes.' Particularly he recommended the Dinsdale water for lead poisoning. As Dr Granville records:

> A man employed in some neighbouring lead-works, who had his upper extremities completely paralysed was sent home quite re-established, after drinking the Dinsdale water and bathing in it six times.

PLATE 79 Engraving of 'Croft Sulphur Springs' near Darlington, 1866

Moving now in part by way of a rope-hauled railway system, the intrepid Dr Granville eventually came to Hartlepool where he describes excavations going on for the formation of a new harbour and docks, according to a scheme devised 'by that able engineer Sir John Rennie'. He goes on to tell us, perhaps somewhat sadly, 'Hartlepool is in a state of transition. It had once its day as a sea-bathing place – once a watering-place of considerable celebrity. That glory is now past . . . We have to record the end of its good days; but we may also report the termination of its degredation. At no distant period we may have to chronicle its rise and new prosperity.' Granville was of course referring to the new docks and harbour which were going to renew the life of Hartlepool. And this they did for another century or so. Going inland from Newcastle, up the Tyne, brought Granville past the new Scotswood Bridge, which he described as being of great beauty. Its construction, he noted, took only two years and the cost was £15,000. He eventually arrived at Shotley Bridge Spa, at the well, which was situated about a mile below the village, in an ornamental garden. The well was protected by a simple round thatched roof, supported by slender rustic trunks of trees, with three circular steps leading down to the well.

The prosperity of this well seems to have been due to the far-sightedness of a Mr Richardson who bought the Shotley estate and then encouraged use of the waters. Granville refers to the growing popularity of this spa and the five hundred strangers who had come to drink the water in the previous year, and this number was growing. A visitor's book recorded these facts and 'Among the names of note contained in the list was that of the author of the *Pickwick Papers*'.

A remarkable series of cures were attributed to the Shotley Bridge Spa, and 'being situated at equal distances from Durham and Newcastle (14 miles) and 12 miles from Hexham, this spa is within reach of three populous cities and districts and requires only to be properly known to be appreciated and resorted to.' In fact Granville went further: 'The immediate vicinity of the Carlisle railroad renders its access easy to the people of the west; and the approaching completion of the great Midland Railway will afford an equally direct and facile line of communication between the southern and central provinces and this highly interesting Spa.'

However, with longer hindsight to set against Granville's foresight, we might think that the coming of the railway, making access easier as it did, also symbolised a new age in which leisure was to play a larger role, though the pleasures of spas were to be replaced by others less concerned with the medicinal properties of water.

HOUSES OF CORRECTION

Durham Gaol, remembered in Tommy Armstrong's once-popular song 'There's nae gud luck in Durham Gaol!', like many of our gaols today, dates from the early years of last century, for until that time prisons were not primarily intended for punishment or for the protection of society, because most offences were punishable by death or transportation. Their main functions were to hold debtors until their obligations had been settled, or else to keep prisoners until they were brought for trial, or until their sentence was carried out. Such prisons were at first contained in castles or large houses and only gradually were special buildings erected.

Transportation may be said to have begun with the Vagrancy Act of Elizabeth's reign, which empowered judges to banish offenders and order them 'to be conveyed into such parts beyond the seas as shall be assigned by the Privy Council'. A later development of the system of transportation (a term first used in the reign of Charles II) took place in 1617 when an act was passed by which offenders who had escaped the death penalty were handed over to contractors who engaged to transport them to the American colonies. The revolt of the American colonies and their subsequent independence in 1776 checked transportation there and British authorities, making a virtue of necessity, decided that the labour of these convicts might be useful to the economy. An Act was accordingly passed to provide that convicts sentenced to transportation might be employed at hard labour at home. Three eminent public men – one of them being John Howard – were set the task of planning a suitable scheme. From this followed an Act of 1778 for the establishment of penitentiary houses. In this Act it was hoped 'by sobriety, cleanliness and medical assistance, by a regular series of labour, by solitary confinement during the intervals of work and by due religious instruction to preserve and amend the health of the unhappy offenders, to inure them to habits of industry, to guard them from pernicious company, to accustom them to serious reflection and to teach them both the principles and practice of early Christian and moral duty'. Truly these form the basis of every variety of prison system since the passing of that Act.

However no immediate action was taken and before the committee was able to agree on a choice of site for the first penitentiary, the discoveries in the South Seas by Captain Cook provided an alternative for convict colonisation.

For many years the numbers shipped out to Australia grew and although concern in England was shown for prison reforms, the lot of those transported was quite overlooked. Eventually however the Colonies themselves made protestations about transportation and the growing population at home forced the British government into further reform. The new solution was clear: it was to be incarceration linked with useful labour.

PLATE 80 Portrait of 'An Habitual Drunkard', from a policeman's notebook: Newcastle upon Tyne, 1903

188

Meanwhile the life and work of Elizabeth Fry (1780–1845) now comes to our notice. This English philanthropist and, after John Howard, the chief promoter of prison reform in Europe, was the daughter of John Gurney, a wealthy Norwich banker and member of the Society of Friends. In 1800 she married a London merchant Joseph Fry. In 1813 she paid her first visit to Newgate prison and gradually became aware of the problems of prisons. She was directly responsible for the Association for the Improvement of Female Prisoners in Newgate Prison, formed in 1817. She described a women's ward like a 'den of wild beasts, filled with women fighting, swearing, dancing, gaming and yelling' which justly deserved its name of 'hell above ground'. Yet within a month of her actions it was transformed said an eye-witness, into 'a scene where stillness and propriety reigned'.

The Prison Discipline Society, formed by a number of responsible and concerned people, worked hard to ameliorate the national situation. It was a direct result of the Society that Acts of 1823 and 1824 were passed which laid down that it was essential to preserve health, improve morals and enforce hard labour on all prisoners. Irons, which had been in common use, were strictly forbidden and it was ruled that every prisoner should have a bed to himself and if possible a separate cell.

In 1834 a Mr Crawford was despatched to study the latest methods of penal discipline in the United States of America. He came back imbued with the value of complete separation and continuous silent isolation, though he could not deny that many prisoners became insane and their health was seriously impaired. In 1839 an Act was passed in which it was laid down that individuals might be 'confined separately in single cells'. In 1840 the construction of Pentonville Prison was commenced and completed within three years, with 520 cells. Within half a dozen years no less than fifty-four new prisons were built on this plan which, it is said, now began to serve as a 'model' not only in England, but all over the world. However, it is relevant to note that a radiating plan for a prison was formulated by the Newcastle architect John Dobson in 1822. His plan is said to have been admired and approved in all official circles to whom he circulated his idea. The Court House and County Gaol at Morpeth, which Dobson designed in 1822, is partially based on this theory and although now mostly demolished, the heavy portentous entrance gate still stands.

The New Gaol and House of Correction in Newcastle, the foundation stone of which was laid on 4 June 1823, was built entirely upon Dobson's radiating principle (the general shape can clearly be seen as Building No. 91 in the very centre of Fig 10). It was completed in 1828 at a cost of about £35,000 and it is interesting to discover how this large sum was brought together, for it was collected by an assessment upon lands and buildings within the town,

not to exceed in the year 1s 6d in the pound of their annual value,

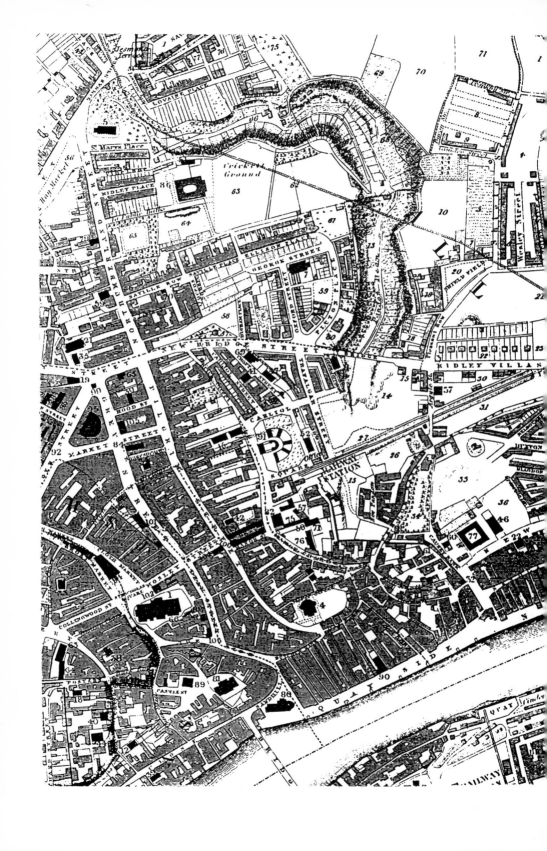

the whole sum raised to be limited to £50,000, the rate to be paid by the tenants and a moiety to be allowed by the landlords and when finished to be vested in the Justices of the Peace for the town and county of Newcastle upon Tyne.

Throughout most of the century hard labour was seen as a necessary concomitant of imprisonment and the treadmill was frequently used. This cumbersome appliance had been designed by Sir William Cubitt in 1818, intended as an efficient means of employing criminals usefully. It was a large hollow cylinder of wood pivotted horizontally in an iron frame, and round its circumference was a series of steps about 7½in (190mm) apart. The criminal, steadying himself by a hand rail on either side, would tread on these steps and his weight, and that of his fellows alongside, would turn the wheel. This mill, with several men working it, was used for grinding corn, pumping water etc. The prisoner worked for six hours per day, fifteen gruelling minutes on the wheel, followed by a short rest of five minutes. In the course of a day's work he would have climbed over 8,600 feet (2,600m).

The treadmill at Durham Gaol was frequently the cause of comments as to its usefulness, for in the *Durham County Advertiser* of February 1824, an extract from the Fifth Report of the Prison Discipline Society pointed out that 'unless it was regulated with great care, it could become, in the hands of some, an engine of terrible oppression'. In the same month the *Durham Advertiser* reported briefly that three men had been sentenced to two weeks on the treadmill for being drunk and disorderly in Claypath. In time it began to be realised that the treadmill was not infallible, or even a very potent deterrent. In 1826 the Durham Visiting Justices lamented that the larger number sentenced to hard labour 'furnished abundant proof of its insufficiency as a preventative'. Two years later they reiterated that the number of recommittals showed 'how little the Terror of the Treadmill operates as a preventative of crime'.

Gradually the use of treadmills was reduced. Yet as recently as 1895 there were 39 still in use in English prisons though these had dwindled to 13 in 1901. More usefully productive work took over, providing goods for public departments: such as blanket-making, hammock and mail-bag making. All these also took over from mat-making which was at one time an exclusive prison trade, having indeed originally been invented by an ingenious prison-master.

Over the early years of the nineteenth century, no standard practice was adopted at the many prisons now to be found around the country. The amount of exercise allowed varied greatly; there was no constant rule as to employment; in some prisons hard labour was insisted upon, in some

FIG 10 Part of a map of the centre of Newcastle upon Tyne by Thomas Oliver, 1844

it did not exist; the cells were of varying sizes and variously lighted, warmed and ventilated. Diets varied from the ample to near starvation.

The failure of the 1823 Act to lay down any dietary standards was criticised by the Prison Discipline Society and the reports of the Durham Visiting Justices indicate some concern in this matter. In 1828 they suggested that the prisoners were having too much salt fish – and as dinner for four days a week this surely was so! Butcher's meat and cheese were to be substituted on some days, they stipulated, though only at an additional cost of a farthing a head.

In 1833, however, when the county was reducing costs everywhere, it was decided that the prisoners' diet was too full and varied: a prison, after all, was meant to be a place of punishment! A plainer diet was accordingly adopted, consisting of one and a half pounds of bread, one and a half pints of milk and one pound of potatoes for each prisoner daily. Three months later the Visiting Justices recommended a further reduction, by removing the potatoes entirely, though on washing days the women were to have an extra four ounces of oatmeal.

Over the next two years further cuts and variations were effected at Durham and one cannot but comment on these comfortably-placed gentlemen so earnestly attempting to avoid giving the inmates of their prison the slightest indulgence.

Eventually the Prison Act of 1865 was drawn up, to codify these and other matters and some of its provisions continued well into this century. Still later it was decided that crime was not merely local and the whole state rather than individual communities ought to be taxed. Hence the Prisons Act of 1877 brought the control of all prisons into the hands of the state and Prison Commissioners were appointed by and were responsible to the Home Secretary.

GAZETTEER OF THE NINETEENTH CENTURY NORTH EAST

This Gazetteer is divided alphabetically into the Counties of Northumberland, Tyne and Wear, Durham and the northern part of Cleveland, thus ranging from Berwick-on-Tweed in the north to Middlesbrough on the Tees in the south. A certain imbalance may appear in that minor items (such as mileposts and small cottages) are mentioned for villages, whereas only the more significant or important buildings or structures are mentioned for towns. This is because some of the minor items may not readily be found unless referred to here, whereas walking through a town permits public buildings and terraces to be observed quite easily. In any case, of course, one cannot possibly claim this Gazetteer to be anything like fully representative.

It is also only right to point out that there is a plentitude of important and interesting buildings, structures and sites of many periods earlier than the 19th century, but these are naturally not referred to in this Gazetteer.

Finally grateful acknowledgment must be made to the very full *Lists of Buildings of Architectural or Historical Interest* published by the Dept of the Environment, used here with permission, where appropriate. Pevsner's *Buildings of England* series has also been useful from time to time. Anyone desiring more information on any particular building should first check in the appropriate county volume by Nikolaus Pevsner and if necessary seek out the relevant D. of E. *List*. Copies of these *Lists* are held by most libraries and archive Departments and a full series for the whole region is held at Beamish, as also is a very useful photographic archive for the region. (Note that, except where otherwise stated, the early photographs used in this book have come from the Beamish Photographic Archive.)

CLEVELAND COUNTY

Egglescliffe · NZ 41 SW · Leyfield House on Urlay Nook Road was a **Railway House,** c 1840, for the S&DR, in dark red brick and bearing a ceramic plate: 19/SD (Stockton and Darlington). Plates of this kind are unfortunately now rather scarce because of demolition and collectors. They are believed to refer to records kept by the Railway Co. (For a list see Atkinson, Frank, *Industrial Archaeology of North East England*, 1974, Vol 2, p 348).

Elwick · NZ 43 SW · One of the few **windmills** of the region. It is a tall brick tapered tower of 6 storeys. The fantail, roof-cap and lower timber floors are missing, but some machinery, including three sets of stones are there, and one of the sails remains.

Greatham · NZ 42 NE · A few **houses** of interest along Front Street, including Nos 2, 4 and 18; also the **Almshouse** (Hospital of God, St Mary and St Cuthbert) of 1803–4 by Jeffrey Wyatt for the Earl of Bridgewater.

An interesting **house** is 'Briarmead' on High Street, of 1833 by Philip Webb, together with its **stable-block.**

Hart · NZ 43 NE · Another **windmill,** in disrepair. This, of early nineteenth century origin, is in rendered limestone rubble. It is a tapered circular tower of three storeys. Most of the machinery is intact, but it lacks stones and has remains of only one sail.

Hartlepool · NZ 53 SW · Effectively the town is made up of Old Hartlepool and the newer West Hartlepool. Together they are now known as Hartlepool, with the older parts described now as the Headland. For convenience and historical clarity, therefore, the older part is here treated first.

Off the east side of Bath Terrace, on the Headland, is a **field gun** of late eighteenth century or early nineteenth century manufacture, mounted on a 2-wheeled gun carriage; captured from the Russian Army at the siege of Sebastopol (1854–6) and presented to Hartlepool Borough Council by Lord Panmore in 1857.

On Durham Street is the **R C Church of St Mary** by J A Hansom of Preston (1850), in Early English style. Also on Durham Street is the United Reformed Church, formerly **Independent Chapel,** dated 1843.

In High Street is a very ornamental **pump** of mid or late nineteenth century, in cast iron, standing in the middle of the road.

The **Municipal Buildings** and former **Market Hall** on the Headland, are on Middlegate, the latter now being a dance hall: the whole of 1865 by C J Adams. Also on Northgate is the **Carnegie Library and Librarian's house**, of 1903. On old Cemetery Road is the **Throston Engine House** of the 1830s. This was the housing for a haulage engine and still contains the bed of that engine, which used to draw coal wagons up a railway incline, to the top of the former coal staithes. The dispute which arose between the railway companies over the use of these coal-shipping facilities, was the major factor leading to the founding of the new town of West Hartlepool in the 1840s (see *Ports and Shipping* in Chapter 7).

Regent Square has, as its name implies, several terraces of the early nineteenth century. These are of painted stucco on brick. Regent Street is similarly favoured, as also is South Crescent.

Southgate on the Headland has several interesting buildings including a **bank** (No 62), now a house and warehouse, of mid to late nineteenth century. Here also was the **Union Tavern**, now a private house, of c 1840.

Turning now to the newer part of Hartlepool, until recently known as West Hartlepool, we begin on Brougham Terrace and the **church** (St Oswald), 1897–1904, by W S Hicks. It is built in Perpendicular style.

In Church Square is a redundant **church** (Christ Church), 1850–54, by E B Lamb of London, in Early English style. Also in this square is a **monument** of 1898 by William Day Keyworth Jr, to the memory of 'Sir William Gray, JP, LL, First Mayor of West Hartlepool, 1887–8. Erected by public Subscription'. It shows a bronze figure in mayoral robes seated and holding plans for the West Hartlepool Municipal Buildings.

Those very **Municipal Buildings** (1886–9) by R K Freeman, are in Northern Renaissance style. Not far away, on Church Street, is the **Shades Hotel**, of mid nineteenth century, but refaced around 1904, in Art Nouveau style. Also on Church Street is the old **Literary and Mechanics Institute**, now a private club; 1851 is shown on a plaque. A little further along is the **Midland Bank** of 1899, by Barnes and Coates of Hartlepool. Parts of the interior still show original features, including moulded and panelled ceilings to the banking hall and the Manager's office.

In the middle of Church Street, Ralph Ward Jackson stands proudly. This donor to the town is remembered by this **monument** of 1897 by Edward Onslow Ford: 'Founder of this Town and First MP for the Hartlepools. 1806 – 1880'.

The **Royal Hotel** or Railway Hotel is on the north side of Church Street, being of brick and built around the middle of the century.

On Clarence Road is the **Public Library** of 1894, designed by J W Brown, Borough Engineer, and not far away the original **Police Station and Court**, now offices. This was built in 1871.

A large **villa** on Elwick Road is now converted to two dwellings. It is dated 1895. Also on this road is a **Park-Keeper's Lodge** at the SE entrance to Ward Jackson Park, of 1883.

The **Church** (St Paul), 1885–6, by C Hodgson Fowler, lies on the south side of Grange Road, in Early English style. Hutton Avenue holds the **R C Church** (St Joseph), 1893–5 by E J Hansom.

On the south side of Park Road is a pair of **shops** with living accommodation above, dated 1898 on a foundation stone, by J Garry (Nos 125 and 127). The interior of 125 has contemporary wall tiles and meat rails.

The **Town Hall** of 1897 on Raby Road was designed by H A Cheers, of red engineering brick, with sandstone dressings.

The **Grand Hotel** on Swainson Street is dated 1899 and nearby is the **Wesley Methodist Church** on Victoria Road, dated to 1871–3, by Hill and Swan. It is currently under threat of demolition, but adds a fine feature to the townscape, with a flight of 12 steps leading up to a Corinthian tetrastyle portico. Just to the east is an ornamental **lamp standard** of 1873, though with a modern top.

Victoria Terrace, now sadly depleted, still holds the old **Dock Offices** of 1846 and the **Ship Hotel** of 1844, converted to the Customs House in 1880 and later to commercial use in 1911.

Finally we should look at the Seaton High Light, a river **navigation tower** of 1838, off Windermere Road, and built for the Tees Navigation Company in magnesian limestone ashlar.

Ingleby Barwick · NZ 41 SW · On the east side of Barwick Lane are two terraced **cottages** (nos 4 and 5), of the early nineteenth century, in brick with pantiled roofs.

Middlesbrough · NZ 41 NE · **The Town Hall**, Albert Road, 1883–7 by G G Hoskins of Darlington, in French Gothic style, with clock tower in NW corner.

Dorman Museum, Albert Park by J M Bottomley, 1903–4.

Public Library, Dunning Street, 1910–12, by Russell & Cooper of London (see *Civic Pride*, Chapter 5).

High School (former), King Edward's Road, by Waterhouse, 1877, with Gothic and later Tudor motifs and a central tower.

Church (All Saints), Linthorpe Road, 1878 by Street.

Parish Church (St Hilda), Market Place, 1838–40, by John Green.

Old Town Hall, Market Square, by W L Moffat, 1846, with simple Italianate front.

Church (St Paul), Newport Road, 1871, by Robert J Johnson.

Custom House, North Street, 1840. One of the early buildings of the first Middlesbrough, having an entrance with two Greek Doric columns.

Queens Terrace still has a few of the 1840s houses, especially the three-storeyed house occupied by Bolckow.

Station, 1877, a stone Gothic building.

RC Cathedral (St Mary), Sussex Street, 1872–8, by Goldie and Child.

Transporter Bridge, 1911, by Cleveland Bridge and Engineering Co.

Church (St Barnabus), 1888–91, by C Hodgson Fowler.
Church (St John the Evangelist), 1864–6, by John Norton.

Norton · **NZ 42 SW** · Like nearby Stockton, it is mostly eighteenth century, but there are several attractive nineteenth century **houses**.

Seaton Carew · **NZ 52 NW** · Apart from the **Church** (Holy Trinity), 1831, by T Pickersgill, with chancel of 1842 by Jackson, most of the nineteenth century buildings of note in this small holiday resort are **hotels**, and **terraces of houses**. The Green has several such buildings, most of them very early in the century, as also has Green Terrace and South End.

Stockton-on-Tees · **NZ 41 NE** · **Church** (St John the Baptist), Alma Street, 1873–4, by William White, in Early English style.
    Bridge Road (No 48) is the original **Booking Office of S&DR**; plain brick cottage with memorial plaque referring to 1825.
    Friends' Meeting House, Dovecot Street, 1816.
    Brunswick Methodist Church, Dovecot Street, 1823.
    Lit. and Phil. Institute, 1839, Dovecot Street (now *Northern Echo* office).
    RC Church (St Mary), Norton Road, 1841–2, by Pugin.
    Congregational Church, Norton Road, 1845, with giant Tuscan pillars.
    Church (St James), Portrack Lane, 1867–8, by Pritchett.
    Church (Holy Trinity), 1837, by J and B Green.

Thornaby · **NZ 41 NE** · **Church** (St Paul), 1857–8 by Mallinson and Healey.

Yarm · **NZ 41 SW** · **Yarm Viaduct**, 1849, in red brick, with high round-headed arches. Above the central pier, in midstream, is what must be one of the largest ever commemorative inscriptions, reading: 'Engineers/Thomas Grainger & John Bourne/Superintendent/Joseph Dixon/Contractors/Trowsdale, Jackson/and/Garbutt/1849'.

COUNTY DURHAM

Annfield Plain · **NZ 15 SE** · **Parish church** (St Thomas), 1840, by G Jackson, in Early English style; restored and much altered 1886. **Carnegie Library**, opened 1908 (see Chapter 5: *Civic Pride*).

Barnard Castle · **NZ 01 NW** · The **Bowes Museum**, looking magnificent but quite incongruous in this small market town, was built for John Bowes by Jules Pellechet and begun in 1869 (See *Life in Society*, Chapter 8).
    The **North Eastern School**, 1886, by Clark and Moscrop of Darlington,

is neo-Jacobean. The **Holy Trinity Methodist Church** is in an ornate 1300s style, of 1894 by Morley of Leeds.

Witham Hall in the Market Place is c 1848, built by public subscription in memory of Henry Thomas Witham (qv) (Plate 60).

Beamish · NZ 25 SW · North of England Open-Air Museum: On a 250 acre site more than 40 buildings and structures relating to the recent past way of life of North East England have been re-erected and restored. Most of these buildings date from the nineteenty century, though they are mostly furnished as from the early twentieth century. They are presented within four areas, and some of the more important are mentioned here:

Colliery
Beamish Second Pit Winder: a tall square building holding the 1855 Joicey vertical steam winding engine, now steamed during summer months.

Mahogany Drift: part original and part recently cut into coal, this drift (or inclined entrance passage into the hillside) offers a glimpse of nineteenth century coal-mining methods in the region.

Francis Street: six houses being part of a terrace of c 1870 pit cottages moved from Hetton le Hole. They are furnished in varying periods from the 1880s to the 1930s.

Home Farm
This **planned farmstead** was the original 'Home Farm' of Beamish Hall and dates to the late eighteenth century and the early nineteenth century. It includes a gin-gan and the chimney of a steam-powered threshing engine. The buildings are in use, and open to visitors; the farmhouse is furnished, and visitors are welcomed by a large coal fire in the farm kitchen.

A **hen-house/pig-sty** has been re-erected here from New Ridley Farm, Stocksfield and a **cartshed** dated 1905 was brought here from Longhirst Lane Farm, near Morpeth, to prevent it being demolished by opencast mining.

Railway
A complete North Eastern Railway Co. station is to be seen here, comprising various appropriate buildings saved from the region:

Passenger station, 1867, from Rowley (west of Consett)
Signal box, c 1880 from Consett
Goods shed, c 1880 from Alnwick
Lime and coal depot, 1834, from West Boldon
Weighcabin, c 1880 from Glanton, Northumberland
Cast-iron footbridge from Dunston Staithes.

There is also an NER class 'C' **locomotive** No 876, built at Gateshead in 1889, the only survivor of its class; and a **colliery locomotive** from the Hetton Colliery Railway ('Lambton Hetton & Joicey Collieries No 14'), built by Hawthorn Leslie of Newcastle in 1814.

Town
Terrace of early nineteenth century houses from Ravensworth Terrace, Gateshead.

The Sun Inn, c 1860, from Bishop Auckland (working!), with brewery stables (and horses!).

Coop stores, c 1870, from Annfield Plain, Co. Durham; a grocer's, a draper's and a hardware shop, all fitted and furnished as in the 1920s.

Bandstand, late nineteenth century, from Saltwell Park, Gateshead.

Several **electric tramcars** are preserved and operate on most days. A notable regional one is a single-decker: 'Gateshead No 10', which originally came into service in 1925, and has been fully restored.

For other material at Beamish see Appendix II (*Museum Collections*).

Bearpark · NZ 24 SW · The **Church** (St Edmund), 1879, by Hodgson Fowler, is in red brick, Early English style.

Belmont · NZ 24 SE · Church (St Mary Magdalen), 1857, by Butterfield: nave and chancel only – no tower or aisle.

Bishop Auckland · NZ 22 NW · In the Market Place is the **Church** (St Anne), 1847, possibly by Salvin, in Early English style, and the **Town Hall,** 1869, rather Gothic.

Bishopton · NZ 31 NE · Church (St Peter), 1846, by Sharpe and Paley.

Blackhill · NZ 15 SW · Church (St Aidan), 1885, by Oliver and Leeson.

Bowes · NY 91 SE · An early nineteenth century sandstone **milestone** stands on the north side of the A66, about 650 metres west of Ivy Hall. It is inscribed BOWES 1 MILE and BROUGH 12 MILES.

Stone Bridge Farmhouse is c 1840, in rendered masonry, with a stone-flagged roof to the front and stone chimney stacks, with various **farmbuildings** of the same general period. Included is a large semi-octagonal **gin-gan.**

A disused **lime kiln** of early nineteenth century, in squared rubble, is just south of Gods Bridge Cottage. It is a large single kiln, partly built into the bankside.

Another **milestone** as above, on the A67 is just west of Milestone House. **Bowfield cottage** on Rutherford Lane, of the early nineteenth century, in squared rubble with stone-flagged roof and stone chimney stacks.

On The Street (north side) is a pair of **houses**, c 1840, in tooled and squared rubble with flagged roof, and nearby is **Annums Farmhouse**, early nineteenth century and similarly built.

Here also is **Dotheboys Hall,** a late eighteenth/early nineteenth house, now divided into seven flats. It is of dressed sandstone, with green slate roofs and stone chimney stacks. This was formerly the Bowes Academy, a private boarding school for 200 boys, run by William Shaw. The school was visited by Charles Dickens, whilst he was staying at Barnard Castle in 1838. He was outraged by its disgraceful conditions and exposed the Academy and its principal (as Wackford Squeers) in his novel *Nicholas Nickleby*, thereby creating a public outcry which forced many such schools (including the Bowes Academy) to close.

Bradbury & The Isle · **NZ 32 NW** · This curiously named parish gets part of its name from a patch of land almost ringed by water: the Skerne and Rushyford Beck flow either side of 'The Isle', before joining north of Darlington. Of interest to us is a small **road bridge** which crosses two tracks of a branch of the Clarence Railway: the former City of Durham branch, and dates to about 1833. It is built in a light red brick, in English garden wall bond, with stone bands.

Burn Hall (2 miles SSW of Durham City) · **NZ 23 NE** · This **Hall** is of 1821–34, by Bonomi, with a giant Ionic portico.

Butterknowle · **NZ 12 NW** · A group of three beehive **coke-ovens**, in rather derelict state, is all that remains of a larger number.

There is a small skew stone **bridge** of 1830.

Castle Eden · **NZ 43 NW** · The first building of relevant interest is a gate **lodge** to Castle Eden Estate, built about 1800 and ascribed to William Atkinson. The single storey lodge is Gothick in design. Not far away, also on the B1281, is an interesting series of two storey buildings, now cottages, which originally formed part of the **cottage industry** complex, of about 1800 and still described as 'The Factory'. On the other side of the road remains part of an old **Brewery**, later a house and now the offices of the modern brewery of Messrs. Whitbread; mid nineteenth century. To the west of the offices is the entrance building fronting the brewery yard, of about 1830.

Whilst the Castle itself, at Castle Eden, is a country house of about 1765 and therefore outside our period, it does have attached to it a **palm house** of 1863 by F R Hicks, as well as a north wing of 1893. Moreover, it also has, attached to the north, a pair of **gate houses** and section of Gothick embattled wall which probably dates to the early nineteenth century.

And just to the west of the castle is an interesting mid-century **glass-house** in limestone ashlar, with cast-iron framework.

On the north side of Stockton Road is Castle Eden **Inn**, a 'pub' of about 1840 in rendered brick, and of interest within the village are the **churchyard gates**: a pair of gates, posts and an 'overthrow' with gas lampholder, of the late nineteenth century.

There are one or two houses in the village worthy of mention, particularly Nos 13 and 14 which probably date to around 1830, though with later alterations.

Castleside · NZ 04 NE · Healeyfield **lead smelt mill** (working 1805 – 1913) remains as a complex arrangement of flues which double-back on the way up the hill. The terminal chimney has been demolished and no trace of the actual smelt mill remains.

Cleatlam · NZ 02 SE · A nineteenth century **milestone** still stands about 600 metres north east of High Barford Farmhouse, made of sandstone. It is a single square-plan stone with rounded top. The lettering is incised sans-serif: BOWES 8 and DURHAM 21.

Cleatlam Hall is a small seventeenth century manor house, but an adjoining **barn, with granary over** and an attached cartshed, are of the mid nineteenth century. The walls are of hammer-dressed sandstone and the roof is of pantiles, with a double row of flagstones at the eaves.

Coatham Mundeville · NZ 22 SE · An interesting **bridge** with a dated plaque: 1861, crosses an old mill pond on Brafferton Lane. It is of squared, rock-faced limestone and about 40 metres long. Nearby is Coatham Mill, now four dwellings. It is of the late eighteenth or early nineteenth century and is a rare survival of a **water mill** in County Durham.

Not far away is a **Deer House** also of the late eighteenth or early nineteenth century in squared limestone, in the Gothick style.

Along Coatham Lane is a former **Crossing Keeper's Cottage**, now a private house. This is of around 1840 and part of the S&DR works, in dressed sandstone.

There is a **flax mill**, disused, but later a corn mill.

Consett · NZ 15 SW · The **Hounsgill Viaduct** was designed by Mr (later Sir) Thomas Bouch and built in 1857, of bricks from Pease's Roddymoor Works. It carried the Stanhope and Tyne Railway and replaced a remarkable pair of inclines, which had been designed by Robert Stephenson.

Copley · NZ 02 NE · Chimney of the Gauntless lead smelt mill.

Cotherstone · NZ 01 NW · Clove Lodge Farmhouse is of the eighteenth century but its attached **barn** and other farmbuildings are of the early nineteenth century, in squared rubble and with stone-flagged roofs.

Off Biscoe Lane is a disused **railway viaduct** over the River Balder, constructed in 1868 for the Tees Valley Railway Co., in sandstone with grey brick arches and cast-iron railings.

There is an early nineteenth century **summer house** of rubble and brick and stone-flagged roof, adjoining Hagg House on the Main Street, built in the Gothick style.

Woodvine Cottages on Main Street are a pair of early nineteenth century cottages in dressed sandstone with flag roof and stone chimney stacks.

Dalton · NZ 43 NW · Pumping Station of the Sunderland and South Shields Water Co., now out of operation, but still holding a non-rotating Cornish engine of 1877.

Darlington · NZ 21 NE · Much of the core of the town may be attributed to the success of the railways, beginning with the S&DR. Its population in 1801 was 4,700, in 1851 it was 11,600 and in 1901 44,500.

North Road Station, now a railway museum, dates to 1842, in plain late Georgian style, with cast iron work inside.

The main **station** on Victoria Road is 1847, probably by William Bell. The **Market and Public Offices**, 1864, by Waterhouse, and the **County Court** on Coniscliffe Road is 1869 in Italian Renaissance style.

The **Public Library** (named after Edward Pease) is 1884 in Perpendicular style, whilst the **Mechanics Institute** on Skinnergate is 1853 by Pritchett.

Mowden Hall, 1881 by Waterhouse lies on Staindrop Road, Cockerton.

The Church of St Cuthbert, whilst too early to mention here, nevertheless contains an unusually good mix of mid and later Victorian **stained glass**.

Other **churches** relevant here are St John the Evangelist (1847–8), by John Middleton, Holy Trinity (1843), by Salvin, and St Hilda (1887–8) by J L Pearson; all of them in Early English style.

There are two **Methodist Churches**, Bondgate (1812), by W Sherwood and Coniscliffe Road (1840), with two good doorways and with Doric pilasters.

The **Friends' Meeeting House** on Skinnergate is of 1834, of five bays with a Tuscan porch.

In South Park is a **memorial** to John Fowler, who designed a double-acting, steam-drawn multi-furrow plough. It is inscribed 'John Fowler, CE, 1856'.

At the Darlington Corporation **Water works** on Coniscliffe Road, the main building is dated 1849 and originally held engines. Another engine (preserved) was erected 1904, by T & C Hawksley of Westminster and built by Teesdale Bros, Darlington.

Statue of Joseph Pease unveiled Sept 1875 at railway Golden Jubilee.

Denton · NZ 21 NW · Around this area there are perhaps half a dozen cast-iron **mile posts** of the late nineteenth century. They are triangular in plan, with a sloping top and a semi-circular back plate. Fortunately they are now cared for, painted white, with the raised sans-serif lettering in black. One stands, for example, on the West side of B6279, about 700m south-east of the junction with New Lane and shows 'STAINDROP 6' and 'DARLINGTON 5'.

On the east side of Dere Street is a late nineteenth century **lime kiln** rather late for such structures, but in nice condition. It is of squared stone with yellow brick arches, being a 'two-cell' kiln partly built into the bankside.

Durham City · NZ 24 SE · There are several **churches** of relevant interest: St Cuthbert, 1858, by E R Robson, in High Victorian; St Cuthbert (RC), 1827, by Ignatius Bonomi; St Nicholas, Market Place, 1857–8, by Pritchett, described at the time by the *Illustrated London News* as 'The most beautiful modern specimen of church architecture in the north of England', and described by Pevsner as 'one of the best churches designed by Pritchett'; Our Lady of Mercy and St Godric (RC), Castle Chare, 1864, by E W Pugin; Congregational Church, Claypath, 1888, by Henry Gradon.

The **Town Hall** in the Market Place is of 1851 by P C Hardwick. The **Shire Hall**, Old Elvet, 1897–8, now University admin. The **Assize Courts** of 180-9–11 are by Francis Sandys; **Bede College** of the University is 1846–7; also **St Hilda**, 1858. **Durham School,** Margery Lane is 1846 by Salvin.

Also in the Market Place is the **National Provincial Bank** of 1876, by Gibson, and the **Equestrian Statue** of the 3rd Marquess of Londonderry of 1861 by R. Monti.

Overlooking much of the town is the long stone **railway viaduct** of 1857.

Frosterley · NZ 03 NW · **Church** (St Michael), 1869, by G E Street.

A triple set of **lime-kilns** on the north side of the road, opposite Rogerley Hall.

At Bishopley Quarry (originally owned by Wear Valley Railway, later S&DR) is an attractive set of **lime kilns**.

Gainford · NZ 11 NE · East Greystone **Farmhouse** dates to the mid nineteenth century, built in sandstone rubble with a pantiled roof.

A nineteenth century **milestone** stands a little distance south of Greystone Hall, with raised sans-serif lettering: BC9 (Barnard Castle) and D7 (Darlington) and another is south of Alwent Farmhouse (cf Cleatham).

There are early to mid nineteenth century farm buildings **barn and**

loose boxes attached to seventeenth century Alwent Hall. There is also a **pigsty with henhouse over** of the same period.

Hollin Hall West Farm also has **stables, cartshed and barn/granary** of the mid nineteenth century.

Nos 10 and 11 and No 23 on the north side of High Green are early nineteenth century.

Tees View (north side) includes (No 5) a large manor **house** of the early nineteenth century with late nineteenth century alterations.

Gilmonby · NY 91 SE · The Grove is a house of about 1840, in squared sandstone, with flagged roof and stone chimney stacks.

Great Aycliffe · NZ 22 SE · A pub now called 'Locomotion No 1' was previously a **railway station** on Heighington Lane. This was an early station and booking office for the S&DR and occupies the site where Stephenson's locomotive engine was put on the rails, for the inauguration of that service. The building dates to about 1835.

There are one or two **houses** of relevant interest in the village, particularly on High Street and **Ricknall Grange Farm** is of about 1840. About half a mile to the south west is a **railway bridge** with twin tunnels of about 1830. It was built to carry a huge embankment of the now disused Simpasture to Port Clarence Railway across the River Skerne, for the Clarence Railway Co.

Greatham · NZ 42 NE · Very long **vaiduct** built 1839–40 to carry an extension of the Clarence Railway to Hartlepool, said by Tomlinson to consists of 92 brick arches, many now hidden under a long embankment.

Haswell · NZ 34 SE · Colliery pumping engine-house (cf Friars Goose, Gateshead).

Headlam · NZ 31 NE · A nineteenth century **milestone** may be seen just south of Killerby Garths, marked D7 (Darlington) and S4 (Staindrop).

An **animal pound,** probably of the early nineteenth century is situated just north of the pack-horse bridge on the Green.

Heighington · NZ 22 SW · There are several interesting **houses** and cottages in this village.

A rare relic is a **hearse-house** of c 1840 in sandstone rubble. This would hold the horse-drawn parish hearse: a hearse of this kind is preserved at BEAMISH.

Off the south side of Heighington Lane is **Trafalgar House,** built around 1815, and amongst the nearby outbuildings is a **dovecot** of the same period. This is a two-storey building with a pyramidal slated roof.

On the north side of High Road is a mid-century **water pump** in cast-iron.

Hetton-le-Hole · NZ 34 NE · **Church** (St Nicholas), 1898 – 1901, by S Piper.

High Coniscliffe · NZ 21 NW · Several more **mileposts** (as described for Denton) are preserved in this parish: one at High Coniscliffe Bridge, another just south of Carlbury Hall (both on the A67), and one a little to the west of Thornton Hall on the B6279 (Staindrop Road).

Here also is the Old **Vicarage**, now a private house, having been built around 1860, in snecked sandstone.

Holwick · NY 92 NW · **Middleton Bridge** over the River Tees was built about 1800, and repaired in 1984. It is of snecked, dressed sandstone, with a segmental arch.

Off the south side of B6277, at Low Farm is the Wynch Bridge, a **suspension footbridge** above the River Tees. It was constructed about 1830 for the Duke of Cleveland. This present bridge replaced an earlier one of about 1741, believed to be the earliest permanent suspension bridge in Europe.

Houghton-le-Side · NZ 22 SW · Off Houghton Bank Lane is the Manor house which is possibly mediaeval, but within its grounds is a **barn and privy** (now used for storage!), of the early nineteenth century. There is also, nearby, a **pigsty with hen-house over**, of the earlier part of the century, of a type relatively common in the region. Other farm buildings also date from the early to the mid nineteenth century.

Hunderthwaite · NY 92 SE · An early nineteenth **summer house** in squared rubble and stone-flagged roof in the Gothick style is near Wooden Croft, similar to one in Cotherstone.

Wildon Grange is of about 1840, in dressed stone with a slate roof but stone chimney stacks. **Barn and byres** are attached to High Birk Hat Farmhouse (itself dated 1741). This farm also has a **field barn** of early/mid nineteenth century of squared rubble with dressed details and a stone-flagged roof.

Nearby is a disused **limekiln** of early nineteenth century in squared rubble.

A **field barn** stands 700 metres east of Hunderthwaite Farmhouse (which is dated 1730). It is dated 1822 and is a rare example of an unaltered field barn.

Hunstanworth · NY 94 NW · A little village on a wooded hillside. Almost the whole: **church, Vicarage** and **school** were built in 1863 for the owner Rev D Capper, by Teulon: an attractive mass, in various coloured sandstones, with little Gothick windows.

Hutton Henry · **NZ 43 NW** · Little of note here except for **Hutton House** built around 1824 for the Rev Thomas A Slater. It is of narrow hand-made red brick with a green slate roof, in two storeys.

Ingleton · **NZ 12 SE** · Holbeck **Farmhouse** on the south side of Front Street is early nineteenth century, in dressed sandstone.

The **Parish Church** (St John the Evangelist) is 1843, by Ignatius Bonomi and J A Cory, in Early English style.

Killerby · **NZ 11 NE** · **Killerby Grange** is c 1800; a two-storey, three bay house in dressed sandstone and with Welsh slates on the front (obviously later replacements) and pantiles on the rear roof. Various outbuildings are of similar date and to the rear is a **water pump** (dated 1804) and trough.

Killhope (Weardale) · **NY 84 SW** · Park Level **portal**: lead mine entrance. Nearby is the large **waterwheel** and building which once housed ore-crushing plant. It has now been restored and incorporates a small museum on Dales leadmining.

Lartington · **NZ 01 NW** · **Deepdale aqueduct** and footbridge crosses the River Tees and is dated 1893. It was built by Head, Wrightson and Co. Engineers of Thornaby on Tees, being of cast-iron and columns, with rock-faced stone and sections.

Deepdale Cottage, along with its range of sheds is c 1840, in squared sandstone rubble, with flagged roof and stone chimney stacks.

Lartington Hall (the home of Henry Witham, qv.) is dated 1635 on the porch doorway, but has an early nineteenth century east wing, possibly by Ignatius Bonomi and a **porte-cochere** and **servants' wing** added 1861–5 by Joseph Hansom. In the garden are **statues** and at least one of these, the Muse of Literature, is signed by R. Borrowdale of Barnard Castle. Other statues include the Muse of Painting, palette in hand, Venus, a lady with a pitcher and a platter of fruit on her head, and a young boy with a bird. Nearby are six flights of steps, also with statues in historical costumes, of c 1867, probably also by Hansom.

Nearby is a small **mausoleum/mortuary chapel** dated 1877 on the keystone. It was built for Monsignor Thomas Witham of Lartington Hall.

A **cottage** known as 'The Nook' is on the north side of Lartington Lane, of about 1830, in dressed sandstone with stone roof and chimney stacks, in Tudor style. And not far away is the former **village schoolroom** and **master's house,** now two dwellings, of mid nineteenth century.

Next, just off Lartington Lane, is 'The Woodlands', the former **railway station**, comprising station master's house, waiting room and ticket office; now a private house. It is dated 1859 and was built for the South Durham and Lancashire Union Railway Company in Tudor Style.

Park House is mid nineteenth century and 'The Beeches' is c 1840, as also is "The Grove".

Finally mention should be made of an outbuilding just to the west of 'The Grove'; formerly farmbuildings, now storage, of early to mid nineteenth century. The interior of part of this was used as a **Methodist Chapel** during the nineteenth and early twentieth century and retains a panelled wood ceiling.

Lunedale · **NY 92 SW** · Just off the north side of B6276 is an early to mid nineteenth century **field barn** in coursed rubble with stone-flagged roof. It stands well in the landscape.

Bowbank House dates to the early nineteenth century in squared and coursed rubble with stone flagged roof.

A late nineteenth century **milepost** in cast-iron is situated near the Grains O' the Beck Bridge. It is small, triangular in plan, with sloping top and semi-circular back plate and in raised sans-serif letters records BROUGH 7 MILES and MIDDLETON 7¼ MILES.

Laithkirk **Parish Church** is said to have been a fifteenth century tithe barn of Lord Fitzhugh, converted and re-roofed in 1826, with further restoration c 1900. It is built in rubble with sandstone dressings and a graduated slate roof. Inside is an octagonal nineteenth century stone font. The **Vicarage**, now a private house, is of around 1845 in dressed sandstone.

At Nettlepot on the B6276 is a stone **trough and cast iron water pump** of the mid nineteenth century.

Thringarth Farmhouse and farm buildings are of around 1840, in squared rubble and with stone-flagged roofs and stone chimney stacks.

A disused **railway viaduct** crosses the River Lune at Laithkirk. It was built in 1868 for the Tees Valley Railway Company.

Mickleton · **NY 92 SE** · This village includes several nineteenth century farmhouses and buildings such as field barns and byres. Of special interest is a **pump house** c 1829 near High Green Farmhouse. Inside is a wood and iron water pump, dated 1829 on a head panel.

Nook Farmhouse on Mill Lane is early to mid nineteenth century with 1845 on a plaque above the doorway, in squared sandstone rubble, with stone-flagged roof and stone chimney stacks. The former Mickleton Church of England **School** is now a private house. It is of around 1840, with 1906 additions. The original building is of coursed rubble, with stone-flagged roof. There is a disused **limekiln** a little to the south of Cote House Farmhouse, of early nineteenth century date.

Middleton-in-Teesdale · **NY 92 NE** · A village which flourished at the height of lead-mining prosperity. **Church** (St Mary), 1886, by Hodgson

Fowler, and in the village is the **Bainbridge Memorial Fountain,** 1877 in cast iron.

The **Baptist Chapel** is 1827 and **Middleton House** is early in the century.

Middleton-One-Row · **NZ 31 SE** · **Church** (St Lawrence), 1871, by Pritchett, with a polygonal turret.

Morden · **NZ 22 SE** · Here is an **accommodation bridge** of c 1830 for the Clarence Railway Co. It was widened and its north face rebuilt in the middle of the nineteenth century.

Off Elstob Lane is a **threshing barn with gin-gan**, the latter with a conical roof and cast-iron finial; of around 1840 and built in engineering brick, in English garden wall bond and Welsh slate roof.

To the east of Holme Mill house is an early nineteenth century **windmill** in dressed limestone. It is of five storeys; a tapering cylindrical tower mill, lacking the cap.

Pelton · **NZ 25 SE** · **Church** (Holy Trinity), 1842, by John Green, in Early English style.

Piercebridge · **NZ 21 NW** · The **Parish Church** (St Mary) dates to 1873, by Cory and Ferguson, in snecked sandstone with ashlar dressings. It is in the Early English style, with a bellcote with spirelet.

Also in the village are several nineteenth century farmbuildings and in particular a **gin-gan** near the Grange farmhouse. This is semi-octagonal, with rectangular piers.

Romaldkirk · **NY 92 SE** · This village includes several nineteenth century farmhouses and buildings such as **field barns** and **byres**. They are generally built of squared sandstone rubble, with stone-flagged roofs and stone chimney stacks.

On the south side of Fell Lane is a stone **trough** with cast iron **pump** in a wooden case, with a lead plaque dated 1866. Another trough and pump are to be seen on The Green, where it provides a village feature.

On the north side of The Green is a large **house** about 1800: 'Beckwath', of reversed E-plan.

What is now known as Hutchinson Terrace (three dwellings) was originally an **almshouse** built in 1674 by William Hutchinson and completely rebuilt in 1829 in Tudor style. In front of the present No 2 is another **water pump**, circa 1830. There is yet another one, somewhat later, near the Rose & Crown Hotel. In front of the Rose & Crown Hotel (which is dated 1733) is a footpath with '1837 VR 1897' picked out in dark cobbles to commemorate Queen Victoria's Diamond Jubilee.

Off the north side of The Square is the old **school**, now a Church Hall. It was rebuilt c 1875, in Tudor style.

Rowley · **NZ 04 NE** · A small **passenger station** of 1867 was built here on what was originally the Stanhope and Tyne Railway. It has now been moved to Beamish and re-erected there as part of a re-created NER passenger and goods station.

Ryhope · **NZ 45 SW** · Two fine **beam engines** here of 1868, were built by R & W Hawthorne of Newcastle, for the Sunderland and South Shields Water Co. They are now preserved by the Ryhope Engines Trust, displayed and put in steam occasionally.

Seaham Harbour · **NZ 44 NW** · (See *Ports and Shipping*, Chapter 7.) The town was laid out for the 3rd Marquess of Londonderry in 1828 by John Dobson, but much altered now by demolition etc.

The **Parish Church** (St John the Evangelist), 1838, by Prosser, in Perpendicular style.

Several '**chaldron wagons**' or 'black' wagons have been saved from here and are to be seen at Beamish. They are marked 'L' to indicate 'Londonderry Coal Co.' and date from the 1880's.

Sedgefield · **NZ 32 NE** · Cole Hill Farm is a **planned farmstead** of the late nineteenth century, in engineering brick in Flemish bond. It is one of a group built for the Sheraton estate and is unaltered and well-preserved.

Sadly there is a redundant **church** at Embleton (St Mary), mediaeval in origin, but largely rebuilt in 1860.

Moving into Sedgefield itself, there is – on Front Street – a pedestal **monument** to Frederick Hardwick of the Iniskilling Dragoons, of 1854 by M Spark.

At the North End is the Hardwick Arms **Hotel**, of early nineteenth century, though with later additions and alterations.

Various **houses** are of relevant interest (such as Nos 3 and 5 North End and Nos 4 and 10 Rectory Row). The **Church** (St Luke) of Winterton Hospital, on Salter's Lane, is by William Crozier Jr and dates to 1884, of engineering brick in English garden wall bonding.

Finally mention should be made of **Sedgefield House**, of the early nineteenth century and with a rear wing added in the middle of that century.

Shildon · **NZ 22 NW** · This is a mecca for railway enthusiasts and fortunately several structures remain from last century. Here we find material from Stephenson's S&DR and at the same time many remains relating to Timothy Hackworth.

The **Parish Church** is by J P Pritchett (1868–9), in dressed sandstone and with green slate roofs; in Pritchett's Early English style.

Of industrial interest here is a group of buildings known as Brussleton Cottages. First is the old **Engine House,** which originally had a stationary steam engine to haul the coal trucks up from the horse-drawn railway to the west. Nearby is the **Engineman's House.** This group dates back to the first days of the S&DR, of 1825 and was converted to dwellings in the middle of the century.

In Burney Gardens is the south **portal** of the Shildon Railway Tunnel which was built in 1842 for the Shildon Tunnel Company (a subsidiary of the S&DR). This Tunnel, originally known as the Prince of Wales Tunnel, was built to by-pass the Black Boy Incline and to serve the Wear Valley.

Daniel Adamson's **Coach House** (c 1831) is on Byerley Road. It is the former coach house of the S&DR and is reputably the earliest surviving railway coach house in the world. In 1827 Adamson pioneered a horse-drawn railway coach, **Perseverance** which ran between Shildon and Darlington.

There is also an **aqueduct** of 1842 built for the S&DR, off Chestnut Close.

Moving now to Timothy Hackworth, we find his **monument** on Church Street: in pedestal form, of 1850. His **birthplace** (No 1, Soho Cottages), of the early nineteenth century, has been restored and set up, with the adjoining cottage, as a museum to the railway history of Shildon. Nearby the former **engine-shed** (part being a fragment of Hackworth's Soho Engine Works) is now a museum housing other railway material; c 1833 and restored in 1975.

Near Low West Thickley is a **bridge** on the original S&DR line of 1825.

Stanhope · NY 93 NE · Unthank Mill, corn mill on the south side of the River Wear: disused, but much gearing remaining; probably mid century.

Summerhouse · NZ 21 NW · A rural area, with several groups of farm buildings and cottages. Especially of interest is square-plan **gin-gan** and a **forge.** The Raby Hunt Inn is c 1835, with earlier wing.

Tow Law · NZ 13 NW · Church (SS Phillip and James), 1869, by Hodgson Fowler is Early English style.

Tudhoe · NZ 23 NE · Two **churches,** both Hodgson Fowler: Holy Innocents (1866), in Early English style and St Andrews (1884) in Perpendicular style.

An interesting group of **workers' houses** was built 1865–70 by Mr Marmaduke Salvin at Tudhoe Grange, but the spacious layout has been infilled and the houses modified.

Ushaw · NZ 24 SW · St Cuthbert's College began to be built in 1803. Later Pugin was involved, building the Chapel (1840–48), though later rebuilt. Various smaller oratories, one by Pugin.

Usworth · NZ 35 NW Church · (Holy Trinity) 1832, by John Green, Early English style; and **Usworth Hall,** c 1800 in five bays and two storeys.

Walworth · NZ 21 NW · Primarily a rural area, and most of its nineteenth century buildings are **farms.** Castle Farm, for instance is early nineteenth century, with **byres, potato shed** and **dove cot.**

To the east of Quarry End is an **ice house** of around 1800.

Warden Law · NZ 34 NE · Site of **stationary coal-haulage steam engine** on line built by Stephenson in 1823, from Hetton Colliery to the Wear. The engine was replaced by the existing one of 1836, by Murrays of Chester le Street; now dismantled and stored at Beamish.

Washington · NZ 35 NW · 1838 **Victoria Viaduct** over the River Wear (see *Railways*, Chapter 7).

West Auckland · NZ 12 NE · Site of **first iron railway bridge,** of four spans over the River Gaunless. Part is preserved in the National Railway Museum at York, and the abutments are in situ.

West Boldon · NZ 36 SE · Site of **coal and lime depot** inscribed 'Stanhope and Tyne Rail Road Company's Landsale Coal and Lime Depot 1834'. Now dismantled and re-erected at Beamish.

Westgate · NY 93 NW · Church (St Andrew), 1869, by R J Withers, in Early English style.

West Rainton · NZ 34 NW · Church (St Mary), 1864, by E R Robson, in High Victorian style. The spire is visible from a good distance.

Westwick · NZ 01 NE · A nineteenth century **milestone** in sandstone near the junction of Darlington Road and Mount Eff Road bears the lettering D14 (Darlington) and BC2 (Barnard Castle).

Ivy Cottage, with attached **smithy** is on the north side of Westwick Road, dating early in the century, with alterations.

Whorlton · NZ 11 SW · Two **milestones** in sandstone are within the boundaries of the village. On the Green is the **Bridge Inn,** of early in the nineteenth century.

211

Whorlton Bridge is an early suspension road bridge crossing the River Tees; built 1829–31 by John and Benjamin Green, with wrought iron suspension chains and links. At the north-west end is the former **tollhouse**, about 1830.

Windlestone Hall · NZ 22 NE · c 1834 by Ignatius Bonomi.

Wingate · NZ 33 NE · **Church** (Holy Trinity), 1840, by George Jackson of Durham, Early English style.

Winlaton · NZ 16 SE · An area once busy with individual craftsmen making chains, locks, clog irons and other ironwork, following the closure of Ambrose Crowley's Iron Works. One small **workshop/forge** is preserved behind the branch Library.

Winston · NZ 11 NW · The **coach house** of Stubb House (itself of the seventeenth century) dates to the early nineteenth century.
A **milestone** is on the B6274, south of the East Lodge of Westholme Hall.
Newsham Hall is of the seventeenth century, but its **coach house and stables** are early nineteenth century.
The former **village school** is now used as part of the Bridgewater Arms. It is dated 1851, in Tudor Revival style.

Wolsingham · NZ 03 NE · **R C Church** (St Thomas of Canterbury), 1854 by J A Hansom, and the **Town Hall** in classical form, dated 1861.

Wolviston · NZ 42 NE · **Church** (St Peter), 1876, by Austin, Joynson and Hicks, Early English style. In the village is the **Parochial School** of 1836 and the **Londonderry Almshouses** of 1838.

Wynyard Park · NZ 42 NW · A splendid nineteenth century **mansion** begun in 1822 by Benjamin Wyatt for the 3rd Marquess of Londonderry. Building took 19 years, but due to two fires, much rebuilt. The facade retains the 1822 design.
In the grounds is an **obelisk** to commemorate the visit of the Duke of Wellington in 1827.

NORTHUMBERLAND

Allendale · NY 85 NW · Planned **farm buildings** are at High Frosthall Farm, early nineteenth century. They include waterwheel etc.
Holingreen Farmhouse is early nineteenth century, in rubble with tooled quoins; **Park Farmhouse** is about 1840, as also is **Beacon Rigg Farmhouse.**
Low Huntwell Farmhouse is similarly early nineteenth century in squared stone and stone stacks with dripstones.

Sipton Bridge is early nineteenth century with a tall round-headed arch. **Sipton Bridge** is dated 1878 with initials W.B.B. It is associated with a mine-road to carry lead from the Allendale Mines near Allendale Common to Whitley Chapel and Hexham.

Another **bridge** dated 1857 is the Blackett Bridge over the River West Allen, 'built by subscription'.

A **Methodist Chapel** in West Allen is **High House Chapel** dated 1859 and there is another at Limestone Brae dated 1825, with Sunday School extension of 1875.

Park Farmhouse in West Allen is dated 1825.

As to industrial remains, there is an early nineteenth century **limekiln** at West Allen, near the Miners' Rest, an early nineteenth century **Bouse-team** at Mohopehead Mine, West Allen and a lead-mine **powder-house** at Sipton.

Allendale Town · NY 85 NW · A **Board School** dated 1879 is still in use. In the Market Place is a **Bank** dated 1873, in seventeenth century style, with Baroque doorcase. There are several nineteenth century shops and houses and on the south side of the Market Place a **wellhead** dated 1849 and inscribed 'ISAACS WELL'. Two inns, the **Golden Lion** and the **Hotspur Hotel** are to be seen: the former probably 1839, the latter dated 1806, restored in 1883.

The **Parish Church** (St Cuthbert) is 1874 by Austin and Johnson, on a mediaeval site, and the **Trinity Methodist Church** is dated 1875 on foundation stone; gabled front to street; many contemporary internal fittings.

By the riverside is the **adit portal** to the Blackett Level (lead mine), 1854. This worked well until 1903, driven to de-water the deep workings at Allenheads.

Allenheads · NY 84 NE · A **Church** (St Peter), 1825, by W Crawhall in squared stone and simple rectangular plan; disused. The Estate Offices are of the middle of the century: one tall storey in ten bays.

The **Hall** of 1854 was built for Thomas Sopwith (q.v.), who possibly acted as his own architect. **Beaumont House** is early nineteenth century possibly built for Lord Allendale's agent.

At the Beaumont Mine are the remains of mid nineteenth century **bouse-teams** where lead ore was stored.

The present **Post Office** (house and shop) has a 'GR' letterbox and original 'Post Office . . .' notice.

At Bridge End, the **bridge** is early nineteenth century, though altered and nearby is the **Friends' Meeting House** dated 1868.

A **Primitive Methodist Chapel** dated 1878 is now a library, in Dawson Place. There are various houses and cottages of interest in this settlement.

Allenheads Farm is a complete house and farmstead of the early nineteenth century. Ranges enclose three sides of a square open to the east; the house being part of the north range.

There are two lead mine entrances: a **portal** to the Beaumont Mine – the Fawside Level – of mid nineteenth century, and the old **horse-track entrance** to Allenheads Mine, in stone and cast-iron. Through this ponies descended a spiral incline at a gradient of 1 in 4 into the lead mine workings. A furnace chamber of mid nineteenth century is on the B6295 (west side), used to draw air up an adjacent mineshaft and thus improve air circulation in the mine.

Allenmill (Allendale · **NY 85 NW** · The **Allenmill Bridge** is early nineteenth century in squared stone with two segmental arches, and nearby is a former **school**, dated 1851 now used as a Holiday Home. This is one of the schools built by W B Beaumont 'for the education of children of all religious denominations'.

Alnwick · NU 11 SE · Church (St Paul), 1846 by Salvin: a large church in Percy Street.

RC Church (St Mary), 1836 by John Green in 'lancet' style. **St James Presbyterian Church,** 1884–5 by Hicks and Charlewood and **United Presbyterian Church,** 1840.

Northumberland Hall, 1826, fronts on to Market Street. The **Duke's School,** 1852–3, by Thos. Robertson of Alnwick.

The **Turk's Head Hotel** is early nineteenth century and the **Old Post Office,** early nineteenth century, with Tuscan porch. The Savings Bank is by William Smith in Gothic style (1835).

Cannongate Bridge is 1821, with three round arches. A **monument** to William the Lion at the entrance to Hulme Park is about 1860. There are two **columns:** the Peace Column commemorates the Peace of 1814 and the Percy Tenantry Column was erected in 1816 to the design of David Stephenson, in gratitude for reduced rents in the years of depression.

Broome Hill Farm: **house** dated WB 1809 (William Burrell); good example for date, with large staircase window.

Various farms in the area with agricultural **steam engine houses, with chimneys** of mid to late nineteenth century: Craster South Farm, Longbank Farm, Woodhouse Farm, Preston Farm and Ratheugh Farm.

Amble · NU 20 SE · In the area are several farms with **agricultural steam engine houses, with chimneys,** Tugton East Farm, Hound Dean Farm and Thirston New Houses.

Angerton Hall · NZ 80 NE · The **Hall** is 1823, by Dobson in Tudor style.

Bamburgh · **NU 13 SE** · Churchyard **Monument** by C R Smith, 1846, to Grace Darling.

Barrasford · **NY 97 SW** · The old **Primary School**, now a house, of 1841 by John Dobson.

Bavington · **NY 97 NE** · **Milestone** two miles west of Little Bavington, about 2ft high with inscription FROM/ALNWICK/XXXII, early nineteenth century.

Beal (near Holy Island) · **NU 04 SE** · **Farmbuildings** east of Beal House are early nineteenth century, four ranges round a cowshed.

Beaufront Castle · **NY 69 NE** · This **Gothic Castle** is 1837–41 by Dobson, incorporating an early Georgian house.

Bellingham · **NY 88 SW** · The **Town Hall** on Front Street is late nineteenth century, with a wooden clock tower.
   The **RC Church** is of 1839 by Ignatius Bonomi.
   The **bridge**, of 1834 is by John Green.

Belsay · **NZ 07 NE** · Two **mileposts** are to be found on the A696 (south side), one at the junction with B6309, the other approx. 440 yards east of Edgehouse. Both are in sandstone, triangular in plan and about 2ft high. The former states TO NEWCASTLE/14 MILES and the other TO OTTERBURN/13 MILES/JEDBRO/42 MILES. The road was surveyed in 1829.
   In this rural area most of the nineteenth century buildings away from the village are farmhouses or outbuildings and the village itself, and its hall, owe their existence to Sir Charles Monck.
   A **bridge** a little to the west of Belsay Castle is early nineteenth century with a single arch.
   Belsay Hall itself was built 1810–17, designed by the owner Sir Charles Monck, with some assistance from the young John Dobson. It is in Greek Doric style and now happily in the hands of English Heritage: the buildings and its grounds and gardens are now open to the public. Behind the Hall the **stable block** in Greek revival style, **pigsty** and **forge** and walled garden with sheds and cottages are all of around the same period and all by Sir Charles Monck. The gardens, once allowed to deteriorate, are now being resuscitated.
   The Hall, in Doric style with pilasters; the third (East) **lodge** dates towards the end of the nineteenth century. It is much plainer, in ashlar with Lakeland slate roof.
   Woodhouse, within the confines of the village, was formerly a **Coaching**

Inn and now a house, built in 1836 for Sir Charles Monck. Nearby is the stable block, necessary for a coaching inn and to the rear a **threshing barn, gin-gan and stable.** The thresher from this barn is now preserved by Beamish Museum.

The village itself comprises three groups of distinctive **houses,** all of the 1830's by Sir Charles Monck, being a **planned village street.** Their ground floors are arcaded with alternate wide and narrow arches. Near the south of the Arcade is a mid nineteenth century **pant** in rock-faced stone.

Here also is the village **school,** c 1870, in Gothic style.

Along Whalton Road is the old **school** and schoolmaster's house, now a house. This is said to be of 1841, though dated 1829 on an interior beam.

Berwick-on-Tweed · NU 05 SW · Church (St Mary), 1858, in Early English style.

RC Church, 1829.

Presbyterian Church, 1858–9 by J D and I Hay of Liverpool, in Decorated style.

Another **Presbyterian Church** on Bank Hall, early nineteenth century.

The **Police and Magistrates' Court** is a free Baroque building of 1899–1901, by R Burns Dick.

Robert Stephenson's **Royal Border Bridge** of 1847 carries the railway across the River Tweed towards Edinburgh.

Early nineteenth century **malthouse** on waterfront; **granary** (1852), still used for grain drying on Bridge terrace, another one on Low Lane and one still in use on Dean's Lane.

Ice house of late eighteenth or early nineteenth century up Bankhill and another half-way up Ravensdowne (on the east).

Various farms in the area, with **steam engine houses, with chimneys:** Shoreswood Hall Farm, New East Farm, Mount Pleasant Farm, Pottery Hill Farm, all of mid to late nineteenth century.

Birtley · NY 87 NE · Catreen Farmhouse and farm buildings, of early nineteenth century.

Black Hall (Hexhamshire) · **NY 95 NW** · A group of **planned farmbuildings** of early nineteenth century is at Black Hall Farm.

Black Heddon · NZ 07 NE · Black Heddon is of 1824, in Classical style, with later byres and shelter sheds, actually dated 1856 on one of the lintels.

Blanchland · NY 95 SE · A few of the **houses** and buildings in the Square are of the nineteenth century (e.g. No 10 and its farm buildings), though the rest are mostly of the eighteenth century, probably incorporating older fabric. Also in The Square is a **Part** dated 1897 ('by public subscription to commemorate the Diamond Jubilee of Queen Victoria'). The Old School, now a private art gallery, is about 1860, probably by S S Teulon.

To the north of the village centre is Shildon and here is a **cottage** of early in the century, rather picturesque. Nearby is the ruined stone **engine-house** of Cornish type, of the early nineteenth century: a tower-like structure with a tall square chimney. The engine, of which nothing remains, pumped water out of Shildon lead mine and is known to have been working by 1840.

To the west of the village is Baybridge and here has been a **house** (now Nos 1 & 2 Grove Cottage) circa 1860, probably by S S Teulon.

A **Chapel** dated 1867, again probably by Teulon, is inscribed 'Wesleyan Providence Chapel' and is in free Gothic style. Nearby the **Miners' Arms Inn** is now houses. It is of late eighteenth century and perhaps earlier, remodelled and extended in the early nineteenth century. The scene of a riot between Cornish and local lead-miners in 1866.

A late nineteenth century shooting box lies over a mile to the north west (933 509) and there are several small boundary stones one or two hundred metres to its north, north east and east, of the nineteenth century in sandstone and each inscribed CT (Crewe Trustees) on the north face and C on the south.

Bolam · NZ 08 SE · **Bolam Hall** dates to 1810, in classical style, built by Robert Horsley for his daughter Charlotte Philadelphia on her marriage to John Beresford, the Baron Decies.

Blyth · NZ 38 SW · **Churches** (St Cuthbert), 1885–93 by W S Hicks, in Decorated style, and St Mary, 1864 by Austin and Johnson.
 RC Church on Waterloo Road, 1862 by A M Dunn.
 Presbyterian Church also on Waterloo Road, 1874–6 by Thomas Oliver.

Branxton · NT 83 NE · **Church** (St Paul), 1849 in Norman style.

Bywell · NZ 06 SE · **Bywell School**, now offices, bears the inscription 'ERECTED BY W B BEAUMONT ESQ 1851' and is in Tudor Gothic style. The former **headmaster's house** is nearby, dated 1832.
 Bywell Bridge is 1836–8 by George Basevi, with five segmental arches.

Cambo · NZ 08 NW · This attractive village is mostly of Wallington estate cottages. The **Church** (Holy Trinity) is 1842 by J and B Green in lancet style.

Capheaton · NZ 08 SW · The Hall was built in 1668 for Robert Trollope, but various outbuildings date to the nineteenth century: the **conservatory** to the middle of the century and the **carriage house** to 1825. The **East Lodge** is 1838, in Tudor style.

Another sandstone **milestone** is just south of East Lodge, similar to those mentioned for Belsay.

In the village **Orchard House** is of around 1830 and the Post Office, with **cottage** attached and adjoining cottage, are all of similar date.

Along Front Street is the former **School house,** now a private house, probably of the early nineteenth century and nearby is a **water pump** of mid century, in cast iron. At Hillhead Farm is a **barn with gin-gan** attached, along with various shelter sheds, byres and stalls, all probably early in the century.

Capheaton Bridge is late nineteenth century, with a single arch.

Various **lime kilns** are to be found in fields around the village.

Carrshield (Allendale) **· NY 84 NW ·** One of Beaumont's **schools,** dated 1851 is now a Schools Expedition Centre (see also Allen Mill).

In the village the present Post Office is a **house with shop** of mid nineteenth century.

The **bridge** over River West Allen is early nineteenth century, with an elliptical arch and nearby the **portal** of an early nineteenth century drainage tunnel: an elliptical-arched opening. The **Carrshields Mine** offices are second quarter of the nineteenth century, and nearby are the leadminers' **'shops'** (living quarters), **forges** etc, of early nineteenth century.

Cheeseburn · NZ 07 SE · The **Grange** is partly by Dobson, after 1813; the higher parts more ambitiously in Gothic style, c 1860 by J A Hansom.

Chollerton · NY 97 SW · Railway bridge on A6079, disused, 1856 by William Hutchinson, with two high round skew arches.

Fell House Farmhouse, early nineteenth century, has a group of **planned farmbuildings** in three ranges round farmyard, with **gin-gan.**

Chollerton Farmhouse is early nineteenth century with farm buildings, cottages and pigsties and cart shed and **chimney** for steam thresher.

Churchyard memorial, 1837 to John Saint, owner of Cocklaw Fulling Mill, showing tools of trade.

Stable and hearse-house, early nineteenth century, near the church.

The **Vicarage** is early nineteenth century, of two builds, largely by John Dobson.

Corbridge · NY 96 NE · In the Market Place is a **cross** of 1814, also the **fountain house** of 1815.

The **Methodist Chapel** is 1867. The **Town Hall** is 1887 by F Emily.

Outside the village is **Walker's Pottery**: two 'bottle' kilns, a circular kiln and two 'Newcastle' kilns.

Shildonhill Farm has an agricultural **steam engine building with chimney**, in brick, with very large stone cap.

Cornhill · NT 83 NE · **Church** (St Helen), 1840.

Cramlington · NZ 27 SW · **Church** (St Nicholas) by Austin and Johnson in thirteenth century style. There is a circular **gin-gan** in stone, with central finial.

Craster · NU 21 SE · **Kippering sheds** of late nineteenth century, with vents near the ridge for outlet of smoke.

Cresswell · NZ 29 SE · **Church** (St Bartholomew), 1836 in Norman style.

Dalton (near Stamfordham) · **NZ 17 SW** · **Broomy Hall Farmhouse** is mid nineteenth century in Tudor style. The **Parish Church** (Holy Trinity), 1836, is by John Green. The former **school and schoolmaster's house** (now a private house) is 1843 in Tudor style.

Dipton Mill (Hexhamshire) · **NY 96 SW** · A **bridge** dated 1822 with single arch.

Dissington · NZ 17 SW · Here is a mid century **bridge**, and at Dissington Red House is an early nineteenth century **gin-gan** with the usual Northumbrian plan.

Doddington · NT 93 SE · A **watch-house** of 1826, in the churchyard; to permit recently buried bodies to be guarded against 'body-snatchers'.
The old **Vicarage**, now a house, is of 1835–6.
The **bridge** over the River Till is hump-backed, early nineteenth century.

Eachwick · NZ 17 SW · The **bridge** is dated 1819; a single segmental arch in ashlar.

Earle · NT 92 NW · **Langleeford Farmhouse** has a group of early nineteenth century farmbuildings. **Middleton Hall** is dated 1807, for the Greenwich Hospital Commissioners.

Earsdon · NZ 37 SW · **Church** (St Alban), 1836–7 by John and Benjamin Green. In the churchyard is the **monument** to the 204 men and boys lost in the Hartley Colliery disaster of 1862 (see *Coal mining*, Chapter 2).

Ellingham · NU 12 NE · **Church** (St Maurice), 1862 by Rev J F Turner. **RC Church**: chapel of Ellingham Hall, 1897 by Dunn and Hanson.

Preston Farm has a good typical terrace of houses along the roadside, with the farm behind, with a **steam engine house and chimney**.

Etal · NT 93 NW · **Church** (St Mary) 1858, by Butterfield, in the grounds of Etal Manor.

The village street, described by Pevsner as 'one of the prettiest in the county' has eighteenth, nineteenth and twentieth century cottages.

Ewart · NT 93 SW · **Sundial** at Coupland Castle, in sandstone with decahedron head with nine bronze gnomons; also a **privy** (now kennels), with two seats.

Various **houses and cottages** and several **mileposts**.

The **Lanton Memorial** is an obelisk, probably erected 1827 to John Davison. A similar obelisk is at Swarland in memory of Nelson.

Felton · NU 10 NE · A magnificent group of **mill and associated equipment**.

Ford · NT 93 NE · A charming 'model' village, built by Lady Waterford. There is a **memorial** to the Marquis of Waterford of 1859, at which time his widow decided to build. The **school** is dated 1860 and this is where Lady Waterford produced her series of paintings (see *Life in Society*, Chapter 8).

The **smithy** has a doorway in the shape of a large horse-shoe dated on the gable 1863.

The **cornmill** on the Till is complete but disused, with two interior undershot wheels.

Fourstones · NY 86 SE · **Gin-gan**, replaced by steam, with **chimney** for this, c 1879.

Gilderdale (near Alston) · NY 74 NW · **Gilderdale Bridge** is dated 1836, with a segmental arch. A railway **viaduct** crosses the Gilderdale Burn (cf Lambley). There are other viaducts on this line at Burnstones and Knarside.

Glanton · NU 01 NE · Disused **railway station** of 1887, on Alnwick to Cornhill line. The **weigh cabin** has been removed to Beamish Museum.

Greenhead · NY 66 NE · **Church**, 1826–8 by Dobson, with plain lancet windows.

Greystead · **Church** (St Luke), 1818 by H H Seward, for the Commissioners of Greenwich Hospital – a sister church for those at Humshaugh, Wark and Thorneyburn.

Gunnerton · NY 97 NW · **Church** (St Christopher), 1899 by Rev Hawes in Arts and Crafts style. (Hawes was curate of Gunnerton, later became RC and emigrated to Australia, where he built several churches.)

Guyzance · NT 90 SW · Semi-derelict **farmhouse**, probably early nineteenth century; farm buildings still in use.

Harbottle · NT 90 SW · **Castle House**, 1829 by Dobson, incorporating seventeenth century parts.

Harle (near Kirk Whelpington) · NZ 08 SW · **Wellhouse Farmhouse**, c 1800, with cottage and byres.

Hartford House · NZ 28 SW · This **House** was built by William Stokoe, much altered. Note the heavy High Victorian iron gates and the lead dome over the south bow-window.

Harwood Shield (Hexhamshire) · NY 95 SW · A **bridge** dated 1832, with one arch, lies south of Riddlehamhope Farm.

Healey · NZ 05 SW · **Healey Hall** was built in 1834 for Robert Ormston, in Tudor Gothic style. There is also a **game larder**, c 1800.
  The **Parish Church** (St John) 1860 is by C E Davis of Bath, in Romanesque style and the **Vicarage** is 1877 by Ewan Christian.
  The **RC Chapel**, 1854, is by Joseph A Hansom, in Decorated style.
  There is a **Mill** of c 1800 and nearby a miller's house.
  Two **gin-gans** are nearby, one at Fotherley Buildings Farm, the other at Low Fotherley, both early nineteenth century.

Heddon-on-the-Wall · NZ 16 NW · To the SW of Close House is a nineteenth century **ice-house**.
  Heddon Banks Farmhouse is around 1850 and a **gin-gan** is attached to barn, byres and granary. The gin-gan is circular, with good roof trusses and an octagonal king post.
  At Heddon Steads is a mid nineteenth century **water tower**, approx 25 ft high.
  Two other **farmhouses** date from early in the nineteenth century: Houghton North (1802) and South Houghton (1826).

Hedley on the Hill · NZ 05 NE · A **Methodist Chapel** is dated 1837 on the porch.
  At Woodhead Farm is an hexagonal **gin-gan** of early in the century, with pantile roof.

Hepple · NT 90 SE · **Church** (Christ Church), 1897 by J Hodgson Fowler, in Perpendicular style.

Hexham · NY 96 NE · **RC Church** 1830, probably by John Green.
Methodist Church, 1909 by Cackett and Dick.
The former **Hydro Hotel**, 1878–9, is in French Renaissance style.
Orchard Terrace is dated 1825; **Queens Hall** 1865–6 is by John Johnston and the **Scotch Church**, dated 1825 has four giant Tuscan pilasters.
Linnels Mill has an overshot wheel and two pairs of stones, all pre-1850 and in good condition. In the area there are several farms with **agricultural steam engine buildings and chimneys**: New Bingfield Farm, Chollerton Farm and Fourstones Farm.

Holy Island · NU 14 SW · **Village cross** rebuilt by H C Selby 1828.
On Marygate is an early to mid nineteenth century **house and cottage** in random rubble and whinstone.

Horsley · NZ 06 NE · **Church** (Holy Trinity) by J and B Green is in Norman style.
A small **house** by Dobson of 1848 stands by the side of Whittle Dene Reservoirs: The Newcastle and Gateshead Water Co (see Plate 43). Also at these reservoirs is a late nineteenth century **sulphurisation building** with nineteenth century machinery inside, including a working beam engine and large cast iron capstan.

Humshaugh · NY 97 SW · **Church** (St Peter), 1819, by Seward.

Ilderton · NU 02 NW · **North Middleton House** is c 1830–40.

Ingoe · NZ 07 SW · **Moralees Farm** buildings include byres, cart shed and **gin-gan**. This latter is circular with square piers.

Kielder · NY 69 NW · A **skew viaduct**, important in the study of civil engineering, is along the Reedsmouth to Riccarton line of the North British Railway, opened in 1862. It stands now at the edge of the huge Kielder Reservoir, but preserved.

Kilham · NT 83 SE · Former **Scottish Presbyterian Church and manse**, now a house and pottery workshop; 1850.
Shotton House, 1828 is by H C Selby.

Killingworth · NZ 27 SE · **Church** (St John), 1869, by E Bassett Keeling, in vari-coloured sandstones.

Kirkharle · **NZ 08 SW** · Former **Vicarage**, now a house; early nineteenth century, known as Kirkharle Manor.

Kirkhaugh (near Alston) · **NY 64 NE** · **Parish Church** (Holy Paraclete), 1869, designed by the Rector Octavius James, on a mediaeval site.

Kirknewton · **NT 93 SW** · **Parish Church** (St Gregory the Great), thirteenth century, but with nave of 1860 by John Dobson, and tower of later nineteenth century.

Farm shelter sheds, early nineteenth century: long range with five projecting ranges, forming four yards, with turnip houses, having hatches opening on to stone feeding troughs in shelter sheds.

Kirkwhelpington · **NZ 08 SW** · **Merry Shiels Farmhouse** is a planned farmstead, early nineteenth century.

Milestone, early nineteenth century, in sandstone, on B6342, 200yd W of A696.

Churchyard memorial of 1833 in ashlar, inscribed to memory of three children who died in 1833 of a fatal fever (William aged 7, Elizabeth aged 4 and Jane aged one month), with 6-line poem ('Our bay trees are blasted . . .').

Bridge of 1819: single arch in ashlar.

Kyloe · **NU 04 SW** · Several early nineteenth century **mileposts** in cast-iron, one for instance, at Kyloe Vicarage: COR/14/MILES (Cornhill) and BEL/5/MILES (Belford).

Lowlynn Bridge, of the early nineteenth century, is a single arch in ashlar.

Lambley (near Haltwhistle) · **NY 65 NE** · **Parish Church** (St Mary and St Patrick), 1885 by William Searle Hicks, in rather a thirteenth century style.

A **railway viaduct**, 1852, probably by Sir George Barclay-Bruce, crosses the river South Tyne, for the Alston Branch of the Newcastle to Carlisle Railway.

Lee St John · **NY 96 NW** · **Church** (St John), 1818 by Dobson, much altered and enlarged 1885 by W S Hicks.

Lilburn Tower · **NT 02 SW** · The **Tower** by Dobson, 1828–43, is in Tudor style.

Loan End · **NT 95 SW** · Union **chain bridge** of 1820: earliest surviving suspension bridge in England.

Longhirst · NZ 28 NW · A **villa** by Dobson, of his best period, 1828.

Long Horsley · NZ 19 SW · **Linden Hall**, c 1813 by Dobson, is a very plain, ashlar house with a four-column porch of Doric columns.
   RC Church, 1871 in lancet style.

Lowick · NT 93 NE · There are several cast-iron early to mid nineteenth century mileposts, one for example near the Red Lion Inn: BEL/11/MILES (Belford) and COR/8/MILES (Cornhill), with FORD 1 on top.
   Barmoor Castle is a country house, largely 1801 by Patterson of Edinburgh, of classical character, but in castellated Tudor style.
   Presbyterian church dated 1821 and restored 1878.
   Holburn Mill (3 miles SSE of Lowick) is an early nineteenth century **corn mill** with overshot wheel and complete mill workings intact inside. Nearby is a **corn-drying kiln** of similar date.
   Vicarage, 1879 in early eighteenth century style.
   RC Church, 1861 by Stephenson of Berwick, with **Presbytery** of 1864.
   Nos 17 to 21 (odd) on Main Street are a **terrace of houses** of early to mid nineteenth century and **Lowick Hall** is a house of 1820–30.

Matfen · NZ 06 NW · **Matfen Hall** is a country house by Rickman, completed by Sir Edward Blackett for himself. Of 'Jacobethan' style, now a Cheshire Home.
   A little to the south is an early nineteenth century **pant and drinking trough** and not far away is a **bridge** over the River Pont, of the early nineteenth century, possibly by Rickman. The West Lodge to the hall is about 1830. **Fenwick Shield Farmhouse** is about 1830. **High House**, about 1840, is in Tudor style. Nearby is a **Dutch barn** of the middle of the century. Farmbuildings include an **engine house and chimney**, barn, byres etc, of 1844.
   A **Wesleyan Chapel and schoolroom** stand redundant, of 1840, in Tudor style.
   At the west end of the village is an early to mid nineteenth century **bridge**.
   The **Parish Church** (Holy Trinity), 1841–2 is by and for Sir Edward Blackett, and just to the east of the Post Office is a **drinking fountain** dated 1886, 'Erected . . . as a Mark of . . . esteem for Sir Edward Blackett'.

Milbourne (near Ponteland) · NZ 17 SW · **Milbourne Hall** is a country house of 1801 by John Patterson. The Church of England **Chapel of Ease** (Holy Saviour) is dated 1868 on the vestry, mostly of Geometric style.
   The **mill** has an overshot wheel and two pairs of stones, being pre-1828.

Mitford · NZ 18 NE · The **Hall**, 1823 by Dobson, has a Greek Doric entrance porch and a conservatory with Tuscan pillars.

Morpeth · NZ 18 NE · On the south side of A1097 is East Mill: an eighteenth century **water mill**, provided in the early nineteenth century with engine and boilerhouse, and extended to a full power-driven mill in 1892. The later part is inscribed along the top floor 'NEW PROCESS FLOUR MILLS 1892'.

New Bridge is 1829–31 by Thomas Telford, with three arches. On Bridge Street is an early nineteenth century **Inn**, the 'Black Bull', in Regency style, and not far away is No 59, a **shop** of roughly the same period, with attractive shop facade.

On Castle Bank is the former **courthouse** and gateway to the former **gaol**, now a restaurant; of 1822, by John Dobson, of ashlar in castellated Gothic style. Pevsner describes it as an 'overpoweringly heavy gateway', with its front and corbelled-out battlements facing the castle hill.

In Castle Square is an early nineteenth century **toll house** of semi-octagonal plan. There are the remains of two **railway stations**. That currently in use by BR is of 1847 by John Green, for the York and Bewick Railway, in Tudor style, with iron canopies added around 1890 (compare with Whittingham). A ceramic map (NER) of 1910 is attached to the wall. The former **Blyth and Tyne Railway terminus** (of 1864) is now a shop and office.

The Parish Church (St Mary) is mostly fourteenth century but its **lychgate** dates to 1861, in Early English style, and in the churchyard is a **watch-house** of 1831, relating to the time when body-snatching for medical purposes was rife.

On Manchester Street is the Boys' Brigade HQ, originally a **Wesleyan Chapel** of 1844, in Perpendicular style.

The **Church** (St James) on Newgate Street is 1842–6, by Benjamin Ferrey in Romanesque style: a large and impressive church.

In the Market Place is a **shop** (No 3) dated 1815, a public **drinking fountain** given in 1855 by Mr Hollon in honour of his wife, in grey polished granite.

Oldgate has various **houses and shops** of interest and the **RC Church** (St Robert) is of 1850, in Early English style.

In the area around Morpeth are two farms with **steam-engine buildings with chimneys**: Shotton Farm and Plessey New House Farm.

Newbrough · NY 86 NE · The **Hall** by Dobson, 1821, has two storeys, with a central pediment.

Ninebanks (Allendale) **· NY 75 SE ·** The **Parish Church** (St Mark), 1871, is by Haswell. Several buildings remain of the former **Ninebanks School**: a central block, the headmaster's house, a southern classroom block and a northern classroom block, all of c 1845, now occupied as dwellings.

Nunnykirk · **NZ 09 SE** · The **Hall** is by Dobson, 1825. Pevsner says 'The finest of all Dobson's early houses'.

Otterburn · **Church** (St John), 1858 by Dobson in Early English style.

Ovingham · **NZ 06 SE** · Churchyard **monument** to a coal-mine overseer dated 1874. Also **tombstones** of Thomas Bewick, noted wood engraver (qv), d. 1828 and his wife Isabella. A memorial stone is preserved in the church porch.

The Tyne **roadbridge** is 1883, in iron with timber flooring.

Plenmellor (near Haltwhistle) · **NY 75 SE** · A group of **planned farm buildings and house** of the early nineteenth century is at Marley Hill. There are three sides of a rectangular cobbled yard.

Two **limekilns** of mid nineteenth century are at Slatequarry Cleugh and near Ouston House, each with twin drawing arches.

Ponteland · **NZ 17 SE** · Westgate **farmhouse** and hind's cottage (now one house) is dated 1835 above the door.

A fine example of a **smithy** stands near the bridge: dated 1822 in good lettering on the lintel.

Berridge Hall **Cottage** is dated 1803 and on the Main Street is the Seven Stars **public house** of early nineteenth century.

Prestwick · **NZ 17 SE** · **Prestwick Hall** is 1815, by Dobson, in Greek Revival style, and nearby is a **bath house** also by Dobson.

Prudhoe · **NZ 06 SE** · **RC Church** (St George) was originally 1825, but now mostly 1886 by J S Hicks, in Decorated style.

Prudhoe Hall, 1878, for Matthew Ridley, is now a hospital admin. block, in High Victorian Renaissance style, with good interior details.

The **railway footbridge** at Prudhoe Station is late nineteenth century, in iron.

Rennington · **NU 21 SW** · **Church** (All Saints), 1831, in lancet style, with chancel and aisle of 1865.

A large masonry block of **limekilns** originally linked to the adjoining line of the railway. The Morpeth to Tweedmouth Railway was opened in 1847.

Riding Mill and Broomhaugh · **NZ 06 SW** · A **bridge** c 1831 runs over the route of the Newcastle and Carlisle Railway. The **Parish Church** (St James), 1838, is by Matthew Thompson in thirteenth century style, with later additions. A **chapel**, originally Baptist, and now Methodist, is dated 1842 and has the inscription BAPTIST/JUBILEE CHAPEL.

226

Riding Cottages are early nineteenth century (Nos 1 and 2) and two are a little later (Nos 3 and 4). **Hollin Terrace** is of 1864 in brick.

Oaklands is a house c 1860, now divided into two. Designed by its owner, Thomas Wilson, it appears to be the prototype for his more grandiose Shotley Hall of 1863.

On the south side of Church Lane is a **drinking fountain** dated 1873. There are two **boundary stones**, one just to the south of the drive to the Glebe and the other a little to the east of Whiteside Cottage. They date to the late nineteenth century; the former is marked WCBB (W C Blackett-Beaumont); the other TWB (Thomas William Beaumont) on its south side and CBG (Charles Bacon Grey) on the north.

The **station-master's house**, c 1832, is at the station, the line being originally the Newcastle Railway. It is probably of 1832 and nearby is a late nineteenth century **passenger footbridge** over the track.

There is a disused **smithy**, with a **wheel-tyre shaping frame** outside (ironwork on a stone upright).

Ridsdale · NY 88 NE · Near the A68 is a large stone building resembling a castle keep. This was the **engine house** of an ironworks, started here in the 1830s and only worked about twenty years. Here also are traces of a blast-furnace site and a double bank of beehive coke ovens.

Ryal (near Matfen) **· NZ 07 SW ·** Here is a **limekiln** of early in the century, with three high triangular corbelled openings.

St John Lee · See Lee St John.

Sandhoe · NY 16 NE · Sandhoe House, 1850 by Dobson, in Jacobean style.

Scremerston · NU 04 SW · Church (St Peter), 1842–3 probably by Bonomi.

The **smithy** has an inscription on its gable, of a horse-shoe and a date (now indecipherable), said to be 1840; has outdoor **tyre-shaping frame**.

Seghill · NZ 27 SE · Church (Holy Trinity), 1849 by John Green, in lancet style.

Shilbottle · NU 10 SW · Smithy in village, alongside 'Farrier's Arms', has a **tyre-shaping frame** outside.

Woodhouse Farm has a good example of nineteenth century cartshed and also a **steam-threshing-engine shed and chimney**.

Shotley Bridge · NZ 05 SE · A **house** of 1863, by the owner Thomas Wilson, in 'playful Gothic' style. This house is exceptionally complete and has a virtually unaltered interior.

The **Parish Church** (St John) is 1836 in thirteenth century style.

Sinderhope (Allendale) · **NY 85 SW** · A **chapel** is dated 1860 and inscribed 'Primitive Methodist Jubilee Chapel'. **Sinderhope Bridge** over the Sinderhope Burn is early nineteenth century with a tall elliptical-headed arch.

A **waterwheel pit** associated with leadmining is in squared stone, built into the hillside, at the Holmslinn Shaft, on the south bank of the River East Allen.

Slaggyford (near Alston) · **NY 65 SE** · The **railway station** of mid nineteenth century served the Alston branch of the Newcastle – Carlisle Railway, opened in 1852 (see Lambley and Gilderdale for viaducts on this line.)

Slaley · **NY 95 NE** · **Parish Church** (St Mary) 1832 by Milton Carr in simple Gothic style.

Spartylea (Allendale) **NY 84 NE** · An early nineteenth century **bridge** in rubble crosses the River East Allen and nearby is a former **Church** (St Peter), dated 1825. This has later nineteenth century alterations in fourteenth century style.

A former **inn**, with adjacent **mill** is now known as Corn Mill Farmhouse.

Stamfordham · **NZ 07 SE** · A pleasant village with an extensive green. At one end is an early nineteenth century **lock-up**. On the north side of the green is a mid century **Presbyterian Church** of one tall storey. The interior has a gallery on iron columns.

The **Heugh Mill Bridge** is early in the century, with three round arches.

Cheeseburn Grange to the south-east is of 1813 by John Dobson, in Tudor Gothic style. **Rose Cottage**, on the estate, is early to mid nineteenth century in Tudor style.

Stannington · **NZ 27 NW** · **Church** (St Mary), 1871, by R J Johnson.

Stocksfield · **NZ 06 SW** · A group of **planned farmbuildings** of the early nineteenth century is at Stocksfield farmhouse, together with a **gin-gan**.

Forge House is c 1850, with forge added later. Various boundary stones, probably nineteenth century are to be found around here, and a milestone near the Broomley Road junction.

Stublick · **NY 86 NW** · Remains of **colliery buildings** with chimney, well-built in ashlar. The buildings are well-maintained and used as farm buildings.

Swinhope · **NY 84 NW** · A **Primitive Methodist Chapel** built in 1845, currently disused, and on the north bank of Black Cleugh is an early nineteenth century **limekiln** with single corbelled arch.

On the south bank of Swinhope Burn is an early nineteenth century lead mine adit **portal**.

Tweedmouth · **NT 95 SW** · **Flour mill** of 1877, now used for malting. Small **engineering works** on the main street.

Wall · **NY 96 NW** · **Church** (St George), 1896 by Hicks and Charlewood, with Gothic tracery.

Wark · **NY 87 NE** · **Parish Church** (St Michael), 1814–18 by H H Seward. **Hearse house** of early nineteenth century, adjoining the church.

On the green is the **Mechanics Institute**, now 'Town Hall' of 1873, with inscription and clock.

High Moralee Farmhouse is early in the century and there are two dated (1843 and 1830) **houses** on North Terrace.

The **pinfold** is early nineteenth century, for the Duke of Northumberland.

Waskerley · **NZ 05 SE** · High Waskerley farm has a group of **planned farmbuildings** of early nineteenth century, with **gin-gan** attached.

West Hartford · **NZ 27 SE** · Good row of early nineteenth century single-storey **cottages**.

Whitfield (near Haltwhistle) · **NY 75 NE** · **Parish Church** (Holy Trinity) 1859–60 by A B Higham of Wakefield and Newcastle, in Early English style.

The old **toll house** of 1832 is on the west side of A686.

Whittingham · **NU 01 SW** · **Church** (St Bartholomew). Sadly an Anglo-Saxon tower was partly demolished and rebuilt in 'bigger and better Gothic' (says Pevsner), by John Green. It is a sad reminder of how the Victorians saw architecture.

Thrunton Farm has **steam engine building with chimney**. Former **railway station**, c 1887 with station house, cottages, coal depot, central platform office, goods shed etc, and iron framework of platform canopy.

Whittington · **NY 97 SE** · **Matfen Piers Farmhouse**, c 1840, with cast iron pump 5ft high and large stone trough.

A **gin-gan and barn** of early nineteenth century near Coombe Cottage, Bingfield. It is circular, with rectangular piers and stone spike finial, in good condition. At New Bingfield is a **house** of 1830–40. A **lime kiln,** early nineteenth century, with three tall triangular corbelled arches stands just west of Shellbraes Farm.

Whittonstall · NZ 05 NE · Church (St Philip and St James), 1830 by Jonathan Marshall.

Wooler · NT 92 SE · RC Church 1856 by George Goldie in Geometric style.
The **police station** dates from 1850, enlarged 1887. Interior has massive iron-clad doors to cells.
House 1820–30 and **bank,** late nineteenth century (Barclays) and several **shops.**
Former **Western Chapel,** and English Presbyterian church, now Masonic Hall, 1818 with porch of 1830–40.

Wylam · NZ 16 SW · Parish Church (St Oswin) is 1886 by R R Johnson, in Perpendicular style. The **Vicarage** is of similar date.
Wylam Hills Farmhouse is early to mid nineteenth century.
The **railway bridge** of 1876 by William George Laws, across the River Tyne, for the NER (part of the Scotswood, Newburn and Wylam Railway): a long single span suspended from two parabolic arches and said to be the earliest use of this construction on a railway.
Holeyn Hall, a country house, of 1851 and addition in 1858, by John Dobson.
The **station and stationmaster's house** are of 1835, the house being in Tudor style. It is one of the earliest stations in the world still in passenger use. The **footbridge** is as for Prudhoe and the **signal box** is late nineteenth century.
The old school, originally the **colliery school** is now Wylam Assembly Church, of 1854.

TYNE AND WEAR

Birtley · NZ 25 NE · Statue (1874) by G Burn of Newcastle; a white marble figure in military uniform on a sandstone pedestal. On pink granite panels is inscription 'Erected to the Memory of Edward Moseley Perks of Birtley Hall, Lt. Col. 1st A D Batt D R V 1874'.
Nearby is the **school house** of about 1860 in snecked sandstone, and the **Parish Church** (St John the Evangelist), built around 1849 by Pickering, in Norman style.

Blaydon · NZ 16 SE · Axwell Park is a fine **Hall** originally built in 1758 by Paine and altered by John Dobson 1817–18. The ashlar and carvings have suffered in recent years from the effects of a nearby coking plant though this has now ceased to work and been demolished. At Axwell Park House Farm is an early nineteenth century **dovecot**: a circular straight-sided tower in coursed rubble. Inside there are pigeon holes around the walls.

The **Parish Church** (St Paul), 1827–9 is by Ignatius Bonomi, with nave, chancel and west tower in Perpendicular style.

A sandstone **memorial** to Thomas Ramsey (died 1873) is by G Burn of Newcastle. The inscription states that it was erected by the miners of Durham, to commemorate his long and self-sacrificing labours in the cause of human progress. The statue is of a man in Victorian dress, beneath a tall gabled and crocketted canopy.

The **RC Church** (St Mary and St Thomas Aquinas) with presbytery is of 1831–2 by John Green, though it was added to in 1848 by Dobson.

Boldon Colliery · NZ 36 SW · Any village having a name like this – quite common in County Durham – clearly has a problem in the twentieth century. Its **Parish Church** (St Nicholas), 1882, was built some twenty years after the sinking of the colliery shafts, to serve the new community. The **Vicarage** is of the same date.

Boldon: East and West · NZ 36 SE · A **lime kiln** which could date to the late eighteenth or early nineteenth century, is to the south east of Down-hill Farm. It is built of roughly squared limestone rubble.

Across the River Don on Follingley Lane is Hylton Grove **Bridge** of around 1800. It is a single arch in sandstone ashlar.

There are various interesting **houses** on Front Street and of particular note, on the northern side, are Nos 41, 43 and 45, originally a large house with service wings. It was built in 1869 for Sir John Fenwick. The principal room on the ground floor has a **ceiling** painted in a formalised pattern of marigolds and crysanthemums.

The **tower mill**: Boldon Mill, is dated 1834 and contains some machinery, though the cap and sails are missing and it is in rather a derelict state.

Although Scots House, in West Boldon, is of the early eighteenth century, its **gatehouse** was built around 1890 for H L Pattinson (qv), the northern chemical manufacturer. This building and its associated walls, gates and gate-piers, are elaborately constructed in brick, with stone dressings and wrought iron gate. There are Pattinson arms in stone on the front gable.

Cleadon · NZ 36 SE · The **Parish Church** (All Saints), 1869, is by R J Johnson, with a later south aisle (1907). It is in Early English style. Across Cleadon Lane is Undercliff, a large **house** of c 1853, now three separate dwellings. It has a large Tuscan entrance porch of two round and two square pillars.

On Sunniside Lane is an early nineteenth century **tower mill** in limestone rubble, of three storeys. It is empty, derelict and lacks cap and sails.

Cullercoats · NZ 37 SE · The **Parish Church** (St George), 1882, by J L Pearson was for the 6th Duke of Northumberland, as a memorial to his father. Nearby is the **Vicarage** probably of the same date.

On Beverley Terrace is a memorial **drinking fountain**, c 1888. It seems, to judge by the inscription, that Lt. Adamson, RN, whom it commemorates, commanded HMS *Wasp* which sailed for Singapore 10 September 1887 'And Was Never Heard of After'.

On the west side of John Street is the **Life Brigade** apparatus house, now a garage. Dated 1867 above the door, it was built for the Cullercoats Life Brigade. This Brigade was only the second in the country, formed immediately after that of Tynemouth of 1864. These Brigades pioneered the technique of rescuing from shipwrecks by rocket-fired life-lines.

The Cullercoats **Look-out house**, now a club, is of 1877–79, built by the Life Brigade.

Earsdon · NZ 37 SW · The **Parish Church** (St Alban) was designed by John and Benjamin Green, relatively early in the century: 1836–7. It unusually contains some early glass in the lancets – possibly by Galyon Hone for Hampton Court. It was restored in 1958 and shows armorials for Henry VII and Henry VIII.

However, more true to our period is the sad **memorial** in the churchyard, 'Erected to the Memory of the 204 Miners Who Lost Their Lives in Hartley Pit, by the Fatal Catastrophe of the Engine Beam Breaking 16th January 1862'. The names of all the dead and their ages are shown on four panels; the youngest being William Davidson, aged 11 (Plate 2).

Bleak Hope House in the village, on Front Street, is early nineteenth century, and its stable and carriage shed are of similar date.

Felling · NZ 26 SE · There are several interesting structures here and in Heworth, which is effectively part of Felling. The **Parish Church** (Christ Church), 1866, is by Anston and Johnson, in Early English style.

On Davison Street, No 35 is a **house and shop** of mid century. The shop frontage is also of interest with a corner doorway.

The **RC Church** is 1893, by C Walker of Newcastle, in an early C14 style, with a good deal of ornament.

An early **house** of 1821 was built for a Mr Swann, who was a sailor, and is known now as Caxton House. On Holly Hill is another **house**, of 1847, built for Thomas Gallon, a paper manufacturer. This was the first house to be built on Holly Hill field.

Of particular interest is the **railway station**, now an urban studies centre. It dates to 1842, served the Brandling Junction Railway, and has recently been restored.

232

Heworth **Parish Church** (St Mary) is 1822, by John Stokoe, in consultation – it is recorded – with John Hodgson who was Rector at the time. It was John Hodgson who wrote the funeral sermon at the time of the Felling Colliery disaster of 1812. The church is of Early English style.

Near the church is an **altar tomb** of 1817 for the Richardson family, in the form of a Doric temple and not far away is an 1824 tomb of the Kell family. This family owned quarries from which the famous 'Newcastle' grindstones came.

Also in the churchyard is a **tomb** of 1864 in granite and sandstone erected to the memory of Thomas Hepburn by the miners of Northumberland and Durham: 'Shorter Hours and Better Education for Miners' is inscribed here.

But most importantly is the **memorial** to 91 men and boys killed in Felling Colliery in May 1812. A sandstone obelisk is placed on a square plinth which bears 4 bronze plaques recording the names and ages of the dead. The youngest was aged 8. (see Chapter 2, *Coal* etc).

On Victoria Terrace is a **house and shop** of mid century, now used as a Post Office. The shop facade is quite attractive, being arcaded with acanthus capitals and leaf-decorated brackets.

Windy Nook **Parish Church** is by Thomas Liddell (1841–2).

Gateshead · NZ 26 SE · There are sadly few buildings of interest left in Gateshead. Of an original 'Listing' of 25 Grade II buildings in 1947, less than half remain. One might be forgiven for thinking that a Listed Building is seen as a challenge! 'Modernisation' is the present keyword in this town which has always suffered from the proximity of Newcastle across the river.

Church (St Cuthbert), 1848, by Dobson, in Neo-Norman style, with Early English tower.

RC Church (St Joseph), 1859, possibly by P P Pugin (? or A H Dunn), in Decorated style.

Walker Terrace (south side only), c 1844: best specimen in Gateshead of a terrace of this kind, though somewhat damaged by inserted windows, etc, and north side destroyed.

Saltwell Towers still standing in Saltwell Park (Plate 70), though deteriorating. Built by Wailes (qv) and sold by him to the Corporation in 1876.

A late nineteenth century **bandstand** once in Saltwell Park, has now been re-erected at Beamish (North of England Open Air Museum), being a good example of cast-iron work manufactured by MacFarlane of Glasgow. It is regularly brought to life once more, by brass band concerts on summer Sunday afternoons.

Ravensworth Terrace (1830–1845), originally down Bensham Bank, but part now rebuilt at Beamish, where it provides part of the urban scene being recreated there. These once-fashionable houses were originally occupied by professional people and tradesmen. J W Carmichael, the landscape and marine painter, lived here, as also did William Collard the engraver and Alexander Gillies, Mayor of Gateshead.

Low Fell was once the high quality residential area not only for Gateshead, but also for Newcastle. Here once lived such men as Leathart, Swan and Spence Watson. There are still some fine **houses** in the area to the east (up the hill) from the site of the old Low Fell station.

Hebburn · **NZ 36 SW** · The **RC Church** (St Aloysius) is 1888 by C Walker of Newcastle, in polychrome brick.

The **Parish Church** (St John) was formerly a wing of Hebburn Hall and was converted to a church by F R Wilson in 1886–87.

A **Presbyterian Church** (now United Reform) is on Church Street, built in 1872 by R J Johnson, in decorated Gothic style.

British Shipbuilders **offices** were originally those of Hawthorn Leslie (c 1890), on Ellison Street, of brick with stone dressings. Various internal details are of interest, including a decorative chimneypiece framing a painting of Hebburn Shipyard in 1883. Andrew Leslie's shipyard was established in 1853 and in 1886 his firm amalgamated with Hawthorn's (manufacturers of ship's engines and railway locomotives), to form Hawthorn Leslie.

The Hebburn **cemetery entrance** on Victoria Road West includes an entrance arch, with wall, piers, gates and railings of 1890, by Frederick West for the Hedworth, Monkton and Jarrow Burial Board. Inside is a linked pair of **chapels** of same date and build.

Howdon · **NZ 36 NW** · The **Bewicke Schools** were built in 1878 by J Johnstone for Wallsend Schools Board. Near these, on the Tynemouth Road, are the Headmaster's house and the school caretaker's house, both now private dwellings, of same date and build.

Jarrow · **NZ 36 SW** · The **Parish Church** (Christ Church), 1869, is by Johnson and Hicks, in Early English style. Its interior furnishings include a Norman-style **font** in Frosterley marble on a pedestal and four columns. The choir stalls, **rood screen**, lectern and altar are in Gothic-style woodwork of high quality.

Jarrow Park, off Sussex Street, has a fine **park entrance** dated 1876. The walls have an inscription along the friezes: 'Given to the people of Jarrow, by Sir Walter and Lady James, September 1876'. Sir Walter James, first Lord Northbourne (1816–1893) was Liberal MP for Gateshead and married the daughter of Cuthbert Ellison of Hebburn. The **entrance lodge**, formerly the park-keeper's home, is in Jacobean style.

On Tyne Street, to the east of the Tyne entrance tunnel, is a **statue** to

Sir Charles Mark Palmer, of 1903 by Albert Toft. It is a bronze figure on a stone pedestal, with bronze panels. One illustrates SS *John Bowes* (first screw-driven collier of 1852), one a coal miner and another HMS *Resolution*. Palmer (1822–1907) founded the shipbuilding firm which caused Jarrow to develop from a village to a town. It was the closure of this yard which led to the Jarrow March of 1936 and to its MP Ellen Wilkinson writing *The Town That Was Murdered* (1939). Note that this statue has been resited from Clayton Street in the town centre.

Lamesley · **NZ 25 NE** · The single-storey **lodge** to Ravensworth Castle lies on the old Coach Road and is dated 1826, and off Cross Lane is the **stable block** of about 1840. In the centre of this yard is a **well** of early in the century.

Also in Lamesley is the old **Vicarage**, now two dwellings, of about 1820. The interior includes Gothick pilasters flanking one of the windows.

Longbenton · **NZ 26 NE** · The **Parish Church** (St John the Evangelist), 1869 is by E Bassett Keeling. Crescents are carved in the copings of the buttresses. They represent the emblem of the Duke of Northumberland.

Monkwearmouth · **NZ 35 NE** · **Church** (All Saints), 1846–9, by Dobson, in Early English style.

Railway Station (now a museum); looking, says Pevsner, 'exactly like a Literary and Scientific Institute or a provincial Athenaeum'. 1848 by Dobson.

Newcastle upon Tyne · **NZ 26 SE** · **Byker Viaduct** (or Ouseburn Viaduct); 1839 by John Green (Plate 68).

Barrack Road: **entrance gate and pair of lodges** to Artillery Barracks; 1806 by John Wyatt.

Barras Bridge: **Hancock Museum**; 1878 by John Wardle.

Barras Bridge: **Parish Church** (St Thomas the Martyr), 1825–30 by John Dobson, in Early English style.

Benton Bank: **Armstrong Bridge** over Jesmond Dene; 1878, designed and built by Armstrong works and presented to the City by Sir William Armstrong. Wrought iron lattice girder bridge on wrought iron box columns: a good example of sound engineering practice for its period, now scarce.

Benwell Lane: **Church** (St James), 1832 by John Dobson in mixed Norman and early English style.

Brunel Terrace: **Church** (St Stephen), 1868 by Johnson in fourteenth century style.

Castle Garth: **Moot Hall,** 1810–12 by William Stokoe: a very early use of the Greek Doric Order.

Clayton Street: one of Grainger's streets, c 1835, probably designed by John Wardle – plainer than Grey Street.

Clayton Street West: **RC Cathedral** (St Mary), 1844 by A W N Pugin.

Eldon Square (remains of), 1826: John Dobson at his best.

Grainger Street, probably by Dobson.

Greenfield Place, c 1824.

Grey's Monument: Roman Doric column on pedestal, with statue of Earl Grey on top. Stair to top. 1838 by Benjamin Green; sculpture of Earl Grey by Edward Baily.

Grey Street, c 1835: claimed to be the finest street in England, mostly by John Dobson and Benjamin Green.

High Level Bridge, 1845–9 by Robert Stephenson and John Dobson.

Hood Street, early nineteenth century.

Jesmond Dene Banqueting Hall, 1860 by John Dobson.

Jesmond Road: **Parish Church,** 1858–61 by John Dobson in fourteenth century Gothic style. **Entrance block to Cemetery;** c 1830: a very good classical design by John Dobson.

Leazes Crescent; 1829 by Thomas Oliver.

Market Street (South side): the most ornamental of all Grainger's street fronts.

Mosely Street (eg Nos 12 and 14); 1891 by A Waterhouse.

Neville Street: **Central Station;** 1848–50 by John Dobson. Has curving platforms with arched roofs of cast-iron, which won a medal at the Paris Exhibition of 1858 (Plate 56).

New Bridge Street: **Lying-in Hospital;** 1826 by John Dobson, now occupied by BBC (Plate 42).

North Road: **Statue of Lord Armstrong** in grounds of Hancock Museum; 1905 by Hamo Thorneycroft (Plate 71).

Osborne Road: **Jesmond Baptist Church;** 1889 by Cubitt in Romanesque style.

St Nicholas Square: **Statue of Queen Victoria,** 1900 by Alfred Gilbert.

St Nicholas Street: (now GPO); 1871–4 by Matthew Thompson.

Scotswood Road; **Market Keeper's house** (now shop), with clock turret; c 1842 by John Dobson.

Swing Bridge; 1876, replacing the old bridge: powered by hydraulic engines, provided by Armstrong.

Town Moor Park: late nineteenth century **bandstand,** octagonal, cast-iron.

Westgate Road: **Literary and Philosophical Society Library,** 1822–25 by John Green. **Neville Hall,** 1870–72 by A M Dunn. **George Stephenson Memorial,** 1862 by John Lough (Plate 61). **Cemetery railings** to Westgate Road Cemetery, 1820 by John Green: have been described as 'magnificent iron railings'; destroyed by vandalism. There is a proposal to restore the iron gates. The masonry piers around the cemetery have recently been restored. **County Court**, 1876 by J Davis.

Westmorland Road: **RC Church of St Michael**, 1879 by Dunn, Hansom and Dunn, in fourteenth century Gothic style.

North Shields · NZ 36 NE · On Albion Road, Rosella Place is a **terrace** of four houses (recently five) of around 1820. A faience tablet on No 2 commemorates it as the birthplace of the artist Birkett Foster.

Also on Albion Road is the **Memorial Wesleyan Methodist Church**, Sunday School and Minister's house of 1889–91, by F R N Haswell. Many of the original fittings survive, though the Sunday School is now a social centre.

On Borough Road is a **Sailor's Home** (now offices), of 1854–6 by Benjamin Green, for the 4th Duke of Northumberland.

At Chirton Green is an **obelisk** dated 1882, inscribed 'Ralph Gardiner/ Chirton Cottage/Author of England's Grievance Discovered/1665/Erected by Subscription 1882'.

Howard Street is particularly rich in buildings of the nineteenth century. No 1, at the lower end of the street, was originally an early (1806–7) **Subscription Library** for the Tynemouth Literary and Philosophical Society, though more recently used as offices. It has a fine Venetian window, with a roundel in the pediment above. At one time this held a clock, as also did the larger roundel in the south gable.

Further along the same (west side) is the **Scotch Church** of 1811 by John Dobson, in Greek Doric style.

Next comes a **Baptist Church**, dated 1846 above the door in Roman numerals.

Crossing to the east side of Howard Street we see a **nonconformist church**, built 1856–7 by Green. It is now the Borough Treasurer's Dept. This church was built for the United Free Methodists, formed in North Shields in 1850 by the Wesleyan Association, the Protestant Methodists and the Armenian Methodists.

With frontages to Howard Street and to Saville Street, stands the old **Town Improvement Commissioner's Offices**, Mechanics Institute, Museum and Police Station. The whole group was taken over in 1849, as Town Hall, built 1844–5. The design is by John Dobson, in Tudor style. Within this structure, on the actual corner site, is the earlier **Poor Law Guardian's Hall,** built in 1837 by Green for the Tynemouth Poor Law Union, in Elizabethan style.

Further down Lower Howard Street, on the east side, is No 105, formerly a **bank** and now a shop. Built in 1882 by F R N Haswell for Hodgkin, Barnett, Pease, Spence & Co, this is a fine three-storey building in Italianate style with a giant Corinthian Order to the upper floors.

Howard Street brings us up into Northumberland Square and here are several fine late nineteenth century **houses**, as well as several built before 1811 (Nos 12–20). On the south side of the square is the **nonconformist church** of St Columba, built 1853–8 by John Dobson for the Anti-Burgher Society; later Presbyterian. It is in Palladian style.

Moving further down towards the shore brings us to the New Quay where the old **Northumberland Arms Hotel**, now offices, has recently been restored. It is a fine building begun in 1800 by D Stephenson, for the Duke of Northumberland, as part of a scheme for a new quay and market place.

On Tyne Street is the 'New High Light': a **lighthouse** dated 1808 on the northern elevation and a rainwater head. The 'Low' lighthouse dates to 1807 and the attached house to 1816.

There are, as the extent of this list might suggest, quite a number of interesting houses, offices and shops within this area: too many to mention here in detail, but the whole provides an interesting visit, though saddening on account of the dereliction and general lack of care.

Penshaw · NZ 35 SW · Monument. Dedicated by the citizens of Newcastle to the first Earl of Durham, the great Liberal politician. Erected in 1844, along the lines of a Greek Doric temple; by John and Benjamin Green. It stands well on a small hill and can be seen from miles around.

Percy Main · NZ 36 NW · The **Parish Church** (St John the Evangelist) on St John's Terrace is of 1862 by Salvin for the Duke of Northumberland.

Ryton · NZ 16 SE · Apart from the early nineteenth century **farm buildings** of the eighteenth century Town Farm, Ryton is the proud owner of four early **lamp-posts** in cast-iron, sited near the thirteenth century church. A little distance away is the 1890s **Parish Church** of Hedgefield (St Hilda) by Oliver and Leeson, in 'Arts and Crafts' Gothic style.

South Shields · NZ 36 NE · Church (Holy Trinity), Laygate, 1833 by Salvin, a native of Durham, in Early English style.

Church (St Stephen), Mile End Road, 1846, also by Salvin.

There are several remaining **terraces** of early nineteenth century cottages, for example in Baring Street and Saville Street.

The casing of **Clarke-Maxim Disappearing Platform** for 6 ins breech-loading gun, 1887. Constructed for trial purposes, in a cylindrical shape approx 21 feet internal diameter in mass concrete. The floating platform (now removed) rose and fell, actuated by air pressure pumps.

It was found to be too slow and the system was abandoned in favour of the quicker and cheaper Elswick hydro-pneumatic mounting. This is an interesting example of late nineteenth century artillery development experiments.

Sunderland · NZ 35 NE · Church (Christ Church), Ryhope Road, 1862–4 by James Murray of Coventry, in High Victorian style.
   RC Church (St Mary), Bridge Street, 1835 in Early English style.
   Presbyterian Church (St George), Ashmore Street, 1890, by J B Pritchett.
   Unitarian Chapel, Bridge Street, 1830.
   Public Library and Museum (1879) by Tiltman.
   John Street, the best of Sunderland's Streets, early nineteenth century.
   Crowtree Terrace, early nineteenth century in local brick on stone foundations.
   Alice Street: a good example of 'Sunderland cottages' (Plate 44).

Tynemouth · NZ 36 NE · This predominantly nineteenth century residential area can only be superficially described here.
   Allendale Place includes two **houses** (Nos 1 and 2) of about 1849. No 3 has been a **bank.** Bath Terrace is an attractive terrace of 11 **houses** of about 1830. Part of Colbeck Terrace is also an attractive group of about 1860.
   The **Parish Church** (Holy Saviour) is of 1839–41 by John and Benjamin Green for the Duke of Northumberland.
   More **houses** (Nos 2–6) in Dawson Square, of about 1860 and, for example, No 55 Front Street is early in the century. No 56, though older, has a nineteenth century **shop front** with slender Gothic pilasters to elliptical-headed windows.
   The **Congregational Church** of 1868 by Thomas Oliver is now a shopping mall; in late thirteenth century style.
   On Front Street is a 1902 **statue** of Queen Victoria (Plate 27) in bronze by Alfred Gilbert. At the east end of Front Street is a small **clock tower and drinking fountain,** in Venetian Gothic style in polychrome brick. There are several nineteenth century tombs around the Tynemouth Priory Church.
   On the Grand Parade is the **Grand Hotel** of 1872 by Thomas Moore of Sunderland.
   Off Howden Road is a particularly interesting **hydraulic accumulator tower** of 1882, built for the Tyne Improvement Commissioners. Inside is hydraulic machinery and an iron staircase. This is the only surviving example on the Tyne of hydraulic machinery, first developed at Newcastle by William (later Lord) Armstrong, in the 1840s.
   Off Pier Road is the great **Collingwood Monument** of 1845, already referred to. The base and plinth are by Dobson, capped by the colossal figure of Admiral Collingwood by Lough.
   Off the south end of Pier Road is the **Watch Club House,** of 1886–7

for the Tynemouth Life Brigade. The **North Pier** (1854–95), of the Tyne Improvement Commissioners, also holds a **Lighthouse** and an **iron crane.**

The attractive old **railway station passenger building** of 1846–7 is by John and Benjamin Green, on the west side of Oxford Street, in Tudor style. It is presently empty and derelict and one must hope that it can be secured.

Tynemouth Station of 1882 is by William Bell of the NER Co. It is in Gothic style. Along the north side of Tynemouth Road are the **Master Mariners' Houses** (Plate 65), of 1837 by J & B Green.

Wallsend · NZ 36 NW · A late nineteenth century **clock** for Swan and Hunter, stands on Buddle Street. Its structure is in cast-iron.

The **Parish Church** (St Peter) on Church Bank is dated 1809 (and restoration of 1892), and was paid for by tontine and partly by the Dean and Chapter of Durham; in Perpendicular style.

On North Road are the **Buddle Schools** and headmaster's and caretaker's houses of 1876 by J Johnson for the Wallsend Schools Board.

There is an **accommodation arch** for the Newcastle and North Shields Railway Co, probably of 1839, by Green, near the junction of Rosehill Road and Marton Road.

East Benton Farmhouse (off Station Road) has an interesting group of **farm buildings,** some around 1800. There is a **byre, stables** and a **granary** with **engine-house** attached. The latter bears a cast-iron plaque dated 1843 and the monogram of J and B Green.

The **Parish Church** (St Luke) 1885–7 is by Oliver, Leeson and Wood, in Early English style.

Whickham · NZ 25 SW · Here is a **memorial** to Henry Clasper (d. 1870) who was a noted oarsman and boat builder (see Plate 76 and *The Common Pleasure* in Chapter 8). This is by G. Burn, and behind is an earlier **memorial** to Clasper's mother, Jane Clasper (d. 1849). This is also in sandstone, but in the form of an up-ended skiff.

Whitburn · NZ 46 SW · Whitburn **Rectory**, 1818 is by Stokoe. The Red Cottage, also on Church Lane, is dated 1842, by Benjamin Green for Thomas Barnes.

Thomas Barnes' house, **Whitburn House**, stands on Front Street, built about 1867.

No 18 has various garden features, especially a former **seed house,** c 1870, in the style of a classical temple.

The Souter Point **lighthouse** was put up in 1871, by Sir James N Douglas for Trinity House, London. This lighthouse actually stands on Lizard Point, but to avoid confusion with the Cornish Lizard Lighthouse, it is named after Souter Point, the next point south! It may claim to be

240

the first lighthouse specifically constructed for electric illumination. The original bi-focal lens is still in use.

Willington · **NZ 36 NW** · The **railway viaduct** was constructed in 1837–9 to a design by John and Benjamin Green for the Newcastle and North Shields Railway Co. It was originally constructed in laminated wood (on sandstone piers): one of the earliest uses in Britain of this technique, but replaced by iron in 1869.

The **Parish Church** (St Mary), 1876, is by Austin and Johnson, in Early English style. Its interior fittings include a high quality **rood screen** commemorating Queen Victoria's Diamond Jubilee.

APPENDIX I
READING LIST

To simplify reference, authors are mentioned by name (with dates where clarification is necessary), thus leading to the alphabetical bibliography. Of course this should only be seen as a guiding reading list, not an exhaustive or definitive Bibliography. Mostly only books are mentioned which still are or have recently been in print, or which can readily be seen in public libraries. Further reading might take one to the British Library with its Parliamentary Papers and other contemporary publications, but this is getting rather deep for a beginner!

Anyone wishing to delve a little deeper than some of the books to be mentioned below should visit one or more of the several Archive Departments, and perhaps look at the publications of (if not join) one or other of the County Local History Societies. The various libraries and many museums (see Appendix for details) welcome serious enquiries and publish booklets, leaflets and so on.

Various books are of broad reference to our subject, notably McCord (1979) and also Asa Briggs (1954), as well as Atkinson (1977 and 1980). Three popular but nevertheless interesting books, full of fascinating facts and illustrations, are by Dougan and Graham (1969), Graham (1979) and McCord and Rowe (1971). An interesting booklet is that of Miller.

Looking first at towns and cities within the region, one must mention Asa Briggs (1963) and Dyos and Wolff. There are many works written from historical or topographical points of view which are of specific relevance including books on:
Newcastle (Middlebrook);
Middlesbrough (Moorson and Anon 1985);
Gateshead (Manders and Rogers);
Sunderland (Bowling and Pickersgill);
Darlington (Sunderland);
Stockton on Tees (Heavisides, and Meynell);
Seaham Harbour (McNee).
Details of these publications are given in the list starting on page 244.

Running now through the book, in chapter order, on the general topic of industrial archaeology, Atkinson (1974) is relevant and also a recent Bibliography on this subject by Greenwood. An authoritative article is that by McCord and Rowe (1977). *Coal mining* is described in Atkinson (1966) and *lead mining* in Turnbull (1975) and in Raistrick and Roberts, reference to regional leadmining, over a greater period than the nineteenth century, is particularly to be found in Hunt and in Raistrick and Jennings (1965). A history of Cleveland iron stone mines comes from Chapman. As to *Engineers and Engineering*, one should mention an interesting publication from HMS Inspectorate of Factories (Anon, 1983).

Moving to *Chemicals*, little is readily available in semi-popular form: though

Campbell has written two useful articles (1964 and 1966). As to *Sunderland Pottery* an attractive and interesting brochure has been published (by Tyne and Wear Museums) by Baker and a useful and attractive work on Tyneside Pottery is that by Bell.

Cottle has written a definitive brochure on Gateshead Glass. And the Tyne and Wear Museums publication on *Wearside Glassmaking* is 'Anon' (1979), and one on *Making Pottery* by Bell, Dixon and Cottle.

Farming in terms of our region and period is not well covered in recent books. In general terms Jewell is interesting and helpful. Northumberland Record Office has produced an interesting if tantalisingly limited catalogue.

As to Urban topics, a history of the Newcastle City Library Service has been written by Knott (1980) and other references will be found within the wider books already mentioned (eg Briggs). Briggs (1963) refers specifically to *Middlesbrough* and both McCord (1979) and Middlesbrook refer to *Newcastle*. Adburgham is helpful on Ladies' shops in general and Pound specifically refers to Fenwick's. Philips is essential in considering early banking in the region.

Turning to life in towns, the subject of *cholera* in Sunderland is covered by a fine teaching set by Miller. The specific styles of regional *housing* described here from Tyneside, Darlington and Sunderland are not well-published, but terraced housing in general is well described in Muthesius.

A booklet on regional *education* has been published by Beamish (1970) and an interesting book by Robson has now been republished (1972).

One aspect of the region's *water supply* history will be found in Rennison and electricity is well covered by Hennessey and by Parsons. Swan's life is described by Clouth.

Railways are naturally well described, though of specific interest are Blackmore, Hoole, Lambert, Mountford, Rolt and Tomlinson. Many could of course be cited in this context.

As to *ports and shipping* one might mention Dougan (1968) and sections within Sturgess (1981). Tyne and Wear Museums (1978) (1968) have produced a useful booklet, and have also produced leaflets on such topics as foyboats and wherries.

Tramcars are another popular technical subject and many publications can be obtained from the Tramway Museum at Crich, Derbyshire. One small booklet which was found helpful is by Wilson. On the small but fascinating subject of cycling, see Sinclair.

On the general subject of *Life in Northern Victorian Society*, one might mention Corder and a booklet on Spence Watson by Staniforth and Hurrell (1985). On various people from the region, Rowland is informative (two booklets without any dates). On the subject of families the Benwell Community Project (Anon, 1978) is informative, if somewhat bitter.

Invaluable for a study of *artists* in the region is Hall (1973). A good example of a specific catalogue is that published by Tyne and Wear (Usherwood, 1984) and another from the Laing Art Gallery is by Stevenson. The work of John Dobson is thoroughly discussed by Wilkes (1980) and his working relationship with Grainger and Clayton is detailed by Wilkes and Dodds (1964).

READING LIST

ADBURGHAM, Alison *Shops and Shopping, 1800–1914* (Allen & Unwin, 1964)

ALLSOPP, B and CLARK, U *Historic Architecture of Northumberland* (Oriel Press, 1969)

ANON *Agriculture and Country Life in Northumberland in the C18 and C19* (Northumberland Co Record Office, 1968)

ANON *A Century of Education: 1870–1970* (Beamish Museum, 1970)

ANON *The Making of a Ruling Class: Two Centuries of Capital Development on Tyneside* (Benwell Community Project, 1978)

ANON *The Maritime Collections* (Tyne & Wear Museums, 1978)

ANON *Glass-Making on Wearside* (Tyne & Wear Museums, 1979)

ANON *The Tyneside Classical Tradition: Classical Architecture in the North East, 1700–1850* (Tyne & Wear Museums, 1980)

ATKINSON, Frank *The Great Northern Coalfield, 1700–1900* (1968: 3rd edn Frank Graham, 1979)

ATKINSON, Frank *Industrial Archaeology of North East England* 2 vols (David & Charles 1974)

ATKINSON, Frank *Life and Tradition in Northumberland and Durham* (1977: 2nd edn Dalesman Publishing Co, 1986)

ATKINSON, Frank *North East England: People at Work: 1860–1950* (Moorland Publishing Co, 1980)

BAIN, Iain *The Workshop of Thomas Bewick* (Bewick Trust, 1989)

BAKER, J C *Sunderland Pottery* (Tyne & Wear Museums, 1983)

BELL R C *Tyneside Pottery* (Studio Vista, 1971)

BELL, R, DIXON, L, COTTLE, S *Maling: A Tyneside Pottery* (Tyne & Wear Museums, 1981)

BEWICK, Thomas *A Memoir of Thomas Bewick, written by himself* (1862). Ed by Iain Bain (Oxford University Press, 1979)

BLACKMORE, J *Views of the Newcastle & Carlisle Railway* (From drawings by J W Carmichael) (Frank Graham, 1969)

BRIGGS, Asa *Victorian People: A Reassessment of Persons and Themes 1851–67* (1954) (New Edn Penguin Books, 1985)

BRIGGS, Asa *Victorian Cities* (1963), (Penguin, 1968)

CAMPBELL, W A *The Old Tyneside Chemical Trade* (Univ of Newcastle, 1961)

CAMPBELL, W A 'James Crossley Eno and the Rise of the Health Salt Trade' *Univ of Newcastle Medical Gazette* Vol LX (1966)

CHAPMAN S K *Gazetteer of Cleveland Ironstone Mines* (Langbaurgh Museum Service, 1975)

CLARK, G Kitson *The Making of Victorian England* (Methuen 1962 & 1980)

CLOUTH, Diane *Joseph Swan* (Gateshead M B C, 1980)

COCHRANE, A *The Early History of Elswick Works* (Mawson Swan and Morgan, Newcastle, 1909)

COTTLE, S *Sowerby: Gateshead Glass* (Tyne & Wear Museums, 1986)

DOUGAN, David *The History of North East Shipbuilding* (Allen & Unwin, 1968)

DOUGAN, D and GRAHAM, F *Northumberland & Durham: A Social Miscellany* (Frank Graham, 1969)

DYOS, H J and WOLFF, M *The Victorian City Images and Realities* (Routledge, 1973)

GRAHAM, F *Northumberland & Durham: A Social and Political Miscellany* (Frank Graham, 1979)

GREENWOOD, J *The Industrial Archaeology and Industrial History of Northern England: A Bibliography* (Privately published, 1985)

HALL, Marshall *The Artists of Northumbria* (Marshall Hall Associates, 1973)

HEALTH & SAFETY EXECUTIVE *Her Majesty's Inspectors of Factories, 1833–1983: Essays to Commemorate 150 Years of Health and Safety Inspection* (HMSO, 1983)

HENNESSEY, R A S *The Electric Revolution* (Oriel Press, 1972)

HOOLE, Kenneth *Regional History of the Railways of Great Britain: VOL IV North East England* (David & Charles, 1965)

HUNT, C J *The Lead Miners of the Northern Pennines* (Manchester Univ Press, 1970)

JEWELL, C A *A Sourcebook of Victorian Farming* (Shurlock, 1975)

KNOTT, J *The First Hundred Years: Newcastle City Libraries* (Newcastle Polytechnic, 1980)

LAMBERT, Richard S *The Railway King, 1800–1871* (Allen & Unwin, 1934)

McCORD, N & ROWE, David T *Northumberland & Durham: An Industrial Miscellany* (Frank Graham, 1971)

McCORD, N & ROWE, David C 'Industrialisation & Urban Growth in North East England', *Internat. Rev. of Soc. Hist.* XXII (1977)

McCORD, Norman *North East England: The Region's Development 1760–1960* (Batsford, 1979)

McNEE, T *Seaham Harbour: The First 100 Years* (Privately published, 1985)

MANDERS, F W D *A History of Gateshead* (Gateshead Corporation, 1973)

MELLOR, G J *The Northern Music Hall* (Frank Graham, 1970)

MESS, H A *Industrial Tyneside: A Social Survey* (Benn, 1928)

MEYNELL, L R *Stockton on Tees in Times Past* (Countryside Publications, 1979)

MIDDLEBROOK, S *Newcastle upon Tyne: Its Growth & Achievement* (Newcastle Journal, 1950)

MILLER, E (Compiler) *Eyewitness: The North East in the Early C19* (Harold Hill, 1968)

MILLER, S *Cholera in Sunderland* (Sunderland Polytechnic, ND)

MOORSOM, Norman *The Birthplace and Growth of Modern Middlesbrough* (Privately published, 1967)

MOUNTFORD, C E *The Bowes Railway* (Industrial Railway Soc, 1976)

MUTHESIUS, Stefan *The English Terrace House* (Yale Univ Press, 1982)

NEVILLE, Hastings, M *A Corner in the North* (1909) (Re-published: Frank Graham, 1980)

NEWTON, Robert *The Northumberland Landscape* (Hodder & Stoughton, 1972)

PARSONS, R H *The Early Days of the Power Station Industry* (Cambridge Univ Press, 1939)

PEVSNER, Nikolaus *Buildings of County Durham* (Penguin Books)
Buildings of North Riding of Yorkshire and *Buildings of Northumberland*

PHILLIPS, Maberley *History of Banks, Bankers and Banking in Northumberland and Durham* (1894)

POUND, Reginald *The Fenwick Story* (Fenwicks, 1972)

RAISTRICK A, & JENNINGS, B *A History of Lead Mining in the Pennines* (Longmans 1965)

RAISTRICK, A & ROBERTS, A *The Life and Work of the Lead Miner* (Beamish and Northern Mine Research Soc., 1984)

REID, Robert *Land of Lost Content: The Luddite Revolt, 1812* (Heinemann, 1986)

RENNISON, R W *Water to Tyneside: a History of the Newcastle and Gateshead Water Company* (Newcastle & Gateshead Water Co., 1979)

ROBSON, E R *School Architecture* (1874) (re-published, Leicester Univ Press, 1972)

ROGERS, F *Gateshead: An Early Victorian Boom Town* (Priory Press, 1974)

ROLT, L T C *George and Robert Stephenson* (Longmans, 1960)

ROWLAND, T H *People and Places in Northumberland & Durham*

——*More People and Places in Northumberland & Durham* (Privately published, ND? 1975)

SINCLAIR, Dr Helen *Cycle Clips: a History of Cycling in the North East* (Tyne & Wear Museums, 1985)

STANIFORTH, F & HURRELL, F E *Robert Spence Watson* (Beamish Museum, 1985)

STEVENSON, B C *Paintings from the Leathart Collection* (Laing Art Gallery, 1968)

STURGESS, R W *The Great Age of Industry in the North East* (Durham County Local History Soc., 1981)

SUTHERLAND, Gillian *Elementary Education in the C19* (Historical Association, 1971)

TOMLINSON, W W *The North Eastern Railway* (1914), (re-issued, David & Charles, 1967)

TURNBULL, L *The History of Lead Mining in the North East of England* (Harold Hill, 1975)

TURNBULL, L & WOMACK, S *Home Sweet Home: Housing in the North East* (Gateshead M B C., 1977)

USHERWOOD, Paul, *Art for Newcastle: Thomas Miles Richardson* (Tyne & Wear, 1984)

WILKES, Lyall & DODDS, Gordon *Tyneside Classical: the Newcastle of Grainger, Dobson and Clayton* (Murray, 1964)

WILKES, Lyall *John Dobson: Architect and Landscape Gardener* (Oriel Press, 1980)

WILSON, Frank E *The British Tram* (Percival Marshall, 1963)

YOUNG, G M *Portrait of an Age: Victorian England* (Annotated edition by G Kitson Clark), (OUP, 1977)

APPENDIX II
SELECTED COLLECTIONS
IN MUSEUMS WITHIN
THE REGION

Most of these museums will be happy to supply a free publicity leaflet and several publish well-illustrated guide books and other more detailed booklets and brochures, as well as postcards etc.

BEAMISH: The North of England Open Air Museum, near Chester le Street, County Durham (Tel: 0207 231811)

See *Gazetteer*, under County Durham: four groups of buildings re-erected on a 250 acre site and restored and furnished in a 'living' way, related to their environment, namely: Colliery, Farm, Railway and Town. Various activities often include a printer at work, baking, proggy-mat making, blacksmith, visit down a 'drift' coal mine etc.
Operating electric tramway.
Herd of Durham Shorthorn cattle and flock of Teeswater sheep being built up.
Considerable Social History and Industrial Archaeology collections from the region, mostly of the nineteenth century and early twentieth century. Replica of 'Locomotion' (S&DR 1825) in steam in summer.
Important collection of North Country Quilts (mostly not currently on display) and costume.
Large Photographic Archive relating to the region and its activities: available for reference on request.

BEWICK BIRTHPLACE MUSEUM, Cherryburn near Stocksfield, Northumberland (Tel: 0661 843276)

A new museum based at the restored birthplace of this famous wood engraver. Already an important collection of Bewick's blocks has been rescued and brought back from the United States with the help of the National Heritage Memorial Fund.

THE BOWES MUSEUM, Barnard Castle, County Durham (Tel: 0833 37139)

See Plate 68 and Chapter 8: *Northern Collectors*
In addition to the French fine and decorative arts and European painting, for which the museum is noted, it also has:

Collection of nineteenth century dress
Display of dolls, toys and models, many of C19.
Victorian period room.
Gallery of nineteenth century Teesdale, with emphasis on farming and lead mining.
A few paintings by J W Carmichael.

DARLINGTON, Tubwell Row (Tel: 0325 463795)

Domestic 'byegones'
Scientific instruments
Photographs of Victorian Darlington
Printed ephemera

Art Gallery, Crown Street
Permanent collection includes late nineteenth century oil paintings and watercolours.
Railway Centre and Museum (Tel: 0325 460532)
Railway material housed in original Stockton and Darlington Railway Station, of 1842.
Several full-size exhibits including loco NER 1463 (1883), S&DR coach (c 1846) and S&DR Locomotive 'Derwent' (1845)
Also signs, uniforms, equipment, printed ephemera.

GATESHEAD, Prince Consort Road (Tel: 091 477 1495)
Many fine Victorian paintings from the original Shipley Bequest and collections of Gateshead glass and other material.

HARTLEPOOL, Clarence Road (Tel: 0429 266522)
The Permanent Art Gallery displays the founding collection of 1920, by Sir William Grey. It includes oil and watercolour paintings, by many late Victorian and Edwardian artists, including J W Carmichael and Thomas Hedley. The collection also includes many topographical works of Victorian Hartlepool.
In the grounds of the building, the development continues of an 'Hartlepool As It Was' display. This already includes a smithy, electric tram office, cottage, brine pump.

MIDDLESBROUGH, Dorman Museum, Linthorpe Road (Tel: 0642 813781)
A permanent gallery 'The Making of Middlesbrough' describes the growth of the town from 1830 to 1930. The Pottery Gallery shows the work of the Linthorpe Pottery and the Middlesbrough Pottery.

NEWCASTLE-UPON-TYNE, City Library (Tel: 091 261 0691)
Holds the very large and important Pease Collection of work by Thomas Bewick: wood engravings, books, printed emphemera etc. It has been added to over the years. Not generally on open display.
The Local Reference Library is obviously the best source for printed information on a large part of the region.

Hancock Museum (Tel: 091 232 2359)
Mostly an important collection and displays of Natural History, but has display
on Thomas Bewick and his work and holds (not on open display) a collection of
watercolours by Bewick, on which he based his wood engravings.

Joicey Museum (Tel: 091 232 4562)
Displays relating to the history of Newcastle.
Small display on Thomas Bewick and his work as wood engraver.

Laing Art Gallery Tel: 091 232 7734)
The North's most important collections of paintings by various artists, as mentioned in the text. See also Plates 1, 58, 68) Also important collections of pottery
and glass from local manufacturers; porcelain and costume.

SOUTH SHIELDS, Ocean Road (Tel: 091 456 8740)
Generally concerned with the overall history of the town. Notable items in the
collections include the mechanism and face of the turret clock from Holy Trinity
Church, an 'Albion' printing press of 1849 (on which was printed the first edi-
tion of the South Shields Gazette), and two lifeboat models, c 1880 and 1887.
There is also a collection of pressed glass from Moore's glassworks (1890s).

STOCKTON-ON-TEES, Preston Hall (Tel: 0642 781184)
The Hall was built in 1825 and occupied from 1882 by the Ropners, a family
of local ship-owners.
Various displays, but most importantly an open-air Victorian street with various
shops and, at certain times, demonstrations by traditional craftsmen, including
blacksmith and Northumbrian Small Pipes Maker. Inside the Hall is a selection
of Victorian Rooms.

SUNDERLAND, Borough Road (Tel: 091 514 1235)
Many aspects of Victorian Sunderland are shown, including 'The Changing Face
of Wearside' which illustrates the development of the town through paintings, maps,
prints and photographs. Also 'The Sunderland Story' features commerce and industry, churches, Sunderland docks and leisure. Major displays feature glass, pottery
and models of sailing and steam ships made in Sunderland, and an 1860s middle
class parlour.

Grindon Museum
Has room and shop interiors of the early 1900s, in a house of the period, built
for one of the Short ship-building family.

Monkwearmouth Museum
A fine building of 1848: one of Britain's finest classical stations. The booking
office, footbridge and waiting shelter have been restored to their original NER
condition at the turn of the century.
Other displays include Victorian and Edwardian bicycles and model locomotives.

Acknowledgements

The larger proportion of the photographs used here has come from the immense collection built up by Beamish, The North of England Open Air Museum in County Durham. A few other sources are identified in the captions, and the following are by the author: 26, 27, 42, 43, 44, 45, 47, 48, 50, 51, 54, 55, 57, 58, 60, 64, 66, 68, 76.

I must particularly thank my colleagues at Beamish, especially Rosemary Allan, Keeper of Social History and Jim Lawson, in charge of the photographic collections. The staff of the Newcastle City Reference Library could not have been more helpful, and my special thanks go to Frank Manders and his colleagues in the Local History section. The services of Newcastle University Library have also been invaluable, as have those of the O.P.L. section of the British Library. The staff of Tyne and Wear Museum Service, especially John Millard and Neil Sinclair, have kindly helped to trace suitable paintings in their collections, for use here. The Newcastle City Surveyor, Mr Arthur Boardman and his staff have also been very helpful, particularly concerning their concealed but all-important sewerage system, and also in lending me an early map of Newcastle by Thomas Oliver.

Professor Norman McCord read through the book in typescript and made several penetrating and informative comments for which I am most grateful.

My wife has put up with my chaos, clutter and cantankerousness in a far more kindly way than I deserve, and Sharon White has come through the challenge of typing out my scrawl and recorded mutterings with flying colours.

Finally my thanks to those scores of people whom I have troubled for odd facts, snippets of information and so on. This book is very much a compendium though I must, of course, accept responsibility for any conclusions and emphasis which I may have drawn or placed.

INDEX

Stephenson, George, 13, 131
Stephenson, Robert, 8, 35
Stepney Bank Pottery, 48
stockbrockers, 84
Stockton & Darlington Railway, 20
Stockton & Darlington Railway Co., 134
stone quarrying, 26
Stone Row, 21
sulphurisation building (waterworks), Horsley, 222
Sunderland cottage, 109
Sunderland Gas Works, 122
Sunderland: library, 71
Sunderland lighthouse (North Pier), 145
Sunderland: Municipal Building, 69
Sunderland ware, 45
Sunderland & South Shields Water Co., 32
Swan Electric Light Company, 123
Swan, Joseph, 122, 164
swimming baths, 179
Swing Bridge, Newcastle, 32
sword dance, 183

tax on soap repealed, 41
Telford, Thomas, 154
Tennant, 41
Thompson & Co., 32
Thompson, Robert, 149
Thornaby, 72
Thorpe Thewles: school established by Marchioness of Londonderry, 115

toll houses: for several, see Gazetteer
Tolpuddle Martyrs, 56
Tooth, Henry, 50
Tower Bridge (hydraulic), 32
Tower Mill, Bolton, 231
Tow Law: coking ovens, 19
Tow Law Ironworks, 23, 25
Town Halls, 62
tramcars, 157
Tramways Act (1870), 157
transportation, 187
Transporter Bridge, Middlesbrough, 196
trapper boys, 14
treadmill, 191
Tudhoe: Ironworks' cottages, 25
Tunstall, Marmaduke, 168
Turbinia, 30
Turnbull, Matthew, 55
Tyneside flats, 103

Union Bridge, 156
United Alkali Co., 4
Urlay Nook: chemical works, 42

Vaughan, 24, 81
Ventilation furnace, 14
viaducts, 197, 204, 207, 211, 220, 222, 223, 240

Wailes, William, 175
Walker, 23
Walker, George: cyclist, 159
watch house (re body snatchers) Doddington (1826), 219; Mitford (1831), 225

Water Babies, 110
watermill: for several see Gazetteer
Waterford, Lady, 175
water pumping station, Ryhope, 32
water supply, 117
waterwheel: Killhope, 33
Watson, Robert Spence, 161
Wearside, 47
Weighton, Professor, 35
Wellington, Duke of, 41
West Hartlepool Harbour & Railway Co., 135
'wet money' re Music Halls, 179
W G Armstrong & Co., 32
wherry, 152
Whittingham: station, 130
Whittle Dene: reservoirs, 119
Whorlton suspension bridge, 173, 212
Willington Quay, 44
Wilson, Joe: song-writer, 181
windmill: for several see Gazetteer
window glass, 52
Witham, Henry T M, 136
Witton Park Ironworks, 23
Witton : Stockton & Darlington Railway, 20
wood pavements, 155
Wouldhave, William, 150
Worship: Census of, 125
Wrekenton Fell: quarry, 29
Wylam Ironworks, 23

Young, Arthur, 56